sociology
REVIEWED

TONY LAWSON

JOHN SCOTT

HAL WESTERGAARD

JOHN WILLIAMS

CollinsEducational

An imprint of HarperCollins*Publishers*

Published by
CollinsEducational
77-85 Fulham Palace Road
Hammersmith
London
W6 8JB

First published in 1993

All articles reproduced from the *Social Studies Review* **and the** *Sociology Review* **by kind permission of Philip Allan Publishers Limited.**

The publishers would like to thank the following for permission to reproduce photographs:

Photofusion for photographs appearing on pages 12, 31, 37, 40, 46, 52, 66, 77, 85, 87, 94, 103, 127; The MacQuitty International Collection for photographs appearing on pages 3, 80, 124, 130; The Hulton Deutsch for the photograph appearing on page 109; Christopher Maguire of the Prison Reform Trust for the photograph appearing on page 72; and Bredero Properties Plc development at Centre West, Hammersmith for the photograph appearing on page 100.

British Library Cataloguing in Publication Data is available on request from the British Library.

ISBN 000 322282 9

Typeset by CG Graphic Services, Aylesbury.
Cover design by Ridgeway Associates.
Printed in Great Britain by Butler & Tanner Ltd, Frome

Contents

General Introduction

Sociology Reviewed builds on the achievements of two A level magazines. The publication in September 1985 of the first issue of *Social Studies Review* and, some six years later in September 1991, of its successor *Sociology Review* represents, in some ways, the coming of age of sociology as an advanced level examination subject. The emergence of the initial magazine meant that there were now enough A level Sociology and Politics students to sustain a publication aimed specifically at these subjects.

Eventually the demand from sociology students alone became too great to ignore, hence the birth of *Sociology Review*. Its success, and that of its predecessor, also points, however, to the need for a publication which keeps Sociology A level students up to date with contemporary developments in society and with emerging debates within sociology itself. The aim of the *Review* is to bring these debates within reach of the average A level student, while stretching the ability of even the most capable student to reflect critically on sociological issues.

The *Review* is widely regarded as being at the cutting edge of developments in A level Sociology. We have tried to demonstrate this in our choice of articles for this collection. We have also highlighted important developments in each topic area of the syllabus. Undoubtedly, some of our readers will be disappointed that their 'favourite' article is not given the new treatment afforded here. We hope this is balanced by the new material which is presented, and by readers seeing pieces from earlier volumes which they may have missed. Perhaps, too, this collection may meet at least some of the demand for back copies of the magazines which are now unavailable.

An equally important development in 1991 was the emergence of a new-style A level Sociology syllabus from the Associated Examining Board (AEB). With by far the largest number of candidates, the AEB syllabus has moved away from a 'traditional' examination which, generally speaking, rewarded the recall of appropriate information, to one in which candidates are rewarded for demonstrating appropriate sociological **skills**. The skills which are now assessed for the AEB syllabus are:

1 **Knowledge and understanding** – the ability to recall studies and debates, with accurate detail and sociological understanding. Students should be familiar with the major sociological studies which have been carried out in a topic area and know the main points that they make. It would also be valuable to understand the context in which such studies were developed and to be able to place them historically. For example, many students describe the work of Goldthorpe and Lockwood when looking at stratification, but do not point out that the research was done in the early 1960s, long before most A level students were born, and that the stratification system has changed considerably since that time.

2 **Interpretation and application** – the ability to interpret material in a variety of different forms and to use studies, concepts, arguments and debates in ways appropriate to the question set. In the examination, candidates will be required to look at items of information and to express their meaning in a different way. For example, from a table of statistical data, the candidate might be asked to identify a particular percentage, or to interpret the trends which the statistics suggest. Candidates will also have to apply their understanding of sociological issues to particular problems. For example, they could be asked to look at some information and suggest what its implications might be for a sociological debate. They will also be required to apply appropriate evidence to support the points made in the course of answering specific questions. For example, if a question was asked about official statistics and the candidate wanted to apply Durkheim's work on suicide to that question, it would not be appropriate to describe Durkheim's four types of suicide in intricate detail. However, it would be appropriate to discuss Durkheim's use of statistics and what problems might be encountered with the way he used them.

3 **Evaluation** – the ability to consider the strengths and weaknesses of studies and arguments and come to a measured conclusion as to their merits. Evaluation is arguably the hardest of the three skills because it involves the student in making judgements about sociological studies and debates. In an assessment at least two sides of an issue should always be discussed, and a conclusion presented in a separate part of the answer. If a question has 'assess' or 'evaluate' in it, and only one side of the debate is given, then a high score cannot be achieved. The conclusion should also emerge from a consideration of the evidence presented in the answer and not just be a personal opinion.

This overt emphasis on skills has been accompanied by a change in the examination format, with Paper 1 now being entirely composed of structured questions, while Paper 2 retains the essay-style format, adapted to incorporate the skills of the new syllabus. Each chapter of *Sociology Reviewed*, therefore, has an example of a structured question or an example of an essay question, as appropriate.

Clearly, the revised AEB syllabus makes new demands on students. In particular it requires that students demonstrate these nominated skills in their examination work. Yet, there has been little opportunity for students to practise those skills until now. One of the main aims of this book is to provide students with practical exercises through which they can test and practise the important skills of interpretation, application and evaluation. Each chapter includes one exercise for each of these skills. By carrying out the tasks we recommend, students should begin to recognise the demands being made of them by the skills approach and they should gain some invaluable experience in responding to exam-style questions in a skilled way.

Finally, another important dimension of the revised AEB syllabus is the introduction of **Coursework** as an optional way for students to demonstrate the required skills. Each chapter of the text includes a Coursework Suggestion so that students can see ways of translating areas of interest into appropriate and manageable research projects.

These are the very direct and practical strengths of *Sociology Reviewed*. Students will be much better prepared for their examinations as a result of following the guidelines and suggestions put forward here. More than that, however, the book is also full of interesting and up-to-date comment and research on crucial sociological debates. We think a book like this should be – and is – fun to read. It should challenge its readers and stimulate new ideas in them. We hope we have some success in this. If we do, it will be down to the hundreds of contributors and thousands of subscribers who have made *Social Studies Review* and *Sociology Review* such outstanding successes.

Thanks to you all!

How to Use this Book

Sociology Reviewed is divided into thirteen chapters, the subjects of which mirror the topic divisions on the AEB A level Sociology syllabus. Part 1 deals with Paper 1 topics, Part 2 with Paper 2 topics. Each chapter includes a short paper by a distinguished sociologist or practitioner as well as **exercises** designed to enable you to test your skills of application, interpretation and evaluation. These exercises relate directly to material in the chapter as well as to additional sociological data. Each chapter also includes one or more coursework suggestions to assist students who opt for this sort of project work as part of their A level course.

At the end of each of the chapters in Part 1 of *Sociology Reviewed* there is also a **structured question** divided into five parts. These questions have been set by an AEB Chief Examiner and so they are very similar to those which students must answer in their examination. Each part of the question relates to material in the chapter. For example, data relevant for answering part (a) of the structured question is highlighted with an A in the margin and is tinted. You should look especially closely at the tinted areas and at the parts of the structured questions they relate to.

At the end of each chapter in Part 2 you will find an **examination essay question** which relates to issues raised by the text or by other data in the chapter. Again, these questions have been set by an AEB Chief Examiner and are very similar to the sort which will confront students in Paper 2 of the examination. In relation to this question, you are provided with *Notes for guidance* which should give you some useful hints on ways of structuring and presenting your answers which will best help you to demonstrate the skills identified in the **General Introduction**.

Remember, the aim of *Sociology Reviewed* is to extend and refine your knowledge of sociology **and** to prepare you better for the difficulties involved in showing your abilities in examinations and *via* coursework projects. Used properly, you should find the book enjoyable and useful.

Introduction to Paper 1 Topics

Paper 1 of the AEB syllabus is composed of five structured questions: a compulsory question on Theory and Methods, and questions on the Family, Education, Work and Leisure, and Stratification, of which candidates have to answer two. Each question has some stimulus material to introduce it and this may include passages of text, newspaper articles, or graphs, tables, pie charts, etc. Attached to these items is a series of questions with varying mark allocations, as indicated on the examination paper. Candidates are required to show the sociological skills identified by the syllabus, as detailed in the **General Introduction**. You may demonstrate these skills in the examination alone or through the coursework option. Considering how you might carry out the coursework suggestions in the text will help you to focus on these skills.

However, the techniques of answering structured questions are different from those employed in essay writing and so it is worth taking some time to think how to go about responding to this type of question. The first thing to notice is that you will need to be familiar with a variety of stimulus material, especially more numerical forms. This does not mean that you have to be familiar with complicated statistical formula, but that you should be practised in interpreting numerical and graphical data. The different types of data in the articles will help you in this area.

Secondly, as you will be given some sociological data to work on in Paper 1 questions, there is less emphasis on the skills of Knowledge and Understanding for that paper. This does not mean that you need no knowledge of sociological studies or arguments to answer questions on Paper 1. Rather you will need to use material given to you on the Paper and material from other studies you may know to demonstrate your skills of **Interpretation**, **Application** and **Evaluation**. Carrying out the exercises in this book will help you to gain some experience in these skills.

Thirdly, the structured question approach requires that each part of the question is targeted on a particular skill or combination of skills and therefore the wording of the questions will give you important clues as to which skill(s) is(are) being asked about. You should be able to work out what skill(s) is(are) required from a careful reading of the questions. Doing the structured questions in each chapter of this text will help you to prepare for this, so that you should be able to spot the form that questions are likely to take.

CHAPTER 1

Theory & Methods

Editors' introduction

Many sociology students seem to consider discussion of 'knowledge' or 'science' to be 'too difficult' or, simply, unimportant compared to the 'real' business of sociology: i.e. research on the patterns and nature of social relationships. In this extract, Hilary Burrage argues that, in fact, science is a central part of modern society and that its relationship to wider political and economic questions has been largely ignored or misunderstood. She challenges the 'taken for granted' approach to the problem of method in the natural sciences and, in the social sciences, she points to the dangers of 'gendering' of knowledge and of the growth of 'funding-led' research. Is it the case that whoever pays the piper calls the tune? Or, do sociological and other researchers have the sort of scientific independence we often assume them to have? In many ways, issues like these underpin the debates about what science is all about.

Here is a very readable and thorough account which should clear up many a confused mind.

The Sociology of Science and the Science of Society

HILARY BURRAGE

Science and Modern Society

It is generally agreed that ours is a technological society. To some extent it is also recognised that this technology is 'man-made' (I use this term explicitly in respect of its gender implications). It is, however, fairly rare to see acknowledged the extent to which science is linked to – and, indeed, through technology is a very major part of – the economies of the most powerful transnational corporations and nation-states the world has ever known.

To understand how science has achieved such a central place in modern societies we need to look at two things: first, the significance in modern times of *rationality*, and second the relationship of science to *technology*.

The roots of 'modern' society are to be found in the Renaissance and the Industrial Revolution. Over the last three or four centuries there have been successive stages in the development of legal and bureaucratic process and of production technology, which can be seen as correlating directly with an increase in rational thought and scientific endeavour.

It may be difficult for those of us born in a technological age to understand, but the link between science and technology is a crucial issue. Only comparatively recently has it been perceived that technology can be developed through natural scientific research, or that technology requires social organisation and bureaucratic processes which are similarly dependent upon, for instance, psychological and economic understanding. For thousands of years it could be said that science existed largely in isolation from technology: technology involved sophisticated techniques in terms of craft skills and social organisation, but these developed by trial and error, and were handed down through the generations by institutions and processes which had very little, if anything, to do with research or academic quests for 'organised knowledge'. (Consider, for instance, the building of Stonehenge, the great medieval cathedrals, or the sixteenth century armadas.) Indeed, during these earlier times 'pure' science, like mathematics, was an extension of philosophy, and was the subject of coffee-house debate rather than of widespread entrepreneurial interest.

One of the most important writers in this area has been Max Weber. Weber's work arose, at least in part, from his enduring interest in science and society, especially the organisation and effects of science in traditional and ancient civilisations. Thus we find that Weber wrote much, for instance, on early Chinese science, and a question which he particularly tried to address is why a sophisticated system of knowledge which existed before the birth of Christ has only in the last century or so become a very major influence on the shape of society as a whole.

The emergence of large-scale industrial societies in the last century or two is, so Weber suggested, due to a merging of economic surplus, capitalistic socio-legal processes, and religious beliefs (principally, the Protestant Ethic) which encouraged an emphasis on the material world and a faith in objective and rational criteria for behaviour. From the eighteenth century onwards we find industry more closely geared to scientific – and hence technical – research. The integral involvement of science in warfare, in business and in modern surveillance techniques and information technology has become taken-for-granted.

But whilst it may seem that science has 'solved' many 'problems' what we next need to ask is, who defines these 'problems' – and who is involved in the work to 'solve' them? Science may not be as 'neutral' and 'objective' as it at first appears. This will lead us, in turn, to examine the implications for socio-political analysis of science in the modern world.

The Politics of Science

Science and technology have in this century become linked in massive transnational and even inter-state enterprises, creating what C. Wright Mills (1959) called the 'military-industrial-bureaucratic complex'. State and corporate power is backed by huge financial resources to develop technical responses to 'problems' which these states and corporations have themselves identified. These responses almost inevitably enhance state and corporate power. In applying the rational methods of science to 'problems' defined by powerful

interests, scientific knowledge becomes 'Big Science' (Sklair 1973). Billions of dollars every year are invested in research and development, and the sums devoted to 'pure' (or more precisely, academic) research are small indeed, compared to the sums allocated to large-scale applied technology.

We can illustrate one way in which this change has a significance for socio-political analysis by looking at the case of medicine and healing. Until the eighteenth century, almost all healing and midwifery was performed by women. These crafts were handed from generation to generation by example and word of mouth, and a considerable knowledge existed both of drugs (herbs and other plants) and of practice (for example, use of the birthing stool). The position of healers and midwives was, nonetheless, precarious. Many thousands of women healers were executed whilst thousands more were otherwise persecuted as witches over the centuries; and one might suppose that this was at least in part because they had a knowledge not shared, and therefore feared, by the men who persecuted them.

But, as Ehrenreich and English (1979) have shown, with the development within the universities of research and science-based disciplines like anatomy and physiology, healing and midwifery soon became 'medicine' and 'obstetrics' respectively. From this time forward such crafts became professions, and thus, given the patriarchal setting of Victorian Britain, the prerogative of men – even to the extent that women were soon judged unfit and inappropriate to carry out those healing tasks which they had for centuries performed.

Once this (white) middle-class and male prerogative in medicine had been established, the economic link

---

Application exercise

What implications does the concept of 'Big Science', as described by Sklair, have for the idea that sociology should follow the model of the natural sciences?

Consider the following questions. If sociology were to become a 'Big Science':

- Who might set the agenda for sociological research?
- What might the role of the state or big business be in funding research?
- How might the status of sociologists be affected?
- Would sociology become more like a natural science?

with the mass manufacture of drugs and other medical materials became inevitable; as, subsequently, did the corporate interests which lie behind the research, development, production and sales promotion of the vast array of items which present-day practitioners of medicine and their patients expect and demand. Thus, the art of healing has become the science and technology of medicine – with all the widespread implications this has had for society in terms of the power and status of medical professionals, and in terms of the organisation of welfare and care

Science and technology as 'organised knowledge' have been geared to meeting the 'problems' of government, the military and large industrial concerns'.

What is Scientific Method?

In the era of 'Big Science', the prestige of the scientist is paramount. For many of us science remains the domain of people whom we suppose to be demonstrably very clever, and to whom we feel we must defer when they make pronouncements about what does and should happen, whether this be in the field of science or elsewhere.

In a very real sense, then, most people in modern societies, if pressed, would reckon that being 'scientific' (or 'rational' or 'logical') is the best way to approach problems and issues – even though every one of us also uses other ways of thinking, based on much older types of response such as personal feeling, religion, cultural mores, etc.

One reason that people may hold scientists and their particular approach to problem solving in high regard is that it is seen in some important sense to *work*. The products of technology, in particular, are proof that science quite literally delivers the goods. It is, we should note, one of the ideologically interesting features of science that its 'positive' effects are popularly perceived as intentional whilst its 'negative' effects are presented as accidental by-products which, with better efforts, can be avoided – even when these latter effects are very significant, for example in terms of hazards or expense. So what, then, is the popular notion of how science operates?

Most people hold in their minds a model of the operation of science as 'objective', that is as both *empirical* and *autonomous*. Science is believed to operate on the basis of 'factual' data alone, and independently of its social setting.

Historical, social and psychological analyses all tell us, however, that this simply cannot be so. We have noted already how science and technology, as 'organised knowledge', have been geared to meeting the 'problems' of government, the military and large industrial concerns. Indeed, we are frequently told by politicians, industrialists, and scientists themselves that this is how science 'should' be. It is clear, therefore, that modern science and technology is to a critically important degree integrated with economic direction and with socio-political definitions of 'problems'.

But what is the significance of this for the philosophy and methods of science? Scientists and technologists usually define what they are likely to discover *before* they even begin their research; indeed, sometimes they even set out to 'find' phenomena which they have already predicted on the basis of, for instance, mathematical calculations. Thus, research methods and findings tend to arise directly from scientists' prior expectations, and are as much the *result* of theory as they are of neutral methods or factual data.

For most of the time, then, scientists work within what Thomas Kuhn (1962) and others call *paradigms* – sets of theory, method, data and instrumentation – which predispose them to address given 'problems' in particular ways. It is only very rarely that really interesting and surprising 'discoveries' are made, quite often by people in some way on the margins of their discipline. It is from these unexpected findings that real shifts in theoretical and methodological understanding tend to arise.

It could be, however, that such 'paradigm breaking' or, in Kuhn's phrase, 'revolutionary' occasions – which are often in any case difficult to identify at the time – become less likely in the present-day context of 'Big Science'. Theories and methods are highly directed, and complex scientific programmes now explore pre-determined technical 'problems' set by corporate and state powers.

Research in the Social Sciences

The discussion so far has taken 'science' as equivalent to the 'natural' sciences: i. e., the physical and life sciences. But what about social science? It will already have become apparent that natural science is *inevitably* ideological. But ideology, of course, has a part in everything which people do, whether or not it is acknowledged, and whether or not this ideology is consistent and coherent. If individuals and groups of people did not have ideas about what they 'ought' to do, and if decisions were not made (also by individuals and groups) to allocate resources to these activities, nothing of any significance would ever happen. To say that science is ideological in this sense, then, is simply to acknowledge social reality. Scientific and technological activities, like everything else, are undertaken by individuals with particular motives and understandings of what they are doing; and these

individuals, in turn, are increasingly likely to work as members of larger, co-ordinated groups.

There is, however, another sense also in which science is ideological. Science, as we have seen, rests fundamentally on a particular set of assumptions about what is appropriate and admissible in terms of evidence and procedure. The natural sciences allow only consideration of demonstrable evidence – i.e., 'hard', and usually quantifiable, data. The ideology of natural science is therefore *empiricist*: natural science is a system of beliefs and knowledge which encompasses only data derived from the natural or material world. It is, at base, a set of theories about natural phenomena arising from what we can observe and test. Similarly, technology is the extension of knowledge about the natural or material world to the development of artifacts, or of things (and processes) created from our understanding of material substances.

Once we perceive science and technology in this light we can see that it is a very precise and special tool in the efforts of humankind to explore and control their world. But it can address only one particular aspect of this world, the *material* world. When natural scientists offer their views on areas of human experience not directly related to the material world, they can do so only on the same basis as other

---

Coursework suggestion 1

Much natural science is conducted in laboratories through the use of the experimental method. You could investigate how the laboratory experiment operates in your own school or college. You would need to build up from reading the sociological literature an 'ideal type' of the laboratory experiment (that is, how such experiments are supposed to be conducted) and then observe how far experiments in the laboratories of your institution conform to this ideal type. There are various issues which you will need to consider:

- Where will you obtain the information to build up an ideal type? When will you know that you have enough information? How complex should you make your ideal type if you are going to compare the real events with it?

- How will you obtain permission to observe laboratory experiments in your institution? How many lessons will you have to observe to obtain a reasonable amount of data?

- You will need to produce an observation schedule, which pays close attention to the students' conduct of and results in the experiments. You will need to examine how the teacher and technician set up the laboratory experiment before the students arrive.

- You will also need a measure of how carefully the students follow the teacher's instructions in carrying out the experiment. How will you know if the students all get the same results?

- How might the concepts of 'logic-in-use' and 'reconstructed logics' help you in carrying out this research?

interested citizens and observers. The views of natural scientists, however eminent, on the 'need' for Star Wars and genetic engineering, for example, are *value choices* which do not follow from their scientific research.

Like natural science, social science is based on observation, but with one very important proviso. For all social scientists, *interpretation* is important at each and every stage of research. Knowledge in the social sciences is not founded simply on 'hard' quantifiable observations. Interpretation is, in one sense, a feature of natural scientific research in exactly the same way as for social scientists. The natural scientist, as much as the social scientist, makes personal choices and judgements at all stages, from the selection of the research 'problem', through decisions to be made about appropriate data, methods, instrumentation, hypotheses, etc., to the final construction and evaluation of explanations and theories to account for the findings of the research.

But, interpretation in the social sciences is of a much wider significance than that in the natural sciences. The social sciences, broadly speaking, are about the behaviour of conscious beings, whilst the natural sciences are concerned with inanimate, or at least non-conscious, 'behaviour'. The social scientist has both the advantage and disadvantage of insight, based on his or her own conscious experience as a social actor – i.e., as a person, as one unit in a network of social interactions.

The advantage of this insight is, as writers such as Weber have recognised, that the researcher often has 'inside information' about what he or she is researching, in a way which is simply not available to those researching the inanimate and non-conscious world; but the disadvantage is that this very insight may be another or additional source of confusion, selective vision or even error on the part of the researcher. These issues cannot be explored fully here, but are central to Weber's notions of *verstehen* (understanding) and value-freedom (Weber 1949).

Conclusion: The Prospects for Science

My examination of natural science research has shown that *all* areas of research are shaped by personal judgements and socio-economic influences. Natural scientific knowledge appears to 'work', to produce the goods, and so is widely regarded as growing in scope and adequacy over time. Social researchers, also, discover new and more sophisticated ways of measuring and developing conceptual links to explain social phenomena, but social science appears to 'work' less well in the sense of providing 'solutions' to perceived social problems. Does this mean that social

scientific knowledge does not 'grow' or 'improve' in the same way as knowledge in natural science? My discussion of the ideological basis of 'Big Science' suggests not. 'Problem solving' is only one criterion of success. For instance, quite often sociological work – and, indeed, some very significant natural scientific work – progresses in terms of theoretical ideas outside, or at most alongside, work 'in the field'. Even here, however, the crucial feature of potentially valid 'science' is that it is open and available in its totality for examination by others.

But whilst 'openness' is the essence of all academic research, it is inhibited by the structure of 'Big Science'. Much natural science research has for some decades involved extremely expensive research teams, each of which addresses only one small aspect of the research area in question, but it is built up around a small number of carefully identified research centres and universities, funded by national government and similar bodies. Because of this, the scope for independent critical analysis of research is perhaps diminishing. Political, economic and professional career interests limit the possibility of critical debate. This is why many people have doubts about secret or quasi-secret military research, or other research which is patented or unavailable for, say, commercial reasons.

So, too, to a lesser extent, with some social scientific research. It is now becoming the practice to have national 'teams' or research workers who liaise through a small number of funding bodies (which are often dependent on governmental support), and who work on issues often identified by these same bodies. As this happens, the number of people with an 'overview of the field' may diminish, and more and more researchers will work on areas which have already been defined in terms of the requirements and beliefs of the government, commercial or military interests which provide the funds.

Because of this *funding-led* definition of issues worthy of research, it is difficult to argue that all interpretations and aspects of such issues are equally open to investigation; and this difficulty is, of course, compounded for both natural and social scientists when, as sometimes now happens, it is also a requirement even of academic and university-based research (as well as of commercial research) that research reports and papers be submitted for approval by funding bodies *before* they are published openly.

Be this as it may, we should not doubt that the clear statement and presentation of perceptions, beliefs, theories, data and so forth is of value. Through careful thought and open debate we *do* come to new discoveries; and through definition and redefinition of whatever we study we are able to extend knowledge and our understanding of how to apply it. What we need to be clear about, in the final analysis, is *why* we want to know about the social (or natural) world, and *how* our knowledge is likely to be applied. At this basic level what are most important are the purposes to which we wish to have our research findings put, and our honesty in reporting these findings. There is no such thing in research as complete value-freedom, but full and honest debate can perhaps exist; and it is in respect of the promotion of such debate that natural and social science researchers (in academic work at least) may have an interest very much in common.

References and Further Reading

Ehrenreich, B. and English, D. (1979) *For Her Own Good*, Pluto.

Kuhn, T. S. (1962) *The Structure of Scientific Revolutions*, University of Chicago Press.

Mills, C. W. (1959) *The Power Elite*, Oxford University Press.

Sklair, L. (1973) *Organized Knowledge*, MacGibbon and Kee.

Weber, M. (1949) *The Methodology of the Social Sciences*, Free Press.

Structure and Action in Modern Social Theory

IAN CRAIB

Editors' introduction

Some of the central practical and philosophical problems facing sociologists involve the examination of a number of key tensions in human experience. How far, for example, are we to understand the relationship between the individual and society? Do human beings freely 'choose' to act in certain ways, or are those 'choices' constrained by external influences? Do people 'make' society or does society shape its members? Or are these oppositions simply examples of an outmoded way of thinking about such relationships, an approach which has been successfully overtaken by new ways of theorising about the social? Ian Craib, a little reluctantly, takes on that old chestnut, the structure and action debate. But he does it in a way which is likely to be attractive to the most apprehensive theoretician. And, in the end, well maybe, there just isn't a sociological problem here after all; at least not one which is resolvable. Now isn't that a comforting thought?

My heart sinks when I hear the words 'structure and action', these days. They bring out the same rather distasteful feeling that comes with the thought of doing the shopping. Just as I would rather do anything else than set off for Sainsbury's, but need to eat, so I would be happy to write about anything other than structure and action, but, since I am a sociologist, I need to think about it.

All sociologists have to think about structure and action. If we are trying to understand the nature of societies and of how people live in societies, then we have to think about something called 'social structure', and something called 'action'. The relationship between the two has been *the* problem for sociological theory. I suspect that some of the difficulties that people get themselves into around this distinction stem from the fact that we tend to assume that because there's a problem, there's a solution. It doesn't follow: as the writer Fay Weldon points out, life is not an arithmetic test set by God.

As a student, I seem to remember meeting this issue in my first theory course. It was presented as a way of distinguishing between different theoretical approaches. It was simply descriptive, offered to us as a way of organising the various theoretical approaches in our own heads. I rather wish it had stayed like that. Social action had to do with what motivates, governs, and directs people's actions, with ideas, values, norms, goals, rationality. From this point of view, what we call 'society' is the result of people acting together. We learnt about Max Weber and the idea that rational social action was what sociology should really be concerned with. This way, we could look at capitalism as the result of a particular way of living, a set of values that were enshrined in Protestantism. We could see Talcott Parsons, who was then well-known and central to sociology as a whole, as a theorist of social action. We knew that because the large and forbidding text that most of us managed not to open was called *The Structure of Social Action*. Symbolic interactionism, rather less important in those days, was another form of 'action theory', dealing in intriguing detail with the way people see the world and relate to each other.

Over the years, theories of social action have grown more complex, usually through sociologists borrowing from philosophy. We can add to the above list something called 'ethnomethodology' and 'phenomenological sociology' which have drawn from linguistic philosophy and phenomenology; and 'discourse theory' and 'post-structuralism'. My own view is that by and large when sociologists borrow from philosophers, the result is a complicated language and a theory which is extremely difficult to understand but often, in practice, very simple. I'm not convinced that these borrowings have led to any major advance in our understanding.

Theories of social structure, on the other hand, were less about values and action than about something else. I'm not sure that I properly understood what a social structure might be. Durkheim talked of 'social facts', something we might loosely call 'society', existing independently of individuals and imposing itself upon them. The meaning was more clear in Marx's case: there was a class structure, and conflict between social classes was built into the economic organisation of capitalism. Classes were forced into conflict with each other not because of different beliefs or values, but through the dynamics of the capitalist system. Indeed, beliefs and values were 'ideologies' produced by that very system.

Views of Action and Structure

Perhaps the simplest way to think of a 'social structure' is as a network of social relationships which is comparatively lasting and does not necessarily change with the particular individuals who make up those relations. In that sense a structure exists over and above people and is imposed on them. We can think about it in terms of role-structures. A school, for example, has the same structure of roles – headmaster/mistress, assistant heads, heads of departments, teachers, students of different ages in different groups, etc. – from year to year some, most or all of the individuals occupying these roles change. We can have larger and more vague ideas of structure – we might just talk about 'society', or the 'organisation' or 'institution'. Or we find, particularly in Marxist theory, the idea of an 'underlying' structure – less a matter of identifiable roles with identifiable occupants than a set of relations that often we don't know about in our everyday lives. When a Marxist talks about a mode of production, or relations of production, he or she is not talking about things that can be pointed to or that we experience in a direct way, yet he or she is saying that these things really exist and affect what happens in the world.

All these views of structure imply that structure *determines*, to some extent, what we think, feel and do. We learn roles through learning what other people expect us to do and acting accordingly – we fit into our place in the structure; or the economic dynamics of capitalism – the tendency of the rate of profit to fall, market competition, the expansionary dynamic of capitalist development – push us into courses of action over which we might have little or no control.

I think distinguishing between action and structure is still a useful way of teaching and learning about the range of theories developed and used by sociologists. It offers a map to guide us through the jungle. It would be nice if we could leave it at that. Unfortunately it does not change the jungle into a landscaped garden and it seems that on the whole, that is what sociologists would prefer to do for two reasons, one I think of as good and the other bad.

The good reason is that when we read any theorist properly, it is clear that if the theory is worthwhile, it goes beyond a simple concern with action or structure. The best are concerned with action and structure. Thus even in his most clearly Weberian work, *The Protestant Ethic*, Weber talks about capitalism becoming an 'iron cage', a system in which people are caught, having to behave in certain ways. In his work on class, status and party, he is clearly talking about a form of social structure as well as social action. Marx had much to say, particularly in his early work, about the goals and values of human beings living together, and Marxist politics is, at its best, suffused with ideas of freedom and choice. Parsons moved directly from an analysis of social action to social structure: he sees structure as a sort of 'solidified', routinised and organised system of action. In fact, Parsons' functionalism is often presented as a structural theory – 'structural functionalism' – a fact which confused me as a student. Even more confusing is the fact that symbolic interactionists, who are often taught as opposing Parsons, have a view of social structure as a role structure which is quite compatible with Parsons' work.

So, any theory worth its salt seems to have something to say about both action and structure. It must somehow deal with both. In fact, this is common sense: we can't think about societies without thinking about the people who live in them; and we can't think about people without thinking about the sort of societies in which they live. The problem is that life gets very difficult for the sociologist. This brings me to the second, bad, reason why sociologists would prefer a landscaped garden.

It is in fact a very human reason. There is something dissatisfying about having to deal with different bits and pieces, having to work with different theories to do the same job. Most sociologists would like to think of themselves as participating in a coherent discipline, and some would like to think of themselves as scientists. Beyond this, particularly during the 1960s and early '70s, when sociology was establishing itself in British universities, there was a sort of imperialist push: sociology can do things better than other disciplines – it can embrace economics, history, psychology, politics and everything else in the human sciences. Yet it could not do this if it were not itself a unified whole.

Attempts at Synthesis

Thus, there is a constant temptation to try to produce a coherent, unified theory which deals with structure and action, and quite possibly everything else with which sociology might be concerned. I want to look briefly at two such attempts over recent years. The first I found particularly stimulating at the time I was coming up to taking my finals in 1970. It was an argument in a book called *The Social Construction of Reality*, by Peter Berger and Thomas Luckmann. The simplest way of describing it is as an attempt to combine Durkheim's argument that social facts have an existence independent of individuals, and Weber's argument that social organisation is a product of individual's social action. Their argument was that both positions are true: people create societies, social

---

Coursework suggestion 2

You could investigate the disparity between the statistical reality of the distribution of household types and how people perceive the reality. You will need to build up a statistical picture of the distribution of family compositions, and for this you should refer to the publication, *Social Trends*, or some other statistical source.

You should then devise a questionnaire to investigate people's perceptions of family household distribution and compare the results with the official statistics. You must also decide on the type of questionnaire which will produce the most appropriate data.

In order to complete the task successfully, you will need to have a very focused research hypothesis, which sets out what you might reasonably expect to find at the end of your coursework. There is no single hypothesis which would be sufficient here. Instead you should consider a number of possible relationships between reality and people's perceptions of reality.

You must also be careful to place this hypothesis within an appropriate theoretical context, perhaps linking the research to the idea that there is a stereotypical view of the family which predominates in society. You will also need some references to published work to support your approach to the issue.

At the conclusion of the coursework, you will need to decide whether the correlation between reality and perception is enough to undermine or support your original hypothesis. You should include an evaluation of your methodology and of whether you could have investigated this issue more adequately in another way.

structures, through their actions and relations. Once created, these structures are experienced by the individuals who make them up as something solid, something which exists independently of the individual and which we have to conform to. Social life is a two-way process: people make societies, societies make people.

We can see this in the example of the family. We can look at a family in two ways. On the one hand it is something which we create: each family member is engaged in a process of interaction and negotiation with the others to find ways of living which can enable us to be as secure as we want to be, as independent as we want to be, and generally to make life bearable and sometimes happy. The compromises we make, the sort of life we create for ourselves, will depend in part on the unique, individual qualities of each family member. On the other hand, from time to time we experience this way of life we have created as a burden: we have to do things for our parents' sake, for our husband or wife or children, or our brothers and sisters, that we don't really want to do: 'the family' pushes us into behaving in a certain way. Usually without realising it, we also develop ways of talking and thinking and sometimes even walking that we learn from our family. As well as producing it, we become its product. There are also quite clear limits on the sort of family we can create: I cannot marry three women, however much I might want to; I cannot marry my sister, however much I might want to. I cannot, as I might do in some societies, take responsibility for my sister's children. Society strictly controls the sort of family I might create. It imposes a family structure on me

There is a more recent approach in the work of Anthony Giddens. It involves a more complex set of ideas than Berger and Luckmann, and here I am presenting a rather oversimplified version. Giddens talks about '*structuration*' and '*the duality of structures*'. The idea seems to be that we cannot isolate structure and action from each other. Or rather, perhaps we can separate them, but only in theory. In social life itself, they are bound together as indistinguishably as hydrogen and oxygen are bound together in water. The ideas of structuration and the duality of structures is an attempt to understand social life as a process, in which 'structure' has a dual nature. On the one hand it is a result of action: we create structures or we maintain existing structures, or we transform them in some way – perhaps we do all of these things in different degrees at the same time. On the other hand, structure is what enables us to act at all. If there were no structure we would be unable to do anything.

Let us return to the example of the family: if there

were no family structure in our society then we would not be able to create families. The existence of a well-established family structure, endorsed and protected by law, opens up the possibility for each of us of getting together with somebody else and, creating a family. When we do this, we are maintaining that already established family structure, as well as creating a new and unique family, and in the way in which we create a new family we might be contributing to some long-term change in family structure. Perhaps we will only have two children and contribute to a long-term change in family size; or perhaps my wife and I will divorce and both or one of us remarry, contributing to another long-term change – the growth of step-families or single-parent families.

Remaining Problems

Both of these approaches are attractive. Both seem to take us a step closer to the well-landscaped garden in which it would be comfortable and pleasant to work. However, perhaps just as even the best-tended garden is only a few steps away from the jungle, reality is constantly proving more complex and difficult than these theories. The real difficulty with both approaches is that there are important ways in which we can see, in the real world, that social structures and human action are not related to each other in any such direct and easy way. We can act in a particular way to change a social structure and find our actions having consequences which are perhaps the direct opposite of what we intended. This need not be through any fault or misjudgement of our own; social structure can have its own laws of development which change the meaning of our actions in a way we can't understand. I might not marry the person I live with because I do not believe in the conventional family form; however, what I produce is a very conventional family; it simply lacks legal endorsement. In fact such common-law relationships are becoming subject to the same legal rights and restraints as formal marriages. In an act asserting my freedom, I might marry for love somebody whom my family rejects. I might still find myself in a family very similar to that of my parents.

This complexity is shown for me quite dramatically in Paul Willis's study *Learning to Labour*. The 'lads'

The simple view.

Action theorists	Structure theorists
Weber	Marx and the Marxists
Symbolic interactions and ethnomethodologists	Durkheim
Parsons when he's writing about social action	Parsons when he's writing about social systems

A more complicated version.

Action creates structure

Weber
Symbolic interactions and ethnomethodologists, phenomenologists
Parsons when he's writing about social action

Structure determines action

Marx and the Marxists
Durkheim
Parsons when he's writing about social systems

Closer to the truth, but still too easy.

Action creates structure and structure determines action

Weber, Durkheim, Marx and the Marxists, symbolic interactionists, phenomenologists, Parsons, Berger and Luckmann, Giddens

with whom he spends most of his time are rebels against a social system in which they are clearly disadvantaged. It is not a case of the system imposing itself on them. However, their very rebellion excludes them from what could change their lives, condemning them to further disadvantage, so it is not a case of action changing structure. At the same time, since they are condemned to something like the lives of their parents, social structure is imposing itself on them; and, since the school system against which they rebel would change their lives, they are in one sense breaking free of structural determination. Clearly something very complex and difficult is going on and Willis has to deploy some very complicated theory to

try to understand it all. Neither Berger and Luckmann nor Giddens can provide him with the tools for the job.

In the end, I think that these apparent solutions are incomplete: they both sound very nice, and they make sense. What they describe actually happens. However, something more complex and contradictory is going on in the world, and neither solution can really make sense of it. It is in fact the complex and contradictory nature of the social world that pushed the founding thinkers of sociology into developing action- and structure-oriented theories in the first place. These days, I tend to think of the action/structure distinction not as presenting a problem to be solved but simply as describing reality, which is perhaps unfortunate for those sociologists who might want a quiet and coherent life.

This complexity results from the fact that the social world contains different types of things. There are the enduring sets of human relations we call structures; and there are people, and the way they work, think and feel and act. Perhaps there are other things as well, but these are enough to be going on with. We need different types of theory to deal with each, since each has its own rules or laws and ways of working, and we cannot understand one without understanding the other. Consequently we are condemned to use different theories which are always cutting across each other in different ways. Action and structure and the difficulties of their relation to each other will be with us all the time.

References and Further Reading

On the founders of Sociology, Anthony Giddens' *Capitalism and Modern Social Theory* (Cambridge, 1971) is a good introduction. Most of the modern approaches (except rational-choice Marxism),are discussed in my own *Modern Social Theory* (Wheatsheaf, 1984). The two solutions I discuss can be found in P. Berger and T. Luckmann's *The Social Construction of Reality* (Allen Lane, 1967) and Anthony Giddens' *New Rules of Sociological Method* (Hutchinson, 1976). Paul Willis' *Learning to Labour* (Gower, 1976) is well worth reading.

My conclusion is based on a comparatively new development in the philosophy of social science, known as realism. The very brave might try looking at Roy Bhaskar, *The Possibility of Naturalism* (Harvester, 1979) – especially Chapters 2 and 3.

Researching Race And Racism

TONY COLE

Editors' introduction

In some textbooks, research is presented as a series of simple steps. In reality it is seldom like that! Actually going out and doing some original sociological research in the field can be a complicated and messy business. Research issues may become even more problematic if the research involves looking at members of minority or marginalised communities.

In this extract, Tony Cole looks at some of the ethical, moral and methodological issues raised by doing research on members of Britain's black communities. He examines documentary research methods as well as those involving survey, interview and experimental techniques.

Perhaps you can consider some of the issues and research problems which might be raised by doing ethnographic research among British people of Afro-Caribbean or Asian origin. If you are black, you might like to conduct similar research in predominantly white communities. Are the problems and research issues the same?

But What is Race? What is Being Researched?

Conceptual clarity and definition of subject matter are crucial to all research and there is an argument that the term 'race' should not be used at all by sociologists or, if used, should always be placed in inverted commas. The explanation for this is that the term 'race' is *associated with* ideas of biological groupings supported by scientific evidence. Biologists today question the validity or value of such theories as means of understanding the human species.

Likewise, sociologists argue that race does not have an objective reality outside people's definition of it; it is a social construct. To say race is a socially constructed phenomenon is not, of course, to say that skin colour, for example, only exists because racists say it does. Rather, in the way that sociologists distinguish between sex (physical) and gender (cultural), it is clear that skin colour is a physical fact but the meaning of this fact is *socially constructed* and socially relative. Being black in South Africa means something different from being black in Britain, though the significance of official and unofficial racism in Britain should not be underestimated.

Notwithstanding these important qualifications, the discussion below focuses on Britain's black population, including how they are seen or treated by whites. By 'black' I mean people of Afro-Caribbean descent and those of Asian origin, regardless of place of birth. These groups experience far more discrimination based on race than other groups and there are also more studies about black populations to draw on for reference.

Numbers, News and Content Analysis

Debates about the size of this group (black Britons) or its pace of change can easily polarise into one in which racists exaggerate the numbers involved and their opponents argue that the numbers are much smaller; this falls into the numbers trap of implying that the smaller the size of Britain's black population, the better it is. Clearly, this kind of argument is framed in terms of an agenda set by racist assumptions.

The key point is, in fact, why such over-estimates are so common. Part of the answer may lie with the mass media. Hartmann and Husband (1972) argue that, in their coverage of race, the media are affected by:

	Total	Whites	West Indians	Asians	Other non-whites
If you saw youths smashing up a bus shelter would you be					
Prepared to tell police what you had seen?	83	83	68	81	76
Prepared to help identify the culprits?	77	78	51	73	67
Prepared to give evidence in court?	71	73	45	66	57
If you saw youths knock a man down and take his wallet would you be					
Prepared to tell police what you had seen?	96	97	89	92	85
Prepared to help identify the culprits?	91	92	75	82	81
Prepared to give evidence in court?	84	85	62	75	68
If you had seen a traffic accident in which someone was badly hurt would you be					
Prepared to tell police what you had seen?	97	97	96	94	95
Prepared to give evidence in court?	91	91	86	87	84
Base: all informants					
(unweighted)	2,420	1,252	511	541	116
(weighted)	13,944	12,428	450	607	459

Source: Police and People in London, Policy Studies Institute, London, 1983.

Willingness to help the police, by ethnic group (%). What problems of validity might you have in collecting data like this?

The news frequently conveys black people as a problem.

(i) an historical legacy leaving Britain with a cultural predisposition to negative perceptions and evaluations of black people

(ii) a set of news values shaping the way the press selects and presents the news. These news values incorporate a frequent reliance on pre-existing stereotypes and an emphasis on the themes of conflict and deviance.

These stories about black people will generally be in terms of some kind of problem, especially for the native white population. Ideas of threat may be implied by emotive language as in the use of words like 'invasion' or 'flood' to describe immigration.

Interestingly, in response to the crisis in China and the suggestion that residents of the British colony of Hong Kong be given the right to come into Britain instead of remaining for the colony's transfer to China in 1997, the British Foreign Secretary said this was not possible, noting that it 'would more than double the ethnic minority population of the United Kingdom' (Sir Geoffrey Howe, quoted in *The Guardian* 7th June 1989). This suggests it is ethnicity, as much as numbers, that is seen as the problem – who they are, not simply how many. Is this an example of racism?

Returning to Hartmann and Husband's research, to illustrate their argument about the media's problematising of black people and, especially the numbers of them, they cite the selective coverage of two stories about race from 1970:

(i) March 1970. Figures from the Registrar General indicated that the birth rate was higher among some immigrant families. Seven out of eight daily papers covered this story, five of them on their front page.

(ii) May 1970. Figures from the Home Secretary showed a low and declining rate of immigration. This was covered by four of the eight papers, only one of them on the front page.

Overall, the first story received five times as much coverage in terms of column inches as the second.

There is another linguistic note to make here, concerning the use of the word 'immigrant'. Though the technical meaning of this word is a person who moves into an area or region, not necessarily from another country, in Britain the everyday usage of the word is often taken to mean only black immigrants from overseas, not white immigrants from countries like Italy or Australia. Indeed, there are times when it is used as a general description of black people, wherever they were born. Consider, for example, if you overheard a snatch of conversation and the word

'immigrants' was used – what image would be conveyed, who would you assume was being referred to? If the answer is 'black people' what does it suggest about attitudes, especially taken-for-granted ones, about black people in Britain?

The research method used by Hartmann and Husband above, that is quantifying and categorising stories or items in the media, is called *content analysis*. Despite criticisms of their overall study (Barrat 1986, pp. 48–50), there is clearly value in looking at the stereotypical portrayal of black people in the media, including in drama and comedy, as well as at their relative absence/invisibility from a range of roles and situations. This method readily lends itself to project-type research.

Documents and their Analysis

For a social researcher in modern, bureaucratised societies, there is often a host of data – statistical and otherwise – in documents and reports produced by governments or other official bodies. Similarly, there may be 'alternative' sources of information from pressure groups or charities who may have different or competing priorities in the collection of data. When sociologists use those sources of data they are generally described as secondary sources because they are not collected primarily for the sociological task in question or by that particular sociologist.

However, *documents* can be used not just for the information they contain and were published for but also – in the manner of content analysis above – to discover their recurrent themes or issues. This use of documents, exploring their latent rather than their manifest content is closer to primary research because it is not the published data itself that is central but the underlying assumptions made in the collection and presentation of that data.

An example of this approach is Solomos's (1988) analysis of official documents on race relations, charting the changing assumptions that have informed and shaped state policies in relation to young black people. In particular, he notes that from the 1960s onwards official thinking about black youth contained two dominant images. The first is the idea that 'second generation' black youth might be a social time-bomb, waiting to explode in revolt against British society. The second, which was more influential in shaping policy, was the idea that black youths were socially deprived both in terms of their background circumstances and their lack of integration into white society, This latter image itself embodies assumptions of pathology about black culture and family life and that integration into British society meant the simple assimilation of British values, a highly problematic idea. The late 1960s brought a change of stance here with some official acceptance that integration could be on the basis of cultural diversity or pluralism. This gave rise to ideas of multi-culturalism.

Solomos discussed these assumptions and the policies they gave rise to in their wider context, arguing for example, for signs of increasing racism in the emergence of new immigration and nationality laws. Though the findings of his document analysis were briefly referred to as illustration of his method, a wider account of Solomos's discussion of these policies is beyond the scope of this article. It is worth noting, however, that content analysis is often used *in conjunction* with information from other sources as a way of making sense of the data produced.

Samples, Surveys and Interviews

The small size of the British black population referred to earlier has significant implications for those wishing to do sample survey research. For example, a representative sample of the British population containing 1000 people would only contain 40–50 black people. Once broken down into Asian and Afro-Caribbean, young and old, male and female and so on, the sample sizes become so small as to be statistically meaningless.

The PSI survey *Black and White Britain* (Brown 1985) overcomes these problems, by carrying out 5000 interviews with black people, as well as 2000 interviews with white people for comparative purposes. Such a sample size is very expensive to achieve and use and it raises the question of funding sources – in this case a mixture of government departments, charitable trusts and the late Greater London Council. Another issue is how the sample is to be made up. There is no list of black people in Britain to act as a sampling frame. Indeed, such a list would be incompatible with the protection of civil liberties. Knocking on doors to construct a list might work in high density black areas but a quarter of the black population lives in low density areas and here it *might* require 24,000 knocks to produce 100 black faces. A different method was used by Brown (1985, pp. 10–11).

Social surveys are aimed at discovering various kinds of data – factual, 'knowledge' and opinion – and it is the latter which raise particular problems (Moser 1968, pp. 220–22), especially on a highly sensitive topic like race. For example, people may be guarded about their views, or have contradictory attitudes involving elements of prejudice and tolerance (not a good word perhaps, because it implies something negative to be tolerated). The possibility of question-wording or interviewer-identity affecting respondents' answers also has to be considered (McNeill 1985, pp. 20–25, 35–36).

Reducing Interview Bias

The strategy employed by Miles and Phizaklea to reduce the impact of the interview schedule on the interviewees in their research on attitudes among white working-class people raised in Willesden, was to ask no direct questions about the topic of race at all. If, in general questions about political beliefs or the local area, respondents introduced unsolicited comments about race these clearly did not come because the researcher put the topic on the agenda. They note, however, that this is likely to underestimate racist beliefs in the area because some with racist views would not have volunteered them. Nonetheless 75% made negative references about black people, very often in terms of categorisations into 'us' and 'them' conflicts over housing and employment.

The question of interviewer identity was raised by the PSI researchers and by Rex and Tomlinson (1979) in their study of Handsworth. The PSI opted for ethnic matching of black respondents and interviewers. Rex and Tomlinson noted that studies in the USA indicated that ethnic matching increases the validity of the research findings. They did not think this would necessarily apply in Britain and they generally used white interviewers. However, one third of their Asian sample were ethnically matched, with no apparent impact on response rate or type.

Sometimes there are sceptical or hostile reactions to surveys of the ethnic minority population or to surveys about race issues. In Rex and Moore's 1967 study of Sparkbrook they found that some Pakistanis were suspicious of their interviewers, believing them to be from the police or the housing authorities. Given the racism in Birmingham Council's housing policies as indicated by Rex and Moore, such scepticism seems quite rational.

Carrying out race-related interviews does not only have implications for the impact the interviewer may have on the interviewee. There are times when it may make the detachment required in the interviewer role harder to sustain, as when Moore recounts an interview in a pub where he had to listen to a drunken white resident, dribbling into his beer, complaining about the blacks lowering the tone of the area. Alternatively, there are times when it calls for special strategies by researchers, such as interviewing in pairs, an approach adopted in the Sparkbrook study after an interview by one of the research team with a council official who made racially abusive comments. These remarks could not be cited or published because there was no corroboration

A more recent example of the sensitivity of race in

The question of interviewer-identity in race-related interviews has been raised by several researchers and studies.

survey research is the issue of whether to include an ethnic identity question in the 1991 census. There was a proposal for one in 1981 but a pilot survey in Haringey had a very high refusal rate to this question and it was dropped. The rationale for the question supported by the Commission for Racial Equality, is to assist the monitoring of racial disadvantage in Britain. However, the reluctance of many people to answer this question may indicate that their experience or perception of government agencies on race issues is a negative one.

Discrimination and Experiments

The reference to seeking to discover the extent of racial disadvantage in Britain conveniently leads on to a brief discussion of the use of experiments for this purpose (Smith 1977). The researchers used actors of four different ethnic backgrounds – Asian, West Indian, white European, white English – and 'gave' them similar and relevant experience and qualifications for a range of jobs they all applied for. Black candidates were found to receive discrimination in 46% of unskilled job applications and 20% of skilled

Coursework suggestion 3

You could carry out a replication of the pilot survey in Haringey by using a 'piggy-back' method. For this you will need to secure the agreement of another sociology student who is already doing a questionnaire survey, which includes information on the names of respondents and further access to them. For the first third of the respondents you could include an open-ended question on ethnicity. For the second third, you could include a 'closed' question on ethnicity, and for the final, no question at all. You could then analyse the refusal rates of each third to establish any differences.

If there are any differences, you will need to follow up the questionnaire with interviews of the 'refusers' to establish whether there is an objection to answering questions about ethnicity, or whether there is some other reason for refusal.

In reporting your results, you should take care to refer to the ethical issues surrounding this type of approach and whether you think it is justifiable in the light of your conclusions.

jobs. The reason why the experiment (i.e. tight control of all variables except the one being tested – race) was possible was because the experimental subjects (employers) did not know they were the subjects of an experiment.

Conclusion – Methodological Diversity?

Though there are many other issues that could have been explored (more on official statistics, e.g. of race/crime or racial attacks, participant observation), a number of research issues have been aired. One general comment needs to be made in concluding the discussion of the above studies. This is, that many researchers in their studies use a range of particular research methods. The Rex and Moore study, for example, used both structured and unstructured interviews, analysis of back copies of the local press, community involvement and participant observations.

It has been argued, in fact, that it is not the norm for there to be a pure match between theoretical position (say, positivism) and research methodology (say, structured interviews) or as singular a use of method in one study as the textbooks suggest (Dale and Clark 1988). Some of the studies cited here would seem to support this.

References and Further Reading

Barrat, D. (1986) *Media Sociology*, Tavistock.
Brown, C. (1985) *Black and White Britain*
Dale, A. and Clarke, C. (1988) 'Theory, Method and Practice' *Social Science Teacher*, Vol. 1 No. 3
Hartmann, P. and Husband, C. (1972) 'The Mass Media and Racial Conflict', Race, Vol. 12 (1970–71), reprinted in McQuail, D. (ed) *Sociology of Mass Communications*, Penguin.
Husband, C. (ed) (1982) *Race in Britain*, Hutchinson.
McNeill, P. (1985) *Research Methods*, Tavistock.
Miles, R. and Phizaklea, A. (1979) 'Working-class Racist Beliefs in the Inner City' in *Racism and Political Action in Britain*, RKP.
Moser, C. (1968) *Survey Methods in Social Investigation*, HEB.
Rex, J. and Moore, R. (1967) *Race, Community and Conflict – A Study of Sparkbrook*, Oxford University Press.
Rex, J. and Tomlinson, S. (1979) *Colonial Immigrants in a British City*, RKP.
Smith, D. (1977) *Racial Discrimination in England*, Penguin.
Solomos, J. (1988) 'Institutional Racism: Policies of Marginalisation in Education and Training' in Cohen, P. and Bains, H. (eds) *Multi-racist Britain*, Macmillan.

Structured question (25 marks)

a) In extract A what is meant by the phrase 'science . . . [is] . . . empirical'?   (1 mark)

b) Give two examples, other than those identified in extract B, of social structures as defined by Ian Craib.   (2 marks)

c) With reference to extract C, why is it important that the survey research includes a representative sample?   (4 marks)

d) Referring to extract A and other information, to what extent do sociologists agree that 'science is believed to operate . . . independently of its social setting'? (9 marks)

e) With reference to Ian Craib's article, evaluate the relative advantages of a structural and an action approach to the study of society. (9 marks)

Evaluation exercise

Assess the usefulness of social surveys in exploring the experiences of black people in Britain.

Begin by making two lists. In the first you should describe the ways in which surveys might be a useful tool for data-collection. This might include the statistical distribution of ethnic minorities, the general categories of their experience and the extent to which they occur. In the second list, describe what surveys cannot tell us about ethnic minorities and their experience. This might include ethnic life 'as it is lived', i.e. the experiences of ethnic minorities described in their own words. If you are yourself a member of an ethnic minority group, does it have any bearing on the question?

Find some evidence from the extract, your notes or any textbooks, which might support the points you make.

In a concluding paragraph, come to some conclusions as to the usefulness of surveys in investigating the experiences of ethnic minorities in modern Britain.

CHAPTER 2

Family

Editors' introduction

It is no surprise that the family remains one of the most popular topic areas for A level Sociology students. After all, we all have our own family experiences to draw upon and, as David Morgan points out below, it is extremely difficult these days to have any meaningful discussion on social policy without first looking at family arrangements.

In recent years, ideas about 'traditional' family arrangements have taken a bit of a hammering from sociologists, especially from feminists. It is perhaps important to point out that it has been the inequalities in these arrangements, and the ideologies associated with the concept of 'the family' rather than the family itself, which have been the main focus for this attack.

Our own lives as parts of families are becoming increasingly unlike those of our parents and grandparents. Rising levels of cohabitation, divorce, births outside marriage and increasing numbers of step-families, give special force to the idea that although the family is always with us, it is constantly changing. Whether such changes reflect greater equality between the sexes remains a matter of debate. As David Morgan implies in his review of recent developments in sociological approaches to the study of the family, evidence for the rise of the much talked about 'new man', who takes his domestic responsibilities seriously, remains rather scarce.

Writing in the *Observer* (23 September, 1990) Patricia Hewitt, from the Institute of Public Policy Research, argued that 'if family policy is to be effective and humane, it ought to be sufficiently flexible to support the family in all its many variations'. Perhaps this issue, and the complexities it gives rise to, coupled with the continuing debate over how partners should divide their family obligations, will be at the centre of sociological and policy debate over the ever-changing family.

Sociology, Society and the Family

DAVID MORGAN

Introduction

Developments in sociological research and theory are frequently stimulated by developments outside the subject itself. The sociology of the family is no exception and there are, perhaps, good reasons why the sociology of the family in particular cannot develop in isolation. Family members are individuals who are often intimately involved with each other over long periods of time. Inevitably such relationships are extremely complex and have important consequences for individual personalities, making these relationships topics of interest to psychologists, psychoanalysts or family therapists. The theories which these specialists develop may – or should – be of interest to sociologists. Similarly, family relationships appear to involve some very basic processes such as those to do with sexuality, human reproduction and ageing. Yet, at the same time, the family is a social institution, shaped by social and cultural conventions and interacting with economic and political institutions within the wider society. As a social institution the family changes over time and varies between different cultures.

There are two sorts of development 'outside' the study of the family that may be seen as having significant impacts:

(a) *Developments in other subjects* – here one might include developments in the study of family history, the growing interest in family law, the growth of marital counselling and family therapy, and so on. But these 'outside' influences are never purely academic and hence we should also stress:
(b) *The impact of political and social movements* – for example, feminism or 'the New Right', these movements themselves reflecting and being part of wider changes within society itself.

Here I shall consider four such influences:

(1) feminist theory and practice;
(2) developments in family history;
(3) developments in the area of social policy;
(4) developments in work and employment and in the ways in which these basic areas of life are being rethought.

This might seem to be a very mixed bag of influences: nevertheless, they are all interconnected in many interesting ways. Moreover, they can be seen as being influenced by studies in the family as much as they can be seen as influencing these studies.

Feminism

There can be little doubt that wider developments in feminist thought and practice have had a major influence upon the study of the family. Of the various possible influences over the past ten years or so, this is probably the most significant. In the first place, and most crucially, it has stressed that gender is a major feature of family living. People do not simply occupy or perform family *roles* – mother, father, son, daughter, grandparent and so on – they are also men and women, boys and girls. Curiously, this rather obvious fact was often blurred in those kinds of theories, functionalist or Marxist, which tended to see the family as a unit within some wider social system or as a social system in its own right. In other words, such theories often tended to view the family as some kind of building block within a larger society and obscured the fact that within this block there were women and

men. This tendency to play down gender differences within the family was also strengthened by widely held and influential theories that argued that marriage in particular and family relationships in general were becoming more egalitarian, more democratic or, in the British version, more symmetrical.

Against this, argued feminists, it should be recognised that families contain both men and women and that gender often has a profound impact on the ways in which individuals actually experience and understand living in families. Moreover, such differences were not to be seen simply as *differences* but also as inequalities; inequalities within families which were possibly more important than class differences between families. Feminists pointed to differences in power and economic status between men and women within the family and argued that, for example, violence against wives was not simply a

---

Application exercise

The article suggests that there has been some movement by men and women towards spheres of activity usually associated with the other gender. Apply the ideas expressed in the article to the argument that marriage in modern British society is a 'partnership of equals'.

Make sure that you take account of the following concepts:

- domestic labour
- the symmetrical family
- domestic division of labour
- the expressive role
- pin money
- the burden of dependency
- community caring
- power relationships
- primary responsibility for childcare
- traditional conjugal roles
- the 'new man'

You will find some relevant information on the **Cuttings** page (p. 25). You should first **define** each of these concepts so that you can apply them to the issue under consideration. Then you should **organize** your ideas so that you produce a coherent argument which applies these concepts appropriately . You need not use only these particular concepts, but you should employ all of them in your argument.

matter of individual, and possibly abnormal, psychology but was shaped by these patterns of inequality between men and women both within the family and within the wider society.

To make this argument a little more concrete, consider the following puzzle. It is well known that the postwar period has been one in which there has been a growing participation of married women, especially mothers, in the labour force. Yet many researchers have also noted that this move of women out of the home has not been accompanied to the same extent by a similar move on the part of men in the direction of greater participation in the home, in housework and in parenting. While there has been *some* movement, it has not been equivalent to the movements made in the

opposite direction by women. Why is this? To begin to answer this, one needs to focus on some very complex processes both within the family and between the family and other areas of social life. For example, in many households the earnings of wives are often regarded as supplementing what are understood to be the main earnings of the husband. Behind this lies the persistence of very widespread notions as to what is appropriate work for women and for men. The way in which these differences are formulated is often in terms of *responsibilities*. Husbands may 'help' – perhaps to a considerable extent – in domestic tasks or with child care, but in most cases the responsibility for these tasks rests with the wives and mothers. Such responsibilities, it should be noted, are not simply in terms of housework or child care, but also in terms of wider caring obligations, particularly in relation to elderly relatives.

Thus, gender remains a major division within families and households. More controversially, it is sometimes argued that the family is the major source of such divisions within society as a whole. Certainly, the family can be seen as a major agency whereby such gender differences are reproduced, that is maintained and transmitted from one generation to another. Also, the family and notions of family obligations remain major sources of resistance to trends towards equality between women and men. But whether the family can be seen as the major or sole cause of gender inequalities in general – in equalities at work or sexual harassment for example – remains more arguable.

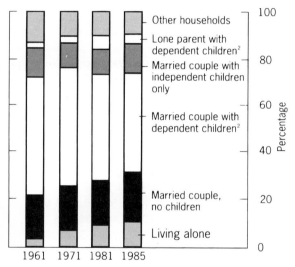

Source: Office of Population Censuses and Surveys
Notes:
(1) Data for 1961, 1971 and 1981 are taken from the Population Censuses for those years; the 1985 data are from the General Household Survey.
(2) These family types may also include independent children.

Figure 1   People in households in Great Britain: by type of household and family in which they live.

Interpretation exercise

Look at Figure 1. What trends can be identified from the data? You will need to refer to different family types across time in your response. Percentages, if given, must be referred to as approximations only.

Another contribution that feminism has made to the study of the family has been in emphasising that the family is not a simple, a natural or a taken-for-granted unit but also something which is ideologically and socially constructed. The 'family' is, in fact, a very complex term and we all use it to cover a wide range of situations and experiences. Sometimes we are referring to households, people living under the same roof, while on other occasions we may be referring to relationships that cut across households, between kin or between parents and grandparents. Yet behind the term 'family', and often influencing all these usages, are certain ideal constructions of what the family is or should be like. The so-called 'cereal packet' image of mother, father and two children is one such image. So too are ideal expectations as to what it is to be a mother or a married couple. Feminist writings have drawn our attention to the contradictions and the relationships between image and reality in understandings of the family – to the ideological dimensions of discussions about 'the family'.

Feminism has, therefore, been a major influence on the study of the family and this influence continues to be felt in numerous studies of different aspects of family living. But can the sociology of the family make any kind of a contribution to feminist theories? The sociology of the family has, in the past, included a variety of studies drawing attention to the complexity of that institution. Studies which were not overtly or explicitly feminist have pointed to the ways in which families are embedded in wider networks of social relationships, the continuing importance of family rituals and the centrality of family matters in the lives of many individuals. More recent surveys have highlighted the continuing importance of the family as a 'central life interest' and have indicated a considerable measure of support for the 'cereal packet' image. If feminism emphasises the continuing tensions, inequalities and exploitations within family living, perhaps the more traditional kind of family sociology may remind us of the persisting importance of family, however defined or understood, in the lives of many people. It is perhaps not feminist thought alone but the continuing debate and engagement between feminism and sociological practice (often conducted by women who are both feminists and sociologists) that will be the important influence.

History

Perhaps one of the most striking developments in recent years has been the growth of family history. Such a growth has not, of course, been all of one piece; it ranges from careful statistical reconstructions of how households in the past were composed to more speculative accounts of how the family might have changed over the centuries. Family history has also derived much from feminist historians, seeking to recover the lives of ordinary women or to explore the roots of the oppressions and inequalities mentioned in the previous section.

This growth in the historical study of the family has had its impact on the sociology of the family and it is now rare to find a book in this area which does not, to some degree, address itself to issues raised by these historians. In many cases it could be argued that here, as elsewhere, the boundaries between history and sociology have become blurred. What, then, has been

Coursework suggestion

It is perfectly possible to carry out a coursework assignment without undertaking any primary research at all. Indeed, some questions are better answered by a search of **secondary** literature than by the use of questionnaire or interview techniques. For example, if you want to know the answer to the question 'How far has feminism changed the sociological study of the family?', it would be difficult to think of a primary method which would allow you to address the issue adequately. In this case, you would have to carry out a literature search, a secondary research activity.

However, conducting a survey of the literature does not mean that you can just do some reading and simply write up what various feminists have said about the family. Instead, you will need to ensure at least two things:

a) Firstly, that you are employing genuinely **sociological** methods in your research rather than simply engaging in common sense speculation. This means that you have to adopt some **systematic** ways of analysing the literature you choose to investigate. This might involve, for example, employing the **comparative method,** in identifying the concerns of pre-feminist and feminist sociologists. Or, it may include some sort of **content analysis** of key texts in order to identify the ways in which different issues are discussed under the impact of feminist research and writing.

b) Secondly, you will need to ensure that you demonstrate all the skills which are identified by the syllabus. It is not enough just to show that you have acquired some **knowledge** of the issue. You will also need to show that you can **interpret** the material you have used and that you can **apply** it successfully to the question you set yourself at the beginning of the project. Also, you will need to employ the skill of **evaluation**, identifying the areas where feminism has made an impact on sociological discussion of the family, and where it has made little headway. Given your original question, you will need to come to a conclusion as to how far feminism has actually changed the sociological study of the family.

the contribution of these historical studies to the sociology of the family, especially in its more theoretical approaches?

This is a complex question, since there often seems to be a considerable gap between the fine detail of some historical studies, often limited to a particular period or geographical area or both, and the somewhat broader discussions that characterise most sociological writings. This contrast, indeed, may underline one of the main contributions of family history: to make us sceptical of some of the more sweeping generalisations about the family as it is now and how it is supposed to have changed. In particular, historical analysis should make scholars wary of some of the more simplified accounts which contrast the family 'before' and 'after' industrialisation. The very phrase, 'the family in industrial society', implies that there is some readily identifiable thing called 'the family' and a readily identifiable process called 'industrialisation' and that there is a close association between the two, with the latter often assumed to be a cause of the former. In place of the grand sweep of this 'before' and 'after' analysis, some historical analysis has reminded us of continuities and similarities between the households of pre-industrial England and present-day households. It has attempted to demonstrate that the process of change was much more complicated than some sociological models suggest and that there was considerable variation between different regions and between different social groups. Perhaps the most important contribution of the new family history has been to show that individuals, as members of families or households, were not simply at the receiving end of some external force called 'industrialisation' or 'social change' but were much more actively involved in the process of social change itself.

In the second place, historical analysis enables us to stand back and to follow the course of individual families and households over time. Most sociological analysis is based upon kinds of snapshots, a survey or an observational study, taken at a particular moment of time. However, family life is essentially dynamic. Individuals, in the course of their lives, move through a variety of different kinds of households, enter and leave a variety of different family relationships, acquiring or losing different kin, friends and acquaintances in the process. Moreover, all the change that takes place in a person's life also takes place against a background of a society which is itself changing, a society which might include world wars, industrial depression and recovery, more long-term trends in unemployment, and so on. Historians, simply because they make use of data which can, in some

cases at least, cover the whole of several life spans, are in a position to help sociologists appreciate this whole process of change in all its different aspects.

Again, it is important to remember that this is a two-way relationship. Moreover, this relationship is not something as crude as maintaining that 'historians provide the facts and sociologists provide the theories'. For one thing, it may be noted that yesterday's sociological studies become today's historical data and that many of the classic sociological studies now provide valuable guides to, and often poignant reminders of, 'the way we were'. More important, however, is the fact that the study of how societies persist over time from generation to generation is something which is at the very heart of the sociological enterprise and it is here that a historical sociology, particularly of families and households, has a central part to play.

Policy Issues

It is rare these days for a major political conference or rally to pass without some, and often quite extended, reference to the family. Of course, the family has always been an important element in political and social thought.

There are probably several aspects of our recent history which have contributed to this 'rediscovery' of the family on the part of political leaders. These would include concerns about levels of public expenditure and the extent of state provision and the desire in some quarters to reduce these; the growth in long-term unemployment and the subsequent assumed consequences for family relationships; rising divorce rates; growing concerns about law and order; and the development of a 'pro-family' lobby especially, but not exclusively, among the 'New Right'. ◀B

All these influences are, of course, interlinked, and the outcome has been a variety of proposals ranging from calls for the appointment of specific ministers or the establishment of departments with a particular family brief, to a more general recognition that practically every piece of social and economic legislation has some kind of family dimension. It is difficult, in other words, to think of any piece of government legislation, especially in the areas of taxation and the payment of social benefits, which does not have some kind of impact on the relationships between husband and wives and/or between parents and children.

The consequences of the elaboration of ideas of 'family policy' for the sociological analysis of the family have been twofold. In the first place, there has been an increasing recognition of the importance of the state, and of politics in general, as an element to be taken into account when discussing the place of the family in society. The sociology of the family has rediscovered the importance of this political dimension and has sought to explore the often complex relationships between the family, the state, class and gender. Here too, it should be noted, there have been important inputs from feminist writings.

Feminists have also been engaged in a second key issue and that is the analysis of the work of 'caring'. This focuses on the difficult, and sometimes painful, questions of responsibilities and obligations for caring between family members and the relationship or balance between these family obligations and the obligations of the state. Feminists have been particularly concerned with these issues because it is often assumed that it is women who are expected to carry out the work of 'caring' or that they are naturally suited for caring activities. For very many individuals these are immediate and practical issues, but these questions also raise further important and profound issues in the analysis of the family about the nature of obligations between family members. In particular, such issues point to relationships between different households across different generations. As we have seen, these are also issues of considerable theoretical importance.

Work and Employment

The long-term and persisting trend in unemployment has had a further consequence for family sociology. In essence this can be seen as a challenge to a conventional and very simple understanding of the family in relation to the economy. Home and work were seen as two separate spheres – work consisted of regular paid employment and was primarily, if not exclusively, the responsibility of the husband/father who was conventionally designated as head of the household. Within the home, there was the typical sexual division of labour. This very simple model informed many functionalist and Marxist approaches to the family. It also had wider implications, for example in the study of social class where class and social mobility were often measured on the basis of the male head of the household and his occupation. In recent years, this simplified model has received a considerable battering from a wide range of sources, not least the actual trends in work and employment within the British economy itself. As a result, it has been replaced by something much less clear cut or straightforward.

Work is no longer seen as simply paid employment; it also includes activities and exchanges both within and between households, some of which will involve money and others of which will not. We have a much broader understanding of economic life, one which includes exchanges within the 'black economy' and the unpaid activities of housework and child care. The 'male breadwinner' part of the model has not been entirely abandoned, but it seems increasingly unreal and much greater recognition is being given to the woman's economic activities outside the home.

Generally, the old categories of 'work,' 'family' and others such as 'leisure' (standard benchmarks of sociology textbooks) have become much less fixed or secure.

For the study of the family this has had two particular consequences. In the first place, much greater attention is being paid to the household – as opposed to individuals – as a unit in society and, on the basis of this, to relationships both within and between households. In the second place, greater attention is being paid to the household as a sphere of *economic* activity. This contrasts with approaches which placed emphasis upon marriage and the family and which focused largely on the emotional or personal relationships between spouses or between parents and children. There is still a lot of work to be done here, for example in assessing the economic activities of children within the household, but the general consequence whereby economic life is, literally, 'brought home' is one that can be welcomed.

However, there remain some difficulties. An exclusive focus upon households and upon the economic activities within them and between them may run the danger of leaving out much of what many people might regard as being crucial to the understanding of family life. This would include an understanding of the emotional ties and sentiments that exist between family members (not necessarily within the same household) and an examination of the ideological significance of the family and the ways in which terms such as 'family' and 'marriage' are heavy with moral, personal and often political significance. We need, therefore, to consider the relationships between household and family and between economic relationships and family sentiments and obligations. And all these, as I argued in the section on history, need to be considered within a general framework that emphasises process and change. It is a formidable task.

Conclusion

I have considered a variety of different influences on the study of the family: feminism, family history, issues of family policy and the reconceptualisation of work and employment. It can be seen that all these influences are inter-related; the influence of feminism, in particular, may be seen as cutting across all these other trends as well as being important in its own right.

I could have considered other influences. In terms of direct theoretical, influence, I could have considered the contributions of phenomenology and ethnomethodology, small but growing. I could have considered more recent developments within Marxism, especially those which have become more sensitive to questions of ideology and culture. I could have considered systems theorising, although this is probably more influential in the United States than it has been in Britain up to the present time.

In terms of more practical concerns I could have considered the influence of the work of family or marital therapists and the theories which have both grown out of and informed (especially Freudian or neo-Freudian theories) these practices. Again, these influences have probably been more pronounced in the United States, although there has been some influence in Britain, especially around the Tavistock Institute and the practice of counselling in, say, the National Marriage Guidance Council (Relate). To date, these theories and insights, dealing particularly with the complex meshes of interpersonal relationships within families and over generations, have had little impact on the mainstream of family research and theorising within Britain. Nevertheless, it is likely that such influences will grow.

Another important influence, although one which has yet to be fully recognised by sociologists of the family, is to do with the variety of ethnic groups and communities within contemporary British society. Much theorising about the family in Western society has been blind to questions of ethnic differences and divisions just as, until recently, it has been relatively blind to gender divisions. Consequently it has tended to have a rather narrow understanding of the range of ways in which family relationships are experienced and understood, the range of possible ways in which family ties and obligations may be used and the range of different relationships between the household and the economy. Moreover, since we should consider not merely ethnic differences but also wider patterns of racism and discrimination, it is important to begin to understand the ways in which family ties can mediate (either through softening or through amplifying) these wider patterns of inequality.

Throughout this brief survey I have emphasised the two-way relationship between the study of the family and wider theoretical and social developments. One cannot pretend that these relationships have always been obvious or smooth. Nevertheless, the study of the family, enriched by opening up to these diverse and complex influences, may itself contribute to the wider development of social theory. The family can be seen as occupying an almost unique position both between the individual and society and, at the same time, across generations or between past, present and future. In other words, it is implicated in some of the most fundamental issues in sociological analysis to do with the relationship between the individual and society, questions of time and change and the persistence of social systems over time.

References and Further Reading

On Feminism
Barrett, M. and McIntosh, M. (1982) *The Anti-Social Family*, Verso.
Thorne, B. and Yalom, M. (eds) (1982) *Rethinking the Family: Some Feminist Questions*, Longman.
Among the many possible case studies see, for example:
Cornwell, J. (1984) *Hard-Earned Lives*, Tavistock.
Dobash, R. and Dobash, R. (1980) *Violence Against Wives*, Open Books.

On History
Anderson, M. (1980) *Approaches to the History of the Western Family*, Macmillan.
Harris, C. C. (1983) *The Family and Industrial Society*, Allen and Unwin.

On Policy Issues
Mount, F. (1982) *The Subversive Family*, Jonathan Cape.
Rapoport, R. *et al* (1982) *Families in Britain*, Routledge and Kegan Paul.

On Restructuring Work
Pahl, R. (1984) *Divisions of Labour*, Basil Blackwell.

On Women and Employment
Dex, S. (1985) *The Sexual Division of Work*, Wheatsheaf.
Dex, S. (1987) *Women's Occupational Mobility*, Macmillan.
Martin, J. and Roberts, C. (1984) *Women and Employment: A Lifetime Perspective*, HMSO.
Yeandle, S. (1984) *Women's Working Lives*, Tavistock.

On Women and Unemployment
Coyle, A. (1984) *Redundant Women*, The Women's Press.
For a vivid case study see:
Westwood, S. (1984) *All Day Every Day*, Pluto Press.

Structured question (25 marks)

a) According to extract A, what is the structure of the 'cereal-packet image' of the family? (1 mark)

b) What are the implications for family life in contemporary society of the 'aspects of our recent history', identified in extract B? (6 marks)

c) How far does sociological evidence suggest that the ideal of a male breadwinner 'has not been entirely abandoned' (extract C)? (7 marks)

d) Assess sociological contributions to an understanding of the role of the family amongst ethnic minority groups in Britain (extract D). (6 marks)

e) Referring to any of the extracts, to what extent do you think sociological discussions about the family are ideological? (5 marks)

Evaluation exercise

David Morgan suggests that the results of historical research can be of great **benefit** to sociological analysis. How far do you agree with this view?

In answering this question, you could organise your ideas into three **sections**. In the first section, you should look for clues in the article which might help you to clarify your ideas about this issue. Though you may produce your own arguments and ideas about the usefulness of historical evidence, you should try to draw general points from David Morgan's article on the family.

However, you do need to be aware that, as Morgan believes that history has a great deal to offer sociologists, he is likely to give a rather **one-sided view** of the value of history. If you are to produce a more **balanced** evaluation, then you must also consider other viewpoints. Even though you may not have easy access to other viewpoints, you can attempt to work them out by asking yourself a series of questions, such as:

- What does history **not** tell us?
- Are all groups in society equally **represented** in historical accounts? If they are not, why not?
- Whose accounts are left out?
- Are historical records **accurate**? And if not, why not?
- Are historical records **unbiased**? And if not, why not?
- Is there more than one version of history?
- Who **produces** history?

You may have come across similar types of questions when you considered whether sociology could be called a science or not.

In the third section you should try to arrive at a conclusion by directly attempting to assess whether history is useful to sociologists or not, drawing on the arguments and ideas you have produced in the previous two sections.

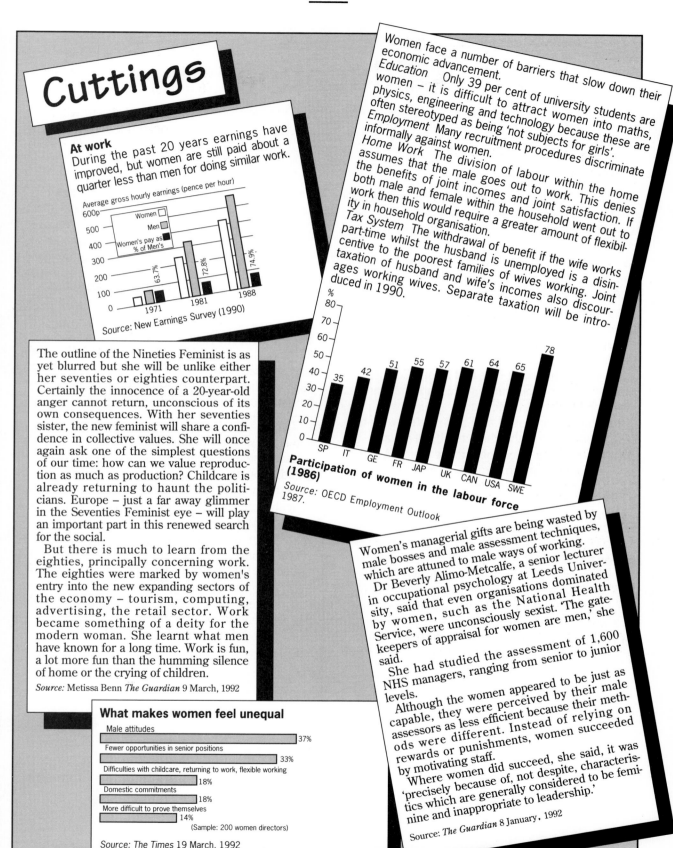

Cuttings

At work

During the past 20 years earnings have improved, but women are still paid about a quarter less than men for doing similar work.

Average gross hourly earnings (pence per hour)

63.7% / 72.8% / 74.9% (1971 / 1981 / 1988)

Women / Men / Women's pay as % of Men's

Source: New Earnings Survey (1990)

Women face a number of barriers that slow down their economic advancement.

Education   Only 39 per cent of university students are women – it is difficult to attract women into maths, physics, engineering and technology because these are often stereotyped as being 'not subjects for girls'.

Employment Many recruitment procedures discriminate informally against women.

Home Work   The division of labour within the home assumes that the male goes out to work. This denies the benefits of joint incomes and joint satisfaction. If both male and female work then this would require a greater amount of flexibility in household organisation.

Tax System   The withdrawal of benefit if the wife works part-time whilst the husband is unemployed is a disincentive to the poorest families of wives working. Joint taxation of husband and wife's incomes also discourages working wives. Separate taxation will be introduced in 1990.

%

Participation of women in the labour force (1986)

SP 35, IT 42, GE 51, FR 55, JAP 57, UK 61, CAN 64, USA 65, SWE 78

Source: OECD Employment Outlook 1987.

The outline of the Nineties Feminist is as yet blurred but she will be unlike either her seventies or eighties counterpart. Certainly the innocence of a 20-year-old anger cannot return, unconscious of its own consequences. With her seventies sister, the new feminist will share a confidence in collective values. She will once again ask one of the simplest questions of our time: how can we value reproduction as much as production? Childcare is already returning to haunt the politicians. Europe – just a far away glimmer in the Seventies Feminist eye – will play an important part in this renewed search for the social.

But there is much to learn from the eighties, principally concerning work. The eighties were marked by women's entry into the new expanding sectors of the economy – tourism, computing, advertising, the retail sector. Work became something of a deity for the modern woman. She learnt what men have known for a long time. Work is fun, a lot more fun than the humming silence of home or the crying of children.

Source: Metissa Benn *The Guardian* 9 March, 1992

What makes women feel unequal

Male attitudes — 37%

Fewer opportunities in senior positions — 33%

Difficulties with childcare, returning to work, flexible working — 18%

Domestic commitments — 18%

More difficult to prove themselves — 14%

(Sample: 200 women directors)

Source: The Times 19 March, 1992

Women's managerial gifts are being wasted by male bosses and male assessment techniques, which are attuned to male ways of working.

Dr Beverly Alimo-Metcalfe, a senior lecturer in occupational psychology at Leeds University, said that even organisations dominated by women, such as the National Health Service, were unconsciously sexist. 'The gatekeepers of appraisal for women are men,' she said.

She had studied the assessment of 1,600 NHS managers, ranging from senior to junior levels.

Although the women appeared to be just as capable, they were perceived by their male assessors as less efficient because their methods were different. Instead of relying on rewards or punishments, women succeeded by motivating staff.

Where women did succeed, she said, it was 'precisely because of, not despite, characteristics which are generally considered to be feminine and inappropriate to leadership.'

Source: *The Guardian* 8 January, 1992

CHAPTER 3

Education

Editors' introduction

The 1992 general election was fought over a number of key issues for a modern economy. One of these was the role of education and training. Over the previous thirteen years, the Conservative Government had sought to make **choice** and the **new vocationalism** the central themes of its education policy. Greater choice in education was provided, it was argued, by increasing the powers of school governors, especially parent governors; by the local management of school budgets; by opening school rolls to reward popular schools with more students and funds; by providing City Technology Colleges (CTCs) to educate outstanding students from inner cities; and by the assisted places scheme which helped to pay the fees of able, but poorer, working-class students to enable them to attend private schools. (Ask your tutor about these changes and look out for information about them in the media.)

But all was not well in the schools. What price 'choice' if resources were lacking? There was talk of 'sink' schools for those left behind in the scramble for exercising choice. The CTCs struggled to raise private funds, and the assisted places programme was discredited by claims that middle-class rather than working-class families were the main users of the scheme. When some Muslim parents called for their own state schools, the drive for greater 'choice' raised wider and more difficult questions.

On the issue of **vocational** education, matters seemed no more clear cut. As youth unemployment rose in the 1980s, schools and colleges were compelled to introduce more courses designed to provide more **relevant** vocational training for young people (TVEI, BTEC, etc.). But how, in an educational sense, should 'relevance' be defined? And, in any case, was this really what education was **for**? Surely, the job market and the state of the economy dictated the sorts of skills required at any point in time, **not** the 'vocationalism' offered at college? But, then, with jobs so scarce for young people, how **were** they supposed to acquire the necessary skills to get a foothold in the workplace? It seemed a joyless circular argument.

In the following article, Dan Finn makes the case **against** the new vocationalism, arguing that its introduction marked the demise of equality of opportunity as the central reference point for education policy in Britain. Finn further condemns the youth training schemes as divisive, exploitative and work-driven, rather than educationally-driven. The article strongly asserts that this new approach is no solution to Britain's skill shortage or the 'crisis' in education. You must weigh up the pros and cons in your answers and coursework projects by discussing just what education is **really** for.

'Education for Jobs': The Route to YTS

DAN FINN

Introduction

At the end of February 1988 there were 402,500 young people participating in the two-year Youth Training Scheme (YTS), of whom 148,600 were in their second year of training. Altogether, 70% of 16-year-old school leavers and 25% of 17-year-old school leavers had joined YTS.

In September 1988 nearly all 16-and 17-year-olds lost their entitlement to basic income support. If they leave school but are unable to obtain a job their only chance of obtaining an independent income is through taking up a guaranteed place on YTS.

This amounts to a radical change in the social and economic position of young people. How has it come about, and what does it mean for the young unemployed?

In this article, I want to examine how a problem about young people not being able to get work was interpreted as a problem about their attitudes and skills rather than a problem about the nature of the labour market. I want to show how the Conservative Government's attempts to manage the political and social consequences of mass unemployment have resulted in the creation of a new economic and social status for young school leavers. I also want to show how these policies have led to the creation of a new tripartite structure of education or training which is thought to be more appropriate to their station in life.

Youth Unemployment

During the 1950s and 1960s the average rate of recorded unemployment was 1.5%; between 1971 and 1975 this rose to 3.5%, and this continued to increase under the then Labour Government until 1977 when unemployment exceeded 1.3 million. There was a slow decline after this until the arrival of the Conservative Government in 1979, following which unemployment escalated. In its first eighteen months of office, the new administration presided over what rapidly became described as the deindustrialization of Britain. The number of people employed in manufacturing industry fell by nearly a million. Between March 1980 and 1981 unemployment increased from 1.41 to 2.38 million and total economic output fell by 10%. In January 1982 the

	Total	Full-time education	YOP/ YTS	Unemployed	Other, mainly employed
1974	1,550	470 (30)	—	47 (3)	1,033 (67)
1975	1,584	495 (31)	—	51 (3)	1,039 (66)
1976	1,624	543 (33)	—	127 (8)	954 (59)
1977	1,664	570 (34)	—	145 (9)	949 (57)
1978	1,718	582 (34)	—	159 (9)	976 (57)
1979	1,767	597 (34)	70 (4)	131 (7)	968 (55)
1980	1,804	613 (34)	72 (4)	129 (7)	990 (55)
1981	1,843	651 (35)	133 (7)	232 (13)	826 (45)
1982	1,867	717 (38)	178 (10)	274 (15)	697 (37)
1983	1,851	739 (40)	235 (13)	283 (15)	594 (32)
1984	1,814	689 (38)	273 (15)	268 (15)	583 (32)
1985	1,769	671 (38)	273 (15)	258 (15)	567 (32)
1986	1,730	663 (38)	272 (16)	241 (14)	554 (32)
1987	1,700	655 (39)	316 (19)	207 (12)	552 (31)
1988	1,672	649 (39)	396 (24)	150 (9)	496 (30)

Source: Employment Gazette, September 1987, p. 460, and unpublished MSC papers.

Table 1   Education and labour market status of all 16- and 17-year-olds in Great Britain in January of each year (thousands, with % in brackets)

unemployment total passed three million for the first time since the 1930s.

Within this overall picture the job and training prospects for young people changed dramatically. In the early 1960s the youth unemployment rate was not dissimilar to that of adults, but afterwards the relative position of young people grew steadily worse. Between January 1972 and January 1977, for example, overall unemployment increased by 45%, but for those under 20 it had risen by 120%. By January 1981 unemployment amongst under-18-year-olds reached nearly 20%, and amongst 18-to 25-year-olds topped 17%. A top level report prepared for the Government in 1981 estimated that by the end of 1983 between 50 and 70% of the labour force under 18 might never have had a proper job (*Time Out*, May/June 1983). By 1983 *Youthaid* estimated that without MSC schemes over half of the country's under-18s and one in four of the under-25s would have been out of work (p. 3).

Youth unemployment itself reflected broader social inequalities. If you were black, a minimum-age school leaver, or if you lived in certain towns or regions, your chances of securing work were more severely curtailed (*Youthaid* 1983).

Youth Unemployment and Comprehensive Education

When unemployment started to escalate in the mid-1970s, the problem of youth unemployment was treated differently from that of adult unemployment. Policy makers, opinion formers and parents began to express their dissatisfaction with the education system which was felt to be placing too much emphasis on personal development and not doing enough to prepare young people for work.

Youth unemployment was treated as an **educational** problem rather than an employment one for political reasons: the Government could not change the labour process and organisation of work to fit existing school leavers, but it could try to fit school leavers to the emerging priorities of employers. Thus with school leavers no longer receiving work experience, schools and training programmes had to become the source of the work ethic. In other words, in the labour market conditions of the late 1970s and early 1980s the state was to be held responsible for the process of work socialisation that had previously been a normal part of leaving school and getting a job.

Since that point, and largely organised by the MSC and the Department of Industry, new **vocational** initiatives and programmes have been introduced across a range of subjects and schools. These innovations, and their funding, have imposed a new agenda on comprehensive schools.

Together, these initiatives and schemes have often

Coursework suggestion

At some stage in your education you are likely to undertake a period of work experience. If you read Dan Finn's article, he suggests that the experiences of young people on such schemes vary enormously, and he provides accounts of the typical experiences reported by young people. Your coursework could consist of a **comparison** between your own experiences on a training or work experience programme and those reported by Finn.

However, this presents you with the problem of how you can make **sociological** an individual account of a set of personal experiences. An important thing you must do is to keep a detailed **field-work diary**, in which you can record your experiences, backing up any comments you make with accurate descriptions of the events. It will not be enough just to record what you were feeling at the time. Instead, you will need to offer some **objective** support for your reaction. This may take the form of corroborative statements from other trainees, documentary evidence from your employer, such as a programme of events, the comments of the liaison teacher, etc.

In **analysing** your results, you will need carefully to compare your experiences with other accounts which you will find, for example, in books, articles and leaflets about youth training schemes. One approach might be to compare your experiences with the claims of the official agencies (in this case, your school or college) about the benefits of work experience programmes. Be careful not to generalise too much from your own experiences as they are, by their nature, likely to be limited.

In your report, you will need to tackle the issue of **generalisability** head on and to discuss how **representative** your results are likely to be.

been described as the **'new vocationalism'**. They represent a new ideology of education, one which signalled the abandonment of equal opportunity as the central reference point of educational strategy. The key element of these schemes is a particular kind of 'realism' and work experience, and the guiding philosophy seems to involve the creation of an appropriate education for certain groups of pupils, to be derived largely from their assumed destination in the workplace. It is not that schools are simply expected to prepare their pupils to get jobs, but that they are now expected to make them intellectually and attitudinally better potential employees.

In combination with the hidden transformation of education that has been wrought by public expenditure cuts and falling pupil numbers, these vocational initiatives have cumulatively undermined some of the achievements of the comprehensive era and are playing a key part in creating a new 'tripartism'. By late 1985, when Lord Young, one of the key architects of the YTS, became the Employment Secretary, he was able to outline very clearly this vision of the educational future. He saw a situation:

> . . . at the end of the decade, (where) there is a world in which 15% of our younger people go into higher education . . . Another 30 to 35% will stay on doing the TVEI (Technical and Vocational Education Initiative), along with other courses, ending up with a mixture of vocational and academic qualifications and skills. The remainder, about half, will go on to two-year YTS. (*Times*, 4/9/85)

In complex ways schooling has been (and continues to be) restructured to legitimise traditional social divisions, instil the spirit of enterprise, and resocialise working-class youth so that it becomes more acceptable to employers. The primary vehicle for securing this latter objective is the two-year YTS.

Youth Unemployment and Employers

Many young workers have always been characterised as casual, irresponsible, poorly motivated and quick to change jobs. What was new in the late 1970s was the scale of the economic recession and a new expectation on the part of many employers that school leavers should have the sense of responsibility and commitment usually produced by work experience. This expectation was partly a result of the employers' power in a buyers' market; more fundamentally, it also reflected changes in the 'labour process', changes in the way that labour was used and controlled at work. Not only was there an absolute decline in the number of jobs available for school leavers, but there was also a concomitant reorganisation of the labour process in those jobs which remained.

By the late 1970s young workers were entering a labour market in which there were fewer openings for either skilled craftsmen or for unskilled casual labourers. The dominant demand was for generalised, semi-skilled labour. The shifting employment opportunities resulting from the rise of service occupations, technological changes in production and the decline of small firms also resulted in changes in the use and control of labour. It was in this context that the young competed unequally with experienced adults. They lacked commitment, discipline and 'realism'. These were the qualities which had to be instilled by the state, as it began to take responsibility

Evaluation exercise

One of the things you may be asked to do in the examination is to **assess** the effectiveness of training for young people. One of the first questions you would have to ask yourself is 'effective in terms of what'? You should begin by drawing up a list of **criteria** against which you can measure the operation of youth training. The experiences of young people themselves might be a useful measure of the success of such schemes. Other measures might involve comparing the operation of the schemes with the government's objectives for them (whether those objectives are stated or hidden) or establishing the effectiveness of the schemes in helping to place young people in permanent jobs.

When you have decided what your criteria are, you will need to gather **evidence** related to each of the criteria, by searching the literature, or your notes, for appropriate arguments and information. You need to undertake the search for evidence with an **objective** approach and you should record all the data whether it supports or undermines the view that such schemes are effective.

Lastly, you will have to **weigh up** the evidence for each of the criteria you have identified in order to come to some conclusions about the effectiveness of the schemes. It may be that some are more effective in terms of one criterion than another and so they may be partially effective. Your conclusions must be supported by appropriate evidence.

for the now lengthy period of transition from school to work (Frith 1980).

It was the MSC which was given responsibility for creating programmes which would both give the young unemployed something to do and make them more attractive to potential employers.

From YOP to YTS

Although its original task was the reform of industrial training, the MSC had, since its creation in 1974, become one of the key institutions acting to reduce and contain the social consequences of mass unemployment. As the recession decimated the apprenticeship system and caused the spectacular growth of youth unemployment, the MSC was required to come up with proposals and schemes which would deal with the problem.

The first comprehensive scheme was the Youth Opportunities Programme (YOP), which was introduced in 1977. It offered six months' work experience with an employer, and the chance to go to college for one day a week for those who wanted it.

YOP was originally defined as an avenue into full-time work, but as this 'promise' soured with the arrival of two, then three, million unemployed, and as fewer trainees obtained jobs, so its credibility was steadily eroded.

The most controversial element of YOP concerned the large number of trainees placed with private employers, usually for six months. In 1981, *Youthaid* pointed out that these trainees were 'concentrated in small, low-paying, non-unionised workplaces'. Rather than friendly employers 'helping' the young unemployed, it began to emerge that many were using YOP to subsidise their recruitment procedures, if not directly exploiting young trainees as cheap labour.

The collapse of youth employment was no simple consequence of the free play of market forces. It seemed that YOP actually made the problem worse:

> State intervention in Britain appears to have accelerated the withdrawal of school leavers' real jobs as employers have seen the wisdom of obtaining young people's services free of charge and adjusted their recruitment.

Simultaneously, work has been transferred from other age-groups thereby ensuring that trainees graduate from schemes to job-starved labour markets. (Roberts 1984, p 9).

The proportion of YOP trainees getting jobs fell as the scheme expanded. At first the proportion getting jobs or places in education, at over 70%, was high enough to sustain YOP's credibility. Over the next few years, however, the success rate fell dramatically. By mid-1981, only 44% of trainees found jobs or places in education when they left the scheme. In areas of high unemployment, placement rates were even lower. Many criticisms were also made of the training quality of YOP, its bad accident and injury record and the sexual and racial inequalities that stopped young girls or ethnic minority youngsters from getting a fair share of the better employment or training opportunities (Cockburn 1987; Cross and Smith 1987).

By 1981, under pressure from voluntary groups, employers and trade unions, the Government agreed to introduce a more adequate training programme – the YTS – which would offer places to all school leavers.

A New Status

Under the leadership of the MSC, and in the form of YOP and the YTS, new relationships between education, training, employers and young people were explored and created. A new educational vocabulary of vocational preparation and social and life skills was to evolve within the programmes. Presented as meeting the needs of the young unemployed, these new ideas in fact defined the young as in need of new forms of provision. Young school leavers were no longer accidental victims of the economic recession. Having been excluded from the proper labour market, they were to be redefined as trainees as an aspect of the state's solution to the recession. Somewhat ironically, the opening paragraph of the MSC document which first outlined the structure of YTS claimed that the new scheme 'is about providing a permanent bridge between school and work. It is not about youth unemployment' (MSC 1982, para 1.1).

	1978–79	1979–80	1980–81	1981–82	1982–83
Work experience (WEEP)	128,200	182,100	304,500	461,500	393,400
(% with private employers)	(84.5%)	(76.2%)	(79.5%)	(80.4%)	(78.6%)
Work preparation	34,000	34,300	55,500	91,500	67,800
Pilot YTS places	—	—	—	—	81,900
Total – all YOP	162,700	216,400	360,000	553,000	453,100

Source: MSC Annual Reports. Note: Average duration of YOP place was six months.

Table 2   Composition of YOP, 1978–83

The Two-Year Youth Training Scheme

Having been suitably differentiated at school, minimum age school leavers were channelled into work through the two-year YTS. This training was expected to make young people better workers in the labour markets of the 1990s.

All 16-and 17-year-old school leavers were guaranteed places on YTS. In their first year, trainees were paid a basic allowance (£28.50 per week) and were placed with an employer for 39 weeks and received 13 weeks off the job training. In their second year trainees got a slightly higher allowance (£35 per week) and 7 weeks off the job training. All trainees were, in theory, given the opportunity of taking a recognised vocational qualification, and were issued with a YTS certificate when they finished.

In 1984-85 some 4,200 training agencies were involved in delivering YTS and they used in excess of 100,000 different workplaces. At any one time nearly 60% of trainees were receiving work experience from external employers. This was usually provided in relatively small workplaces, with over half having less than 10 employees at the sampled workplace. Nearly all these establishments were in the private sector (*Employment Gazette*, August 1985). Only a minority of trainees were directly employed or enjoyed the benefits of high-quality vocational training along the lines of a conventional apprenticeship.

Government sponsored research found that when they were in the workplace less than a third of trainees were receiving systematic on-the-job training. Forty per cent were helping adult workers do their normal jobs, and one in three were doing the same jobs as other workers. A 1987 study estimated that while only a small minority of trainees had their allowance increased, or 'topped-up', by their employer, many of these young people were adding substantially to the output of their workplaces. The value of their output varied from £18 a week in mechanical engineering and £21 a week in construction to £36 per week in repair of consumer goods and vehicles and £33 in retail distribution (Deacon and Pratten 1987).

YTS had become an obvious way of screening young people for recruitment. Over half the managing agents, and nearly three-quarters of the other work experience providers have said they use the scheme in this way. In return for providing rudimentary training, employers are able to pick and choose their recruits from a pool of cheap trainees.

The latest follow-up survey shows that of the young people who left YTS between April 1986 and September 1987, 59% were in work, 22% were unemployed, and 16% were in education or other training (11% of these had joined another YTS

scheme). Those trainees who were most likely to become unemployed were living in inner cities or the depressed regions. They were likely to have fewer qualifications, and to come from ethnic minority backgrounds.

YTS was expected to make young people better workers in the 1990s labour market.

The Experience of Trainees

In the first year of YTS 350,000 places were taken up, less than three-quarters of the anticipated number. One in five trainees dropped out of the scheme prematurely, a third of whom became unemployed. Between April 1986 and September 1987 64% of those who left finished with YTS more than four weeks before the end of their course. A quarter of early leavers complained about their schemes, and one in five blamed the low level of the allowance. At least 10% of eligible unemployed school leavers were not participating in YTS (Horton 1986).

Interpretation exercise

Look at Table 3 in Dan Finn's article (p. 32). Prepare a report which discusses the **priorities** of employers in deciding whether or not to take part in youth training.

	% of establishments
Advantages to the employer	
Screening for good employees	42
Savings on labour costs	32
Help with training budget	9
Personal or business obligation	7
Good for employer's image	6
Other advantages	18
Social Reasons	
Wanted to do something to help young people	45
Seriousness of youth employment problem	22
Obligation to society to help deal with serious social problem	15
Obligation to the industry to play part in training	10
Other social reasons	7
Number of employers surveyed	**1,000**

Source: Employment Gazette, June 1986, p. 197.
Note: Percentages add up to more than 100% as respondents could give more than one answer.

Table 3   Employers' reasons for taking part in YTS

By December 1984 Mrs Thatcher was indicating that her Government wanted to stop the young unemployed claiming benefit. As far as she was concerned, 'young people ought not to be idle', and 'should not have the option of being unemployed'.

Following the 1987 general election, the Government passed the relevant legislation and from September 1988 very few minimum-age school leavers were able to gain an independent income unless they joined YTS. According to the Secretary of State for Employment, in October 1987, 'The only option which is being taken away from young people is the option to spurn the offer of a training place and live on benefit. That is not a good option for young people.'

However, the lack of enthusiasm for YTS displayed by many school leavers was not the product of irresponsibility or feckless idleness. Despite the attractive images of MSC publicity, there were enormous variations within the scheme. Some employers offered good training, with the chance of a job at the end, but other sponsors clearly offered what school leavers saw as an extension of YOP and experienced as a spell of cheap labour. Those who refused to join the scheme often saw it as a poor substitute for a job and dismissed it as 'slave labour', doing menial work which offered no real training (Fawcett Society 1985, p. 32-33; Roberts and Kirby 1985; Horton 1986; LMNI 1987).

A New Social Condition

Many young people have been sceptical about YTS and have rejected the ideology going with it, but they have negotiated their labour market realities and opportunities for education and training in a variety of undramatic ways.

Increasing numbers of young people have chosen to continue their full-time education and, as Ken Roberts has pointed out, many school leavers experience unemployment only intermittently. Rather than a particular group being condemned to permanent idleness, in many districts the joblessness is spread around and 'absorbed within sub-employed biographies'. As the jobs available in their local labour markets are frequently monotonous and low paid, young people settle for working sporadically; a 'common view is that neither work nor unemployment are tolerable for long unbroken periods' (Roberts 1984, p. 65).

	June 1984– March '85 15% follow up	April 1985– March 86	April 1986– August 87
In full-time work with same employer	24	28	26
In full-time work with different employer	31	25	30
In part-time work	na	4	3
On another YTS scheme	6	6	11
Unemployed	32	28	22
Doing something else	3	6	4
Percentage early leavers	52	50	64
Usable sample	63	59	60
Total	**na**	**223,500**	**250,111**

Source: 100% follow up of YTS leavers survey.

Table 4   Destination of YTS leavers: June 1984– August 1987

In the last two years registered unemployment and youth unemployment in particular have fallen rapidly. While this is partly due to some recovery in the economy, and to the expansion of YTS, it has been exaggerated by the ways in which the statistics have themselves been changed and by the dramatic fall in the number of young people coming on to the labour market (Unemployment Unit 1987). While registered unemployment amongst 16-and 17-year-olds has fallen from 217,000 in 1983 to 135,000 in October 1987, the number of 16-and 17-year-olds fell by 200,000 in the same period. This dramatic demographic decline will continue. Between 1987 and 1994 the number of people in the 16 to 19-year age group will fall from 3.5 million to 2.6 million: a fall of 26%.

Nevertheless, in January 1988 there were still 119,400 unemployed 16 and 17-year-olds, and a further 773,900 unemployed 18-to 25-year-olds. Of these, 157,600 had been out of work for more than six months, and 214,800 had been out of work for over a year. This long-term unemployment is concentrated in certain areas and regions and it is in these places that the old transitions to adulthood and economic independence may now be shattered. Once youth unemployment rises above 30%, as it has done in may inner city areas and on many housing estates, long-term unemployment spreads rapidly (Roberts 1984, p. 7).

A comprehensive report prepared for Wolverhampton City Council has argued that it is in these area that we are witnessing the emergence of what it calls a 'new social condition' (Willis 1984). They found that the young long-term unemployed were becoming increasingly pessimistic and had been left in a state of 'suspended animation', cut off from anticipated futures of leaving home, material consumption and marriage.

In this changing world some of the young unemployed were developing new ways of growing up working-class. In her 1980s experience on the road to Wigan Pier, for example, Beatrix Campbell (1984) found a baby boom and what she called a wave of 'dole queue mothers'. Single parenthood got these young women off the unemployment register and cut out the demoralising failure to find a job. It could end the monotonous experience of badly-paid work or provide a way out of the parental home. Significantly, the young women were living on state benefits and creating a future which no longer presupposed dependence on the male wage. Single parenthood offered young women maturity, some independence and the positive experiences of motherhood. Their new independence, however, could also produce its own isolation and oppression. For one group of young mothers:

> . . . instead of the gradual move from schoolgirl to worker, to fiancée, to wife and finally to mother, they were suddenly ripped away from their friends and their existing way of life and flung into the blurred existence of the single mother. For them it was a feeling of lost youth, of not being part of something they should have been, or of growing old too quickly. (Presdee 1984)

The dominant experience of long-term unemployment is still that of poverty, social isolation and depression

Application exercise

Finn's article details ways in which the growth in the number of long-term unemployed may affect individuals and families. You should also consider the implications for society as a whole of an **increase** in unemployment.

To do this, you will need to **apply** the information supplied in the article. You should consider the following issues:

- What are the **social control** implications of an increase in unemployment? Is there any evidence that public disorder or unrest has increased as unemployment has increased?
- What is a possible increase in public disorder likely to mean for the political fortunes of any government which oversees a growth in unemployment? Is unemployment a **political** issue?
- What are the **financial** consequences of an increase in unemployment, in terms of tax revenues, social security payments, etc. How might this affect a government's ability to carry out its policies?
- Does an increase in unemployment have any implications for rates of homelessness, suicide, or mental illness? How might any increase in these phenomena be **visible** in society?
- How might the consequences of an increase in unemployment vary in terms of **region, gender, ethnicity** or **age**? For example, what are the implications likely to be for society as a whole of a possible increase in the number of so-called 'dole queue mothers'?

both for the unemployed and their families. It is often a world punctuated by social crisis, by domestic breakdown, violence, ill-health and even suicide. Temporary training and employment schemes are the only lifeline which the Government extends to this lost generation.

Conclusion

The double and partly contradictory aim of the YTS, and increasingly of the MSC's other measures, especially the new adult Employment Training Scheme (which will prioritise the recruitment of 18-to 25-year-olds), is to produce a generation of young people who are basically skilled and willing to work, but who can also maintain these qualities in suspended animation through any periods of unemployment they experience. Having been suitably differentiated at school, these new model workers are to be instructed, through their training and work experience, and through the discipline of unemployment, to transcend the narrow trade practices and occupational loyalties of a now unwanted division of labour. They will, it is hoped, become highly mobile and individualistic, infinitely adaptable to technological change, possessing all the traditional virtues of the work ethic.

Characteristics of entrants	Number of entrants	Percentage of total entrants
Male	204,500	57
Female	155,500	43
16-year-old school leavers	323,100	90
17-year-old school leavers	35,900	10
18–21-year-old school leavers	1,000	—
White	342,700	95.2
Black/African/Caribbean descent	6,400	1.8
Indian sub-continent descent	5,400	1.5
All others	2,300	0.6
Preferred not to say	3,300	
Total entrants	360,000	

Source: Youth Training News, MSC, September 1987, Issue 40.
Note: The analysis relates to young people entering YTS for the first time in 1986–87.

Table 5   YTS: main characteristics of entrants, 1986–87

Through the two-year YTS, minimum-age school leavers will be given their first lessons in the economic and political realities of 1980s Britain. As the Chancellor of the Exchequer expressed it in his 'Budget for Jobs' speech in 1985, the Government is investing its resources in training schemes not only to produce a workforce with the right technical skills, but also to create one which is 'adaptable, reliable, motivated and is prepared to work at wages that employers can afford to pay'.

References and Further Reading

Campbell, B. (1984) *Wigan Pier Revisited: Poverty and Politics in the 80s*, Virago.
Cockburn, C. (1987) *Two-Track Training: Sex Inequalities and the YTS*, Macmillan.
Cross, M. and Smith, D. (eds) (1987) *Black Youth Futures: Ethnic Minorities and the YTS*, National Youth Bureau.
Deakin, B.M. and Pratten, C.F. (October, 1987) 'Economic effects of YTS', in *Employment Gazette*.
Fawcett Society and the National Joint Commission of Working Women's Organisations (1985) *The Class of '84: A Study of Girls on the First Year of the Youth Training Scheme*, 150 Walworth Road, London.
Frith, S. (1980) 'Youth and the labour process', in M. Cole and B. Skelton (eds), *Blind Alley: Youth in a Crisis of Capital*, Hesketh.
Horton, C. (1986) *Nothing Like a Job: A Survey of Unemployed School Leavers (1983–1984) Who Could Have Gone on the Youth Training Scheme But Did Not*, Youthaid.
LMNI (1987) *Report of the National Labour Movement Inquiry into Youth Unemployment and Training*, available from TURC, 7 Frederick Street, Birmingham B13.
MSC (1982) *Youth Task Group Report: New Training Initiative.* Presdee, M. (1984) 'The twilight zone', *Youth in Society*, National Youth Bureau, Leicester.
Roberts, K. (1984) *School Leavers and their Prospects: Youth and the Labour Market in the 1980s*, Open University Press.
Roberts, K. and Kirby, R. (Spring 1985) 'YB on YTS: why not?', *Youth and Policy*, No. 12.
Unemployment Unit (1987) *Hidden Unemployment: The True Measure of Unemployment in London*, Youthaid, 9 Poland Street, London, W1V 3DG.
Willis, P. (1984) 'Youth unemployment: a new social state', *New Society* (29 March).
Youthaid (1981) *Quality or Collapse? Youthaid Review of the Youth Opportunities Programme*, Youthaid, 9 Poland Street, London, W1V 3DG.
Youthaid (1983) *Youth Unemployment: A Background Paper*, Youthaid, 9 Poland Street, London W1V 3DG.

Structured question (25 marks)

a) In extract D, suggest one other ethnic category which might be included in the 'All others' option.   (1 mark)

b) What is meant by 'sub-employed biographies', as used in extract B?   (2 marks)

c) To what extent do sociologists agree that schools should be expected to make pupils 'intellectually and attitudinally better potential employees' (extract A) ?   (8 marks)

d) How do sociologists suggest that pupils are 'differentiated at school' (extract C)? (5 marks)

e) Using the information from any of the extracts and from elsewhere, assess the impact of youth training schemes on the experiences of young people.   (9 marks)

CHAPTER 4

Work & Leisure

Editors' introduction

Much research in the sociology of work – and, indeed, in other areas of sociology – has focused its attention on **male** workers. Women have not figured centrally in the principal theories in this area, as is particularly clear when sociologists have tried to use work and employment relations as central elements in theories of stratification: the class position of a woman, for example, is often defined by the occupation of her husband or male partner. Throughout the post-war period, however, women have entered the labour market in ever greater numbers. Feminist writers have been in the vanguard of attempts to describe and explain patterns of women's work and to explore the implications of these patterns for conventional sociological theories. Their writings have now begun to have a significant impact on all research into work and employment.

Rosemary Crompton examines some of the features which are specific to women's work. It is, for example, frequently located in or associated with the home, and it is generally low paid. Women's work is tightly constrained by conventional social norms of motherhood and domesticity, leading to a characteristic 'bi-modal' pattern of employment : there are peaks of employment before the birth of the first child and after the end of the child-rearing period. She argues, however, that the proportion of women in employment will continue to rise and that women are increasingly getting 'better' jobs. Crompton concludes by considering some of the implications for patterns of domestic care. Who will do the caring work previously undertaken, unpaid, by women?

Women and Work in the 1990s

ROSEMARY CROMPTON

Both men and women work, but the structure of women's work is different from that of men's. More of women's work takes place in the home or domestic sphere. This work will not, usually, be associated with wages or other formal payments, and it is not regulated by trades unions, employers, or the state. It is, rather, governed by informal (and changing) ideas and norms relating to motherhood and domestic responsibilities more generally. Men, too, work in the home but proportionally more of their work takes place in the sphere of employment and the public marketplace.

During the Second World War, there was a mass mobilisation of women, including married women, into employment as part of the war effort. After the war, most of these women returned to domesticity. However, both the state and private employers were also generating an increasing demand for women as paid workers, as the post-war economy entered a period of boom at the same time as the expansion of the welfare state was creating jobs in the education, health and welfare services. Through the 1960s and 1970s, increasing numbers of married women returned to the labour force, often after their youngest child had reached school age. It was still assumed, however, that women would take the major responsibility as far as home and domestic life was concerned, and, as a consequence, many of the jobs the women returned to were designed to accommodate this.

Part-time working was widely regarded as enabling the optimum combination of domestic work and paid employment, and other innovations such as the 'twilight shift' (when a husband was assumed to be available to look after children) were developed in order to enable women to fulfil their 'two roles' – home and work.

By the end of the 1970s, a distinctive pattern of women's employment in Britain had emerged. The employment profile of the female labour force was 'bi-modal': an early peak amongst young women was followed by a trough as women of childbearing age left the labour force, to be followed by a second peak (at its maximum around the age of 45) as women re-entered the labour force when their children were older (Hakim 1979).

Women were and are also concentrated into particular jobs as, conversely, are men. This extensive occupational segregation by sex is summarised in Table 1.

It shows that men tended to predominate in professional and managerial jobs – except those in health and welfare – and women in lower-level clerical jobs. Men predominate in manufacturing, transport and construction, whereas women are in 'service' jobs such as catering, cleaning, hairdressing and selling. These jobs are also likely to be part-time, in contrast to the rather better-paid clerical jobs. Part-time work might be convenient for women, but it is not a particularly advantageous form of employment. Many part-time jobs are classified as unskilled, and have only low wages. Jobs which have careers attached to them, in industries like banking, or the civil service, are more usually full-time. Cleaning and catering, and other 'caring' jobs reflect the nature of work done by women in the home. Table 1, therefore, shows the massive impact of domestic work on the pattern of paid employment of women, in relation to both the hours they work and the kind of jobs they do.

Women, the Family and Work

Although women's work is concentrated in relatively low-level and less skilled occupations, it might be argued that this arrangement is of maximum benefit to men, women, and their families. Some economists have suggested that in households with two adults, it makes sense for one to specialise in 'domestic' work and the other in 'market' work, and to exchange their relative surplus product. These arguments are echoed in the functional analysis of the family by the American sociologist, Talcott Parsons. He argued that in the modern family, women fulfil 'expressive' (i.e. caring) roles, whereas those of men are 'instrumental' (i.e. breadwinner) roles. In support of these kinds of views, it might be pointed out that girls have had equality of educational opportunity with boys since the Second World War, that sex discrimination in employment has been illegal since 1976, and that equal pay for women also dates from the same period. Have women, therefore, chosen low-level, part-time work, in order that they may fulfil their 'two-roles'?

There have, not surprisingly, been extensive criticisms by feminists of these kinds of arguments. Liberal feminists, who have campaigned for equality of rights and opportunities for women since the nineteenth century and before, have argued that

Occupation	Full Time	Part Time	All Women	All Men
Professional & Managerial	8	1	6	24
Professional in Health, etc.	16	10	13	5
Clerical	41	22	33	6
Catering, Cleaning, Selling	16	54	32	7
Manufacturing, Transport	17	10	14	51
Other	2	3	2	6
	100	100	100	100

Source: adapted from *Women and Employment, A Lifetime Perspective* (1984).

Table 1   Occupations of full- and part-time working women and working men (percentages).

despite recent legislation these ends have not yet been achieved. In particular, they have argued that the continuing domestic demands made of women make it difficult, if not impossible, for women to achieve equal status with men, despite a formal equality of opportunities. Women do not choose poorly paid, part-time work but, rather, have it thrust upon them.

Radical feminists have taken these arguments further. They have stressed the significance of *patriarchy* – that is, the systematic oppression of women by men. Men keep women out of the better jobs, and the subordinate position of women in employment serves to reproduce the structure of male power and domination in society. Both liberal and radical feminists would agree, however, that one important reason for the low status of 'women's work' is that it is often *culturally* defined as inferior, that is, that the value it is given reflects the low status of women in society.

Throughout the 1980s, therefore, feminists have not only continued to fight for equal opportunities for women in employment, but also to transform the status of 'women's work'. In 1984, the Equal Pay (Amendment) Act came into force, which established the principle of equal pay, not only for the same work but also for work of equal value. Equal values cases are difficult to establish, and procedures are laborious, but nevertheless a number have been won. In 1989, for example, seven female secretaries, typists, and

The majority of doctors in training now are women.

clerk/typists claimed that their work was equal to a male bank messenger's, and won their case against their employer (Lloyds Bank plc). Even the threat of action can have an impact. There has been recent publicity concerning the pay up-grading of jobs dominated by women, following an equal value referral in the retail sector. Marks and Spencer have recently announced a three-year pay deal worth 26.4% for sales assistants (largely women) while freezing pay for warehouse staff (largely men). Changes are also taking place in the nature of the female labour force itself. In particular, women's levels of educational qualifications have been rising – for example, the majority of doctors in training are now women. More women are qualifying as accountants and lawyers, and gaining work-related qualifications such as the Institute of Bankers and Insurance examinations.

Coursework suggestion

Many students of A level Sociology have part-time jobs. If you have a part-time job it could provide you with an opportunity to carry out a covert **participant observation study** of gender relations at work. For such a study, it is essential to have a clear focus for what it is you wish to observe and a strategy for recording instances which are important to your research question. You will also need a time limit for the collection of your data.

Some observations may be statistical, for example, counting the number of men and women in supervisory positions in your workplace. Others will be more qualitative, examining inter-relationships between men and women in the work context. You will need to be careful here not to allow your own biases or experiences at work to influence how you interpret what you see. The more detailed an

account of any interaction you can provide, the more convincing your analysis of it may be to a reader of the research.

You will also need to be honest with yourself, reflecting on whether you have influenced interactions by your presence.
It is perfectly valid to draw upon your own experiences in work, because part of the attraction of participant observation is its ability to allow the researcher to stand in someone else's place and experience what s/he has experienced. But you will need to support those personal experiences by other evidence that what you are going through is what others in the same position are also experiencing. You should address these issues directly in an evaluation of your project.

Women and Caring

These changes in the way women's work is valued, and in the nature of the female labour force, are taking place against the background of what has come to be known as the demographic 'time-bomb'. A government report published in 1988 noted that the most radical change in the labour force during the 1990s will be the decline in the number of young people in the labour market (*Employment for the 1990s*, HMSO). The numbers aged 16-19 in the population will have fallen by over 1 million between 1983 and 1993; in the labour market this means that the number aged under 25 is projected to fall by 1.2 million between 1987 and 1995 (Figure 1). The report argues that this shortfall in young people may be offset, in part, by the increased recruitment of women, and argues that, in order to achieve this, 'Employers must recognise that women can no longer be treated as second-class workers. They will need women employees, and must recognise both their career ambitions and domestic responsibilities' (p. 8).

However, there have been other aspects of government policy throughout the 1980s which might

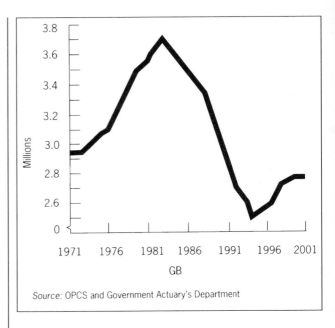

Figure 1   Population aged 16–19; 1971 to 2001.

work against these convenient assumptions. During the last decade, there has been a shift towards 'community care': '. . . people who are affected by problems of ageing, mental illness, mental handicap or physical or sensory disability need to be able to live as independently as possible in their own homes . . . The Government is firmly committed to a policy of community care . . .' (*Caring for People: Community Care in the Next Decade and Beyond*, HMSO 1989). As the White Paper notes, 'the OPCS study of informal carers identified about 6 million carers in Great Britain . . . the greater part of care for most people at most times of their lives continues to be provided by their families and friends . . . (pp. 62, 92) rather than by statutory bodies. The majority of such carers are women.'

As feminist work in the area of social policy has emphasised, much of the (unpaid) work of caring has always fallen on women, and an official shift in policy in the direction of 'community' care means more of such work. Writing in 1983, at a time of high levels of unemployment, Rimmer noted that existing public expenditure estimates of the costs of care had been kept low by ignoring the contribution of informal carers, and posed the question as to whether this effective subsidy could be relied upon when the situation in respect of unemployment changed. As we have seen, it has done. Women have also been prominent in the voluntary 'caring sector' which has been identified by the Government as a central element in community care – but in 1989, the Charity

---

Application exercise

The article states that 'the White Paper on employment is explicit that it is employers who must provide the facilities to enable women to remain in employment'.

What arrangements or policies can employers make to meet women's needs as workers?

In answering this question, you should draw upon the article itself to give you some ideas as to what employers can do to recruit women workers, to retain their services and develop their career opportunities. This should include a recognition of the likely domestic responsibilities of female employees. Begin by writing down as many things as you can think of that employers could do to help female employees , and then divide them into appropriate categories. These might be, for example, **Recruitment**, **Retention**, **Careers**. Or alternatively, **Dealing with female workers' domestic responsibilities** and **Dealing with female workers' career ambitions**. Then turn your points into paragraphs, so that your answer is well structured.

Evaluation exercise

If you were asked to assess the likely impact of the government's Community Care Programme (CCP) on the lives of many women in work, how would you go about the task?

Firstly, you could look at the article carefully to find out what the CCP consists of and for some clues and/or questions about its likely impact. Your task would then be to produce a **realistic** account of how it might affect women in work. There are also factors not referred to in the article but which you can apply to this issue, such as demographic trends, and the growth of private provision for the dependent population.

As you are asked to assess the likely impact, you should think about how these developments **might** affect women workers. The effects will probably not be uniform for all women workers and you should therefore provide a variety of possible outcomes. The assessment task is to evaluate which of the outcomes you have identified is most likely to occur, based on the arguments you have put forward.

The following questions might help you to generate some ideas:
Who has traditionally undertaken the caring role?
Who is likely to take up the burden of care for the elderly in the future?
What alternative arrangements for the elderly might be developed?
What is the role of choice in accepting responsibility for care?
Would a change in government affect the CCP?
Can employers do anything to help women workers who also have caring responsibilities?
Does the development of the 'new man' make a difference?
Does the CCP generate new jobs?
Are they mainly for women?

Aid Foundation had already identified a 'manpower' crisis in the voluntary sector due to the increased number of women going to work.

We have, therefore, a paradox. On the one hand, women are being identified as a key element in the labour force, in order to make up the reduction in the supply of labour given the decline in the number of young people. On the other hand, the unpaid labour of women is a key (if under-emphasised) element in the continuing shift to Community Care. As Table 2 indicates, the trend towards the increasing employment of women shows no sign of slackening.

Women are now 46% of the labour force, and the Government's own projections assume that by 1995 the female labour force will increase by over three-quarters of a million (*Employment for the 1990s, op. cit.*). Table 2 (p. 40) suggests that, whereas the proportion of women who worked full-time fell slightly during the 1970s, it has risen somewhat during the 1980s. Perhaps this is a consequence of the increased 'quality' of women's labour as represented by their education and training – for, as we have seen, the better jobs tend to be full-time. More women are getting higher level jobs. The increase in women gaining professional qualifications has already been described, and figures supplied by a major clearing bank show that in 1990, 25% of those on managerial grades aged under thirty were women. This figure might seem low, and, indeed, under ten per cent of all of the same bank's managers are women – but there were no women at all in bank management in the 1970s. The finance sector in particular is extremely anxious to recruit and retain women workers, and is in the forefront of the development of career breaks, childcare schemes, and so on – the Midland Bank, for example, has set up around two hundred day nurseries for its employees.

Diverging Households

It is likely that the proportion of women in employment will continue to increase, and this trend may also increase the material gap between households in this country. In 1984, Pahl argued that 'A process of polarization is developing, with households busily

Interpretation exercise

What trends in male and female employment can you identify in Table 2 (p. 40)? You should refer both to absolute numbers and to proportions in your response, as well as carefully distinguishing between full-time and part-time workers. Make sure that you do not just repeat the figures in the table but actually interpret them in terms of trends. These should be expressed by describing increases and decreases, with perhaps a limited number of figures to illustrate the trends you identify.

	Males (thousands)	Females (thousands)	Females % of total	% Females full-time	% Females part-time
1971	13,424	8,224	38.0	25.3	12.6
1976	13,097	8,951	40.4	24.3	16.3
1981	12,278	9,108	42.6	24.7	17.8
1986	11,643	9,462	44.3	25.2	19.6
1988	11,978	10,096	45.7	26.2	19.5

Source: Department of Employment Gazette.

Table 2   Trends in men's and women's employment 1971–1988

engaged in all forms of work at one pole and households unable to do a wide range of work at the other'. The proportion of dual-income households among married couples has increased from 55% in 1976 to 67% in 1986, and the trend identified by Pahl is likely to be exacerbated. Women in good jobs tend to marry men in good jobs, thus increasing the gap between the higher earning households and those at the bottom – which will include a high proportion of carers and cared for, reliant on state benefits.

A work-place nursery in Tower Hamlets, London.

The trends reviewed in this article suggest that more women will be moving into better jobs during the 1990s, but that this positive development might be accompanied by a crisis of caring in the community, as well as an increase in material inequalities between households. What steps, therefore, might be taken to avoid these negative outcomes? It is not possible simply to turn back the clock and force women to return to the home, and it is not physically possible for women to assume the double burden of paid employment and caring work. Ungerson (1987) has argued that ' . . . what is needed is high-quality and easily available domiciliary and day-care *services*, combined with equally high-quality forms of flexible residential care, including permanent sheltered housing for protected independent living and regular respite care for those normally cared for informally' (p. 155).

The question remains, who will provide such care? Present Government policy is committed to a proportionate reduction of state expenditure on social services. The Government White Paper on community care recognises that 'demographic trends will have implications for the future availability of carers' (p. 63) but makes no suggestions as to how these implications might be met. As we have seen, the White Paper on employment is explicit that it is *employers* who must provide the facilities to enable women with families to remain in employment. Is it realistic to anticipate that employers will extend their support to finance the kinds of facilities described by Ungerson? Will the banks provide granny flats as well as creches? These questions will have to be answered during the 1990s.

References and Further Reading

Beechey, V. & Perkins, T. (1987) *A Matter of Hours: Women, Part-Time Work and the Labour Market*, Polity Press.

Caring for People: Community Care in the Next Decade and Beyond (1989) Cm. 849, HMSO.

Crompton, R. & Sanderson, K. (1990) *Gendered Jobs and Social Change*, Unwin Hyman.

Employment for the 1990s Cm. 540, HMSO.

Hakim, C. (1979) *Occupational Segregation*, Department of Employment Research Paper No. 9.

Martin, J. & Roberts, C. (1984) *Women and Employment: A Lifetime Perspective*, HMSO.

Pahl, R. (1984) *Divisions of Labour*, Basil Blackwell.

Rimmer, L. (1983) 'The economics of work and caring' in Finch, J. & Groves, D. (eds) *A Labour of Love*, Routledge & Kegan Paul.

Ungerson, C. (1987) *Policy is Personal: Sex, Gender and Informal Care*, Tavistock.

Structured question (25 marks)

a) What do sociologists mean when they refer to 'domesticity' (extract A)?   (1 mark)

b) Describe the patterns of occupational segregation between men and women, as shown in extract B.   (4 marks)

c) Assess the extent to which the Equal Pay Act, as amended, has succeeded in equalising male and female incomes.   (6 marks)

d) To what extent does sociological evidence support the idea expressed in extract A that 'it [is] still assumed . . . that [working] women [will] take the major responsibility as far as home and domestic life is concerned'. (7 marks)

e) Assess the validity of the concept of patriarchy in describing the position of women in work (extract C).   (7 marks)

Cuttings

The Family Policy Studies Centre in London published a critical review of the changing roles of men and women, *Inside the Family* (1987). These were its main findings.

- The home domain is still very much a female one. Women are still primarily responsible for domestic and caring tasks, although 50% of couples claim to share child care equally.
- While women are mainly or solely responsible for almost three quarters of all housework, men are primarily responsible for over 80% of household repairs.
- While women have become increasingly active in the labour market, for many this is still largely secondary to their roles as wives and mothers – most married women with children who work do so part time.
- Men spend less time at home, but generally work longer hours in their jobs. Even women employed full time rarely work as many hours as their male colleagues.
- Female employees (both full- and part-time) generally have less free time at home than males. While spending fewer hours at work (or travelling to and from work) they spend much longer on domestic work, shopping etc: while full-time male employees have around 10.2 hours of free time per weekend day, and 2.6 during the week, for full-time female employees the respective figures are 7.2 hours and 2.1 hours.

Domestic tasks and women's employment

		Full-time working women %	Part-time working women %
Household shopping:	Mainly man	4	4
	Mainly woman	52	64
	Shared equally	43	32
Preparation of evening meal:	Mainly man	11	4
	Mainly woman	61	79
	Shared equally	26	15
Household cleaning:	Mainly man	6	1
	Mainly woman	61	83
	Shared equally	33	15
Washing and ironing:	Mainly man	4	—
	Mainly woman	81	95
	Shared equally	14	5
Repairs of household equipment	Mainly man	83	74
	Mainly woman	5	13
	Shared equally	12	11

Source: Jowell, R and Witherspoon, S. (eds) (1985) *British Social Attitudes* p. 57, Gower

People in households: by type of household and family in which they live

Great Britain				Percentages
Type of household	1961	1971	1981	1989[1]
Living alone	3.9	6.3	8.0	10.2
Married couple, no children	17.8	19.3	19.5	22.4
Married couple with dependent children[2]	52.2	51.7	47.4	42.2
Married couple with non-dependent children only	11.6	10.0	10.3	11.4
Lone parent with dependent children[2]	2.5	3.5	5.8	5.8
Other households	12.0	9.2	9.0	8.0
All people in private households[3]	100	100	100	100

1 1989-90 data. The General Household Survey changed from calendar years to financial years in 1988.
2 These family types may also include non-dependent children.
3 The number of people in each census was 49,545,000 in 1961, 52,347,000 in 1971 and 52,760,000 in 1981. The sample size of the General Household Survey in 1989-90 was 24,997.

Source: Office of Population Censuses and Surveys

Child care

Places available in publicly-funded child care (for children aged three to compulsory school age) as a percentage of all children in that age group

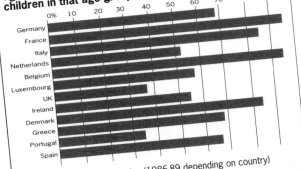

Source: European Commission (1986-89 depending on country)

CHAPTER 5

Social Stratification

Editors' introduction

Social stratification is central to all the major theoretical perspectives in sociology. For Marxists, the division of society into opposed **classes** leads to 'class struggle' which, in turn, is seen as a fundamental driving force in social change. For functionalists, on the other hand, the organisation of society into a hierarchy of **statuses** is the basis, through their varying 'functional importance', of social stability. Behind these competing views is a difference in terminology (class *versus* status) and a difference in theoretical focus (change *versus* stability, or conflict *versus* consensus).

Malcolm Hamilton reviews these varying approaches and the concepts that they employ. In addition to Marxist and functionalist theories, he examines the work of Weber and the conflict theorists. His aim is to clarify the important theoretical differences which separate the writers associated with the various approaches. The purpose of this clarification, however, is to outline the basis for a **synthesis**. He examines the work of Lenski, which tries to synthesise the ideas of 'power' and 'function', suggesting some problems with the argument.

Can you identify further difficulties with Lenski's claims?

Inequality and Stratification

MALCOLM HAMILTON

Three different types of *inequality* can be distinguished, namely privilege, prestige and power. *Privilege* concerns the distribution of valued goods, services, rewards, opportunities and 'life chances' in general. *Prestige* involves the evaluation of characteristics and actions in terms of their social worth or admirability. *Power* occurs when one person is able, for whatever reason, to get another to do what that other would not otherwise have done.

These three types of inequality are connected in a variety of ways. Privilege may form the basis upon which power rests while power in turn may be used to generate privilege. Both power and privilege may generate prestige, while, conversely, prestige may give access to *either*. Writers on stratification have devised alternative ways of describing these elements of inequality. I shall consider the work of Marx and Weber, the functionalist theory and conflict theory.

Marx and Class

The idea of *class* is most closely associated with Karl Marx, who was largely responsible for introducing the concept to sociology. Marx believed that all historical societies, that is societies above the level of the primitive mode of production, are divided along class lines. In each major type or mode of production, two main classes are important for understanding how inequality is generated. Marx did not, however, define class in terms of privilege and wealth, income, birth, occupation, and so on, but in terms of relationship to the means of production and position in the social organisation of the means of production. One class owns the means of production and as a result is able to exploit the other, propertyless and subordinate class. In the ancient mode of production the two main classes were the slaves and the slave owners. In the feudal mode of production they were the landed nobility and the semi-servile peasantry. In the capitalist mode of production, with which Marx was particularly concerned, they are the *bourgeoisie* who own the major means of production (industrial capital) and the *proletariat* who have nothing other than their capacity to work, their labour power. In order to live, the proletariat must sell their labour power to the owners of the means of production, the sale of labour in the market providing the wages on which they depend.

Class, of course, while not defined in terms of income or wealth, does determine to a very large extent, Marx believed, the distribution of income and wealth. The proletariat are exploited and therefore relatively poor while the bourgeoisie are able to use their property to accumulate wealth and power. Wealth tends to 'pile up at one end of society' as Marx put it. Wealth and power generally also determine lifestyle and, therefore, prestige and status in society. Finally, occupation is to a large extent correlated with class, if not entirely so.

Marx's conception of class is, then, a dichotomous one. There are, in any class system, two main classes which are interdependent and, because one exploits the other, they are also antagonistic to one another. It is this antagonism, in a capitalist society, which provides the driving force for social change and the transformation of capitalism into socialism or communism.

Marx's ideas have been subjected to a great deal of criticism. Here we shall review the most important points. The criterion of class consciousness means that, in principle at least, classes in the fullest sense may not actually emerge in capitalism, or the proletariat may never become a class in this full sense. Some critics, including Max Weber, have questioned whether classes typically do become class conscious. According to this view, class consciousness is something that may arise in definite and specific circumstances, but which neither necessarily nor very readily does so. It is an empirical question as to which circumstances do promote the development of class consciousness.

A second criticism of the Marxian conception of class concerns the application of the concept to real historical situations and to real societies. It is obviously a very considerable simplification of a reality which is far more complex than the Marxist picture makes it seem. Marx was well aware that social reality, including class structure, is complex, but he believed

that what mattered was to identify the main 'fault lines' in society, however much they may be masked by details and superficial appearances. There were, in Marx's day, many individuals and groups who did not fit neatly into his two-fold categorisation of proletariat and bourgeoisie: small independent farmers, tenant farmers, independent self-employed craftsmen, small traders, shopkeepers, professionals, and so on. Marx, however, believed that, as capitalism developed, society would polarise increasingly between the two main classes. Those who stood outside the dichotomous class system would be sucked into it. The existence of such groups was explained in terms of capitalist development. They were seen as survivals from pre-capitalist society and destined to disappear as capitalism matured beyond this early stage. Other groups, such as professionals, would remain marginal and relatively insignificant from the point of view of understanding the mechanics and dynamics of capitalism.

The reality of the development of capitalism has not, however, confirmed this picture of polarisation and dichotomisation at all. If some of the groups that Marx saw as transitional have, indeed, disappeared, new ones have arisen and proliferated. One of the most striking things about the development of capitalism in the 20th century has been the tremendous expansion and diversification of the middle classes – the white-collar, administrative and managerial sectors. There has been much debate in recent years, in Marxist circles, about this development and how these classes might be fitted into the Marxist model, but the essential point here is that the Marxist conception has run into grave difficulties in its application to contemporary society as a result of the rise of the middle classes.

If the two main types of criticism of the Marxian conception of class discussed above are valid then Marxist class theory is of little use. Yet, despite the problems and difficulties there does seem to be something in it. It certainly continues to provide many Marxist theorists with a tool which they feel gives them considerable insight into the workings of contemporary society.

Non-Marxists too have generally retained something of the original idea in their redefinitions and reformulations of the concept. Indeed, it is significant that later writers and theorists have not entirely abandoned the notion, but have rather sought to redefine, modify and reformulate it in such a way as to make it more applicable. It seems to touch upon many aspects of contemporary capitalism too closely to be abandoned outright. Political divisions have, for example, frequently reflected class divisions and political parties have always drawn their support disproportionately from different classes. Industrial relations and conflict have to some extent followed the lines anticipated by Marx's analysis.

Weber: Class and Status Group

Weber also used the concept of class, but he defined it rather differently from Marx. He also believed that systems of stratification could not always be seen in terms of class, but were often based upon status criteria producing systems in which the major social divisions were *status groups* rather than classes.

Classes, Weber argued, are the major social divisions in societies dominated by market exchange of goods, services and labour. A class for Weber is a *category* of persons who share a similar position in the market, in so far as this position determines opportunities for those things which are desired (life-chances). Class is a question of market power. Classes are not *necessarily* groups with a sense of identity, common interest and purpose.

A key determinant of class position, according to Weber, is the ownership of property which can be used to earn a return in the market. Like Marx, he considered the division of society into property owners and non-owners as of fundamental significance. However, Weber distinguished between various forms of property ownership and associated type of return. As well as the employers of labour, Marx's bourgeoisie, who earn profit, there are the owners of land and of buildings which they let or lease in return for rent, and there are the finance capitalists who lend money in return for interest. These groups may not always have common interests, or may have conflicting interests at any particular time.

Weber also distinguishes between various types of labour that are sold in the market place. He makes a fundamental distinction between non-manual, educated, skilled labour on the one hand and manual labour, which may be skilled or unskilled, on the other. The sellers of labour, then, like property owners, do not form a homogeneous group which necessarily has a common interest. Weber's conception of class, then, is not a dichotomous one. Classes, therefore, do not necessarily stand in a relationship of exploitation and antagonisms towards one another.

Status groups, unlike classes, are inherently groups which have a sense of identity and common purpose. They are, to use Weber's terminology, communities. The members of a status group share a common situation *vis-a-vis* life-chances determined by some positive or negative social estimation of their worth or honour. Status groups have certain rights, privileges, opportunities, etc., not because of their position in the market – their market power – but because they have certain characteristics or attributes evaluated in terms of worth, prestige or the lack of it, and so on. Slaves, for example, do not, for the most part, have poor opportunities in life because of their market situation but because they are *slaves*. That is to say their status as slaves determines their opportunities, prevents them from doing certain things, commits them to subordination to the will of others, and so on.

Whenever jobs, offices, opportunities for income, trade, access to education, etc., are restricted on the basis of birth, background, ethnicity, race, religion, kinship, and so on, one has a status group rather than a class, according to Weber. Status is usually expressed in terms of distinctive habits, lifestyle and restrictions upon interaction with non-members. Speech, dress, manners, residence, marriage patterns, all may become expressions of status group membership.

Class and status can be interlinked and usually are. Weber says that property is not simply a determinant of class position, but may also be a criterion for membership in a status group. On the other hand class and status can cut across one another. Indeed, Weber points out that status nearly always repudiates mere class position as a sufficient criterion for membership of a status group emphasising the type, manner of acquisition of wealth and how long it has been in the family.

Despite the linkages and contradictions between class and status group that may exist in any given system or society, Weber's main concern in defining these concepts is to characterise the stratification systems of societies as either class-based or status-based. As noted above, industrial, capitalist society is predominantly class-based. Earlier forms of society have often been status-based.

Some would question whether Weber's concept of status group is really necessary. The idea that major life-chances are determined in any society by status position is one that might be challenged. In a feudal society, for example, while there may have been many rights and privileges associated with aristocratic status, the main reason for aristocratic privilege was control of land, a form of property. Aristocrats were, therefore, a class. Many slaves in ancient societies had poor life-chances, it is true, because they were the property of someone else. But again we have a property owning *class* and a class of those who are *themselves* property.

The Functionalist Approach

The best known exponents of the functional theory of inequality are Kingsley Davis and Wilbert Moore who set out their views in a seminal article in *The American Sociological Review* in 1945. It stimulated much subsequent debate in the pages of this and other journals for many years thereafter.

We may set out the essential points briefly (see Banton, 1987).

(1) All societies need to attract the right people, with the appropriate skills, into functionally important positions and to motivate those who occupy such positions to fulfil their duties effectively.

(2) The appropriate skills are often in scarce supply.

(3) Society must use differential rewards to encourage people to acquire the skills and attract them to the positions.

(4) The greater the uniqueness of a position the more functionally important it is.

(5) The more central the position, that is the more other positions depend upon it, the more functionally important it is.

(6) The more important a position the more highly rewarded it will be.

(7) The more scarce the skill the more highly rewarded it will be.

The main criticisms of the functionalist approach may be summarised as follows:

(1) It is not empirically true that the more important positions are always the most highly rewarded and vice versa.

(2) Those who are best qualified do not always succeed in getting the better rewarded and most important positions because of imperfections in the mechanisms of recruitment and placement *which are themselves the consequences of inequality.*

(3) It is not functionally necessary to reward important positions more highly since these positions often entail intrinsic gratifications, such as interest, the opportunity to exercise authority, to take decisions and enjoy responsibility, which are sufficient to attract the more able.

(4) The notion of functional importance is vague and unclear. Is it what helps society to survive? What does it mean for a society to *survive*? Is it what helps a society to function smoothly? What does function mean in this context – to continue existing and operating in the same way? But societies change and develop.

(5) Uniqueness is no guarantee of functional importance.

(6) Centrality should not be equated with importance. Most positions are dependent on many others and 'central' positions are as dependent upon other positions as other positions are upon 'central' positions.

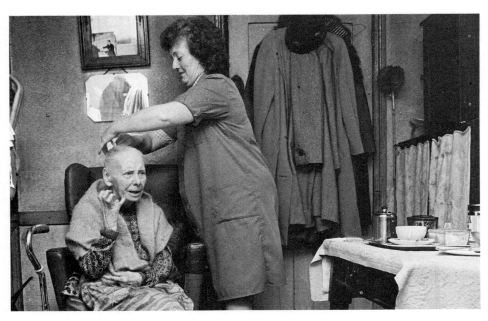

A home help in Battersea. Functional importance is not the only determinant of income.

Coursework suggestion 1

One of the ways in which you can explore how individuals see class structure in modern Britain is to present them with a series of statements and then ask them to agree or disagree with each of the statements. This is called a **structured interview**. You will need to have an idea of the range of views which sociologists have suggested exist in the population at large. The Hamilton article provides some useful information but you will also need to read other literature on the theory of class.

Begin your coursework by developing a hypothesis. For example, you might wish to test the hypothesis that **'The majority of people hold a conflict view of society'**. Firstly, you must be clear what is meant by a conflict view of society. Secondly, you will need to generate a series of statements which are clearly linked to a conflict view, for example, 'Society is divided into the **haves** and **have-nots**'. To test your hypothesis properly, you must also include statements which offer alternatives to the conflict view of society. You will need to ascertain whether non-conflict views are more commonly held than conflict views, or vice versa.

You should 'pilot' your statements by asking other sociology students which of the statements you have prepared indicate conflict views of society and which do not. If they cannot tell which are which, then you probably need to rethink your statements.

When you have finalised your statements, you can introduce a measure of how far respondents might agree or disagree with them. This is usually done on a five-point scale ranging from 'strongly agree' to 'strongly disagree'.

You will need to make a number of very important decisions as to how many interviewees to ask and how to select them so as to produce a random sample. These decisions will be influenced by your chosen method for analysing the results: if you are going to do your statistical analysis by hand, a large sample will take a long time to analyse; if you can use computer spreadsheets you will be able to use a larger sample. Once you have a random sample of the appropriate size, you can interview individuals using your structured interview schedule.

Finally, you will need to analyse the resulting statistics for their implications for your hypothesis. It is not enough to simply describe the results in terms of the numbers of people agreeing with various statements, you must show their significance in relation to your original hypothesis. Be careful not to include material which has no bearing on your hypothesis. A good rule to follow is: if you are not going to use a table or chart directly to examine your hypothesis, then you probably don't need to include it.

You should note that many criticisms have been made of the structured interview approach adopted here. You need to be aware of these and you should incorporate them in your evaluation of your project.

(7) By focusing exclusively on *positions* the functionalist approach ignores important processes in the generation of inequality which involve individuals winning, creating, achieving, etc., rewards for themselves by actions which do not fit into any pre-determined pattern. In short they create new 'positions' in the process of pursuing rewards.

(8) The functionalist approach ignores the use and operation of power in society.

Some critics have seen in the functionalist approach an incipient supply and demand model of the process of the generation of inequality. Scarcity is clearly the supply side of a such a model. Functional importance could be seen as the demand side. The members of a society may demand what is functionally important, as well as many things which are not. On the other hand, society may not demand what is functionally important – it is not always the case that people demand what is good for themselves, let alone for society as a whole. So rewards go to those who supply the demand whether or not what they supply is functionally important. Other things being equal the higher the level of demand the higher the price.

If one accepts that the strengths of the functionalist position are better expressed in terms of a supply and demand model then in many ways one could go further and replace it with a power model, since the former can be seen as a kind of power model. Those who have power in the market place or in the system of exchange will get the higher rewards. Those who control strategic resources in the system of exchange will get the higher rewards. It is to power or conflict theories that we now turn.

Theories of Conflict and Power

Modern theories of power and conflict, such as those of Rex and Dahrendorf, have their origins in the works of Marx and Weber. Marx's theory of the creation of inequality in society is clearly a power theory. In pre-capitalist societies, it is largely the coercive power of slave owners and landowners which compels slaves and serfs to work for the owner. In capitalist societies, employers are able to exploit workers because workers are highly dependent upon selling their capacity to labour to employers. The owners of the means of production are in a position of power relative to those who are excluded from this ownership. Because of this, workers are forced to alienate all rights in their product. That is to say, they alienate their rights in what their own labour creates – they alienate their own creative capacity and the value that it generates. This is the source of the capitalist's profit and the reason why labour is exploited.

Marx's theory has been criticised for the failure of the predictions it made about the development of capitalist society. Exploitation and the increasing polarisation of society into a proletariat and bourgeoisie would lead to the emergence of a class-conscious, revolutionary, working class which would seize power and transform capitalism when an opportunity resulting from the inevitable crises and failures of capitalism presented itself. Marx's predictions have not come about. In the more advanced capitalist societies, workers did not develop a revolutionary class consciousness or revolutionary outlook but supported democratic socialist and social democratic parties. Society did not polarise between bourgeoisie and proletariat, but rather a complex class structure emerged characterised by a large and diverse middle class.

As we have seen, Weber's view of class can perhaps deal more effectively with this complexity, but he also considered inequality to be largely a matter of the exercise of power in society. Both class and status

> ## Evaluation Exercise
>
> Closure theory argues that recruitment to the professions is controlled in order to maintain the scarcity value of the service provided. What explanation have functionalist sociologists offered for the existence of professional associations? Which explanation do you find the more convincing and why?

groups are phenomena of the exercise of power. That class is a question of market *power* for Weber is quite clear; but status groups also, he points out, can enjoy their privileges only if they have the power to enforce the rules of exclusion and maintain a monopoly of access.

Closure theory is a relatively new, alternative approach to the Marxist one. It borrows from Weber but emphasises *exclusion* and exclusionary practices as the primary means by which groups manage to reserve for themselves various privileges and opportunities (Parkin 1979). This is clearly reminiscent of Weber, but closure theory attempts to subsume class and status under a common framework. It treats both property and the use of qualifications and credentials by the professional middle classes as forms of exclusionary practice or closure. A clear example of this is professionalisation, where recruitment is regulated by a professional association and numbers are strictly controlled in order to maintain the scarcity value of the service provided. Other groups in society will, naturally, attempt to prevent exclusionary closure.

The main problem with closure theory seems to be that, while exclusionary practices are a very common way in which groups attempt to monopolise opportunities, it is somewhat misleading to think of property ownership or credentialism in this way. Property rights are a means of defending the property one has, not of excluding others from owning property. They are a way of preventing others from taking or using one's own property. Credentials may be a way of competing for desirable positions but are not in themselves means of excluding others from acquiring the credentials. To say they are means of exclusionary closure is rather like saying that a runner who trains very hard is operating an exclusionary tactic designed to keep others out of top-class racing. Closure theory, then, conflates rather different things – restriction of access to opportunities to a group of eligibles on the one hand and specific advantages, inherent or acquired, in the competition for opportunities and rewards on the other.

The Function of Power and the Power of Function

Is it possible to put the insights of the functionalist and the power theories together into a synthesis? Lenski in *Power and Privilege* attempts to do so. Lenski argues that two laws govern the way goods and services are distributed in a society. The first law states that in societies at the subsistence level of development the social product is distributed on the basis of need since in such societies everyone is dependent upon the survival of everyone else for their own survival. It is *functional* to distribute the social product in this way. In societies which produce a 'surplus' above subsistence needs, that surplus is distributed on the basis of power. It follows that the more productive and technologically advanced a society is, the greater will inequality be, since there will be a greater surplus to distribute unequally.

Two factors mitigate this tendency, however. Firstly, the military participation ratio – that is the proportion of the population which typically bears arms and fights to defend the society – affects the level of inequality. The greater this proportion the less inequality there will be since the dominant groups will have to ensure the loyalty of the population by buying them off with more of the surplus than they would otherwise have as a consequence of their power. Secondly, the extent to which the dominant groups need to legitimate their power and rule affects the level of inequality. No dominant group can rule by coercion alone, it must seek legitimacy, which may be at the expense of yielding up some of the surplus they might otherwise be able to monopolise. The extent to which dominant groups need to legitimate themselves in this way and the amount they must yield to do so, vary according to circumstances and, therefore, the degree of inequality also varies. That is why in contemporary industrial societies, which rely heavily upon legitimacy for social order, the evolutionary trend towards greater inequality is arrested and, perhaps, reversed to some extent.

Lenski's theory may be questioned as a true synthesis on the grounds that the alleged distribution of the social product according to need in societies at the subsistence level of production masks a power process. In such societies, if everyone is dependent upon everyone else, and roughly to the same extent, one might say that everyone has about the same amount of power as everyone else and therefore everyone receives about the same proportion of the social product as everyone else. When, however, the social product falls below subsistence level, as it may do at times, power is clearly seen to determine the distribution of society's resources. Anthropologists have observed the behaviour of people in such societies at times of famine and shortage and have often found that stronger and more powerful groups will drive out weaker groups.

Finally there is one way in which one might acknowledge the importance of both power and function in understanding patterns of inequality in society. Those who perform important functions for society may as a result be in a powerful position which enables them to appropriate a larger measure of the social product. The privilege they are able to enjoy would in this case be a consequence of their power and not a reward required to get them to perform the function; but their power is in turn the consequence of the fact that they do perform an important function. This, then, could be *one* source of power, alongside many others in society, which contributes to the generation of inequality.

References and Further Reading

Banton, M. (1987) 'The Davis-Moore Theory of Inequality', *Social Studies Review*, Vol. 3, No. 2.

Giddens, A. (1980) *The Class Structure of the Advanced Societies* (Chapters 1 and 2), Hutchinson.

Hamilton, M. and Hirszowicz, M. (1987) *Class and Inequality in Pre-Industrial, Capitalist and Communist Societies* (Chapters 1 and 2), Wheatsheaf Books.

Lenski, G. (1966) *Power and Privilege*, McGraw-Hill.

Parkin, F. (1979) *Marxism and Class Theory: a Bourgeois Critique* (Part 1), Tavistock.

What is Happening to the Working Class?

GORDON MARSHALL

Editors' introduction

The major theoretical frameworks for the study of social stratification – Marxist, functionalist, Weberian, and conflict theory – are often discussed at a very abstract level. Malcolm Hamilton's aim was to highlight their use as general accounts of social development. However, a theory proves its values though its relevance to research on what is happening in particular societies. In this manner, Gordon Marshall takes up a central research question – the social and political role of the working class – and tries to clarify the relevance of Marxist and other theories.

Marshall reviews the arguments of 'post-industrial' theorists who draw on a functionalist approach and see the working class as becoming ever more similar to the middle class. They describe this as the process of 'embourgeoisement'. By contrast, Marxists see the working class as subject to ever greater exploitation and degradation: a process of 'proletarianisation'. He suggests that neither theory can be accepted without qualification. Looking at evidence from studies of voting behaviour, he concludes that the working class has experienced neither embourgeoisement nor proletarianisation, but 'restructuring'. Britain remains a class society, but it is not in a state of endemic class warfare. Sociologists must, therefore, employ the concept of class as a central explanatory concept.

A great deal of stratification research in Britain is focused on the 'working class'. In recent years the debate has been fuelled by discussions of a number of alleged changes to the class structure. These include the decline of traditional proletarian occupations and communities; the expansion of working-class 'affluence'; the growth of service-sector and white-collar employment; the professionalisation of certain non-manual occupations and routinisation or deskilling of others; and the increasing participation of women in paid employment.

There is a long-standing tendency among sociologists to interpret these changes within one or other of two quite different theoretical frameworks. One perspective is typified by the work of post-industrial theorists such as Daniel Bell (1976). The image that is presented here is one of societies in which the labour process is increasingly less proletarianised, requiring a higher proportion of workers with technical expertise, in occupations demanding less routinisation of tasks and more responsibility. Tendencies intrinsic to production itself are thus seen to accord workers greater control over their conditions of work and more freedom within it. Workers adopt more of a 'middle-class' outlook: they experience 'embourgeoisement'. The other framework is more distinctively Marxist in provenance and has most recently been evident in debates about the work of Harry Braverman (1974). This perceives changes in the labour process as being almost the complete opposite of those outlined by the post-industrial theorists. Work is regarded as becoming generally more proletarianised; real technical expertise is thus confined to a smaller proportion of the labour force, routinisation of activities is more pervasive and responsibilities are less meaningful. Far from the material basis of alienation being undermined, it is argued here that deskilling is prevalent and alienation correspondingly intense.

Different conclusions about the nature of 'working-class consciousness' follow from these contrasting accounts. Liberals, such as Bell, argue that consciousness of class is steadily declining: workers are becoming more individualistic, more consumer-oriented, and correspondingly less inclined towards collective strategies for improved welfare. In meritocratic post-industrial societies they pursue pleasure and status in a strictly personal fashion. Marxists, on the other hand, maintain that the newly proletarianised workers of late-capitalism will be pushed to collective resistance against the managerial strategy of deskilling tasks and policing the labour process ever more closely. In their view, work (and in particular the process of production) is still central to the creation of class-based images of society, and so to the development of oppositional social consciousness.

To some extent, the contrast between these frameworks merely reflects the changed economic circumstances of the long postwar boom as compared with those of the recessionary 1970s and 1980s. As the age of affluence has given way to economic stagnation, so the liberal perspective has become less fashionable among class theorists. In part, however, the contradictory interpretations arise as a consequence of determined efforts by the two groups of social theorists to shackle the activities of the working class to their own socio-political goals. For this reason the two perspectives actually converge in their logic – despite wide-ranging and explicit substantive disagreements. Both have taken the Western working classes as the essential means to achieving liberal or (conversely) socialist political and social goals; both are prone to implicit historicism, since they share a common tendency to view present events as part of a predetermined long-term historical trend; and, in consequence, both are inclined to wishful rather than critical thinking in the interpretation of empirical materials.

Embourgeoisement, Proletarianisation and Restructuring

For those with no particular political axe to grind, the picture seems somewhat more complicated than is allowed for by straightforward arguments about 'embourgeoisement' or 'proletarianisation'. Indeed, recent research in this area has tended to converge on the alternative thesis that class conflict has been somehow restructured.

This argument has been cogently summarised by Steven Lukes (1984). Lukes argues that technological change, the increased participation of women in paid labour, and 'politicisation of the market' via state intervention in economic processes, together with the shift from manufacturing to service industries, have made the distinction between manual and non-manual labour largely irrelevant. Indeed, with the rise of mass production and consumption, labour or work itself has become less central to the identity and consciousness of workers. More and more, the working class is concerned with issues of consumption – of housing and of state benefits, for example. According to Lukes, recent research shows Britain to be a society divided against itself in new ways: those with a stake in private property and those without; the self-sufficient on wages versus welfare claimants; the populations of declining regions against those resident in economically buoyant areas; those in relatively secure occupational or company career-ladders against the unemployed and subemployed who are on the economic margins of society. These new sectional interests are reflected, it seems, in the growth of instrumental, pecuniary, egoistic (in short, capitalist) values and attitudes, and in a corresponding decline in older forms of solidarity based on community, unionism, or class itself. British workers, having come to terms with the acquisitive society, have settled down in a mood of quiet disillusionment to seek their private satisfactions at home and in leisure and to pursue conflicting sectional demands in the workplace.

The Marxist historian Eric Hobsbawm, in a controversial and much debated volt-face, has arrived at similar conclusions based on a review of British labour history (Hobsbawm 1981). In his account the solidarity of shared lifestyle and common political objectives among the traditional British working class has been undermined since the 1950s by the growth of public-sector employment and of multinational corporations. These twin developments mean that the majority of employees in this country now bargain for wages under conditions other than those imposed by strictly market criteria. This development, together with the increased but uneven participation of women in paid labour, the expansion of non-manual employment, and postwar immigration from the new Commonwealth, has encouraged 'a growing division of workers into sections and groups, each pursuing its own economic interest irrespective of the rest.' Everywhere, according to Hobsbawm, solidaristic forms of political consciousness has given way to 'the values of consumer-society individualism and the search for private and personal satisfactions above all else.'

Both Hobsbawm and Lukes attribute the breakdown of class politics, and in particular the recent poor showing of Labour at the polls, to the new sectionalism and self-interest. In this they would seem to be supported by a number of psephological studies which suggest that the electorate is now fragmented politically along unfamiliar lines. As Ivor Crewe pointed out (Crewe 1985), there is some disagreement as to whether working-class support for Labour has been undermined specifically by partisan dealignment, by the segmentation of economic interests (female secretaries working for a Japanese-based multinational in Milton Keynes have little in common with elderly male colliers in Fife), or by the development of sectional consumption cleavages (home owners versus council tenants). In each case, however, structural shifts in the ordering of stratification are seen somehow to have generated new schisms that undercut the solidarities conventionally associated with social class.

A Breakdown of Class Politics?

From even this brief account it is clear that the central themes in the thesis of restructured class conflict are those of *sectionalism, instrumentalism* and *privatism*. Although proponents of the argument interrelate these ideas in different ways, their common perception is one of recent changes in social hierarchy (in particular changes in the occupational structure), and in social values, associated with the rise of a diffuse individualism embracing lifestyle, politics, and ideology. The heterogeneous working class of contemporary Britain has absorbed capitalist economic values: it takes an instrumental stance towards class organisations (the trade unions and Labour Party) so that a pecuniary and sectional self-interest has undermined worker solidarity; and it has retreated from class politics into the privatised world of home and family. Distributional conflict now centres on consumption and status rather than production and class.

These arguments have a familiar ring. Although they are in the main rooted in studies of the impact of economic recession on class processes, it can be argued, with only slightly oversimplification, that they seem merely to endorse the principal findings of the Affluent Worker Study, carried out by Goldthorpe and his colleagues in Luton as long ago as the early 1960s (Goldthorpe et al. 1969). The objective on that occasion, it will be remembered, was to study the impact of economic affluence on working-class life.

The authors of the Luton study argued that 'traditional proletarian' and 'traditional deferential' world view were declining in the face of 'privatised instrumentalism'. They found may of their respondents sharing in an instrumental (or money-maximising) orientation to work and a privatised (or home-centred and family-centred) lifestyle. The resulting 'pecuniary' model of society, where class divisions were seen in

Has the sale of council houses any bearing on class solidarity?

terms of differences in material possessions or income, was gradually replacing older images of society within which classes were viewed as conflicting groups in a struggle for power (traditional proletarian imagery) or as hierarchically ordered status groups (the perspective of traditional differentialists).

Of course, these findings were, at the time, considered controversial. John Westergaard (1970), for example, was not surprised by the fact of workers' pecuniary attitude to work but was surprised by the interpretation that the Affluent Worker Team placed upon this. He argued that workers tied to their jobs merely by a 'cash nexus' were displaying minimal cooperation with management and, therefore, retained a potential for militancy which, properly orchestrated, could become socialist radicalism. Westergaard was clearly unconvinced by arguments about privatisation or by more general conclusions about the strictly sectional distributional struggles (competitive wage demands) which followed from these. Nevertheless, recent literature on the supposedly novel aspects in a restructuring of distributional conflict during the present recession seems to have arrived at precisely the same conclusions as were reached by Goldthorpe and his coauthors; in other words, it offers a sort of 'Affluent Worker Through the Looking Glass'.

The Continuing Relevance of Class

Where, then, does this leave the debate about the working class? The consensus seems to be that workers in contemporary Britain are neither incorporated, as liberals would maintain, nor nascently revolutionary, as Marxists would seem to hope. Instead, we are witnessing the demise of social class as an important factor structuring social processes in this country, and the emergence of new forms of sectionalism based on (among other things) cleavages rooted in the sphere of consumption. Is this in fact the case?

Together with two colleagues I carried out a study that attempts (among other things) to answer precisely this question (Rose et al, 1987). Our research forms part of a larger international project investigating class structure and class consciousness in a dozen or so countries throughout North America, Australasia and Europe. The project aims to replicate questions about work, home and political life in different national contexts, so as to provide for strictly comparable analyses of class processes in separate countries. The British results come from a national sample survey of men and women aged between 18 and 65, yielding 1,770 useable responses, with each interview lasting approximately one and half hours.

Our findings cover all of the fairly extensive arguments summarised by Lukes and Hobsbawm. Clearly they cannot all be summarised here. Instead, I have included two tables from our final report, simply to illustrate our most significant single finding: namely, that class processes continue to be the major factor structuring contemporary British society.

Table 1 shows the voting intentions of our respondents, according to social class, controlling for self-assigned class. Interviewees were asked whether or not they normally thought of themselves as belonging to a particular social class and, if so which one. The actual class categories themselves – service, intermediate and working – are those devised by John Goldthorpe in the 1970s for his well-known study of social mobility in England and Wales (Goldthorpe 1980). The service class comprises all professionals, administrators and officials, managers, and supervisors of non-manual employees. The intermediate class is made up of routine non-manual workers (clerical and sales personnel), lower-grade technicians, supervisors of manual workers and the self-employed. The working class encompasses both skilled and unskilled manual wage labourers. This table shows the impact of class identification on voting intention and confirms that social class retains is salience as an important source of social identity. Class identification is

particularly important for the Labour vote since, even among those presently in the relatively privileged service-class positions, Labour has a majority at the polls – providing these individuals identify themselves as working class.

But what is the relative importance of social class as compared to sectoral cleavages in the explanation of social schism? Is it true that housing tenure, for example, is a better predictor of attitudes and values than class itself? The data in Table 2 (p. 54) bear directly on this question. Voting intention is once again taken as the dependent variable. As one would expect, class, housing tenure and vote are heavily interrelated. Not only is it the case that vote is associated with both class and housing tenure; housing tenure and class are themselves strongly correlated. (For example, fewer than 8% of the service-class respondents in our study lived in council houses as compared with 36% of working-class interviewees.) Given this degree of interconnectedness, a three-way cross-tabulation is called for. In fact this demonstrates that social class is still strongly associated with vote, even when a control is introduced for housing tenure. The table also reveals some of the interaction between these three variables. The association between vote and class is not uniform across housing tenures. Among owner-occupiers and those renting privately, there is a significant class-vote relationship that seems largely unaffected by housing tenure. Local authority tenants, on the other hand, seem to be more influenced by housing situation than by objective social class. Here, the Labour Party is most popular, irrespective of class position. Almost 57% of all council tenants would vote Labour. But, of course, the majority of council tenants are (as we have seen) working class.

This would suggest that, in so far as sectoral cleavages in housing are associated with voting intention, these are merely surrogates for social class. Or, to put the matter another way, class voting is mediated by housing tenure. Only among council tenants is the basic class–vote pattern significantly

(a) Those who felt Upper or Middle Class				(b) Those who felt Working Class			
	ACTUAL SOCIAL CLASS				ACTUAL SOCIAL CLASS		
	Service	**Intermediate**	**Working**		**Service**	**Intermediate**	**Working**
VOTE Conservative	58	53	34	VOTE Conservative	28	38	19
Labour	14	13	40	Labour	36	35	59
Alliance	23	23	18	Alliance	25	17	15
Would not vote	5	11	8	Would not vote	10	11	7
Total	100	100	100	**Total**	100	100	100

Note: Percentages may not add up to 100 because of rounding.

Table 1   Voting intention by actual social class and self-assigned class

| | | | SOCIAL CLASS | |
		Service	Intermediate	Working
(a) Owner-occupied housing	Conservative	51	49	25
	Labour	19	22	50
	Alliance	24	21	17
	Would not vote	6	8	8
(b) Local authority, rented housing	Conservative	17	22	15
	Labour	39	50	63
	Alliance	26	16	13
	Would not vote	17	12	9
(c) Privately rented	Conservative	50	39	34
	Labour	32	16	53
	Alliance	14	21	13
	Would not vote	5	25	0

Note: Percentages may not add up to 100 because of rounding.

Table 2   Voting intention by social class and housing tenure.

altered. This group is more likely to vote Labour whatever its class situation. But these tenants are overwhelmingly found among the working class. It is reasonable to conclude, therefore, that the association between housing and vote is simply a proxy for the familiar class–vote linkage. The argument for sectoral consumption cleavages would seem to be mistaken – at least as far as the important factor of housing is concerned.

Application exercise

What are the implications of Marshall's findings for the idea that the working class in Britain is fragmented? In your response you should address the following issues:

What is meant by 'fragmentation' of class?
Which two issues does Marshall focus on in examining voting behaviour?
What are Marshall's conclusions concerning housing tenure and voting behaviour?
Does Marshall argue for or against the idea that class is still an important factor in modern Britain?
Does his conclusion support or undermine the idea of fragmentation? Find a quotation from the article to support your decision.
Do you know of any counter-evidence which might be applied to the fragmentation debate?

Conclusion: Class and Collective Identity

Of course, these tables are simply illustrative, rather than conclusive, but they do tend to suggest that Britain remains a class society rather than a 'post-industrial' or a 'post-class' one. Class is still a common and salient source of collective identity. Naturally, class identities do not constitute class consciousness, at least in the sense that most Marxists would intend. Britain is not a nation of class warriors resolutely involved in a power struggle to achieve specifically class objectives. Nevertheless, our research does confirm that class is still a crucial factor in the understanding of social change in contemporary Britain. It is not, as many accounts of the restructuring of distributional conflict would have it, an obsolete concept.

References and Further Reading

Bell, D. (1976) *The Coming of Post-Industrial Society*, Penguin Books.
Braverman, H. (1974) *Labor and Monopoly Capital*, Monthly Review Press.
Crewe, I. (1985) 'Can Labour rise again?', *Social Studies Review*, Vol. 1, No. 1, pp. 13–19.
Goldthorpe, J. H. et al. (1969) *The Affluent Worker in the Class Structure*, Cambridge University Press.
Goldthorpe, J. H. (1980) *Social Mobility and Class Structure in Modern Britain*, Oxford University Press.
Hobsbawm, E. (1981) 'The forward march of Labour halted', in M. Jacques and F. Mulhern (eds), *The Forward March of Labour Halted?*, New Left Books.
Lukes, S. (1984) 'The future of British socialism?' in B. Pimlott (ed), *Fabian Essays in Socialist Thought*, Heinemann.
Marshall, G, Rose, D. and Newby, Y. (1987) *Social Classes in Modern Britain*, Hutchinson.
Westergaard, J. H. (1970) 'The rediscovery of the cash nexus', in R. Miliband and J. Saville (eds), *The Socialist Register*, 1970, Merlin Press.

Class and the Elderly

SARA ARBER

Editors' introduction

A person's class position is generally defined in terms of their occupation or position in the labour market. So how can sociologists identify the class location of those who have no occupation? When theories pay particular attention to employment relations and paid work, those who are unemployed, in education, or those who have retired cannot be placed easily in terms of the conventional categories.

Sara Arber has addressed the class position of the elderly, focusing on the relationship between class and age. She shows that people's life chances **after** retirement are determined by their labour-market position **before** retirement. She also shows that class and age stand in a complex relationship to

gender: there are important differences between elderly men and elderly women, but both show the influence of class location.

Arber looks at the key theories of class and age: proletarianisation theory and labour-market continuity theory. The former theory, linked with the Marxist theory discussed by Marshall, depicts the elderly as members of a deprived 'underclass'. Arber rejects this theory. Using data on income and employment, she shows that there is considerable support for the labour-market continuity theory. This holds that inequalities among the elderly are based on their previous labour-market position.

The elderly have been largely ignored in analyses of social stratification, mainly because paid work has predominated as the basis for studies of stratification. This practice can no longer continue. In the 1990s, men may spend almost as many years in retirement as they do in paid work, because of the growth of early retirement and high levels of unemployment among older workers. This paper will examine how position in the labour market influences the financial resources of older men both prior to statutory retirement age and during retirement.

The lack of consideration given to later life in stratification theory is part of a more general neglect of whole groups of people without paid employment. Until the last decade, for example, women had been largely neglected. This was because not all women are in paid employment, and because women's work was considered subsidiary to that of their husbands (Goldthorpe 1983). There is now a growing literature on alternative approaches to integrating women into class analyses (Scott 1987; Arber, Dale and Gilbert 1985), and a wide-ranging theoretical debate about the relationship between patriarchy and stratification theory (Crompton and Mann 1986). This has not been

matched by an equal concern about the social-class position of the unemployed, the early retired and the elderly – three increasingly large groups excluded from studies of class because they lack a current occupation.

The Elderly in Sociology

Most research and writing on the elderly has a 'social problem' focus, and is located within a social policy tradition. The underlying assumption is that the elderly are a problem for society. The growing proportion of the population who are elderly is emphasised, and particularly the burden of the number of 'old' elderly (i.e., over seventy-five years old) and 'very old' elderly (over eighty-five) (Thompson 1987). The latter two groups are conceptualised as a burden on the state because they are high users of health and welfare services. They are also seen as a burden on women because policies of community care and the gendered nature of kinship obligations mean that most community care for the elderly is done by women (Finch 1987). The recent attempt to abolish SERPS (the State Earnings Related Pension) and the debate about whether the cost of

SERPS could be borne by the working population is another example of this problem-oriented view of the elderly.

The elderly are primarily conceptualised as a homogenous group, and attention is given to *age relations* rather than class or gender differences *among* the elderly. Phillipson (1982; Phillipson and Walker 1986) and others discuss the 'social construction' of old age and the social construction of dependency (Townsend 1981). Writers more concerned with labour-market issues discuss the elderly as a 'reserve army' and the 'peripheralisation' of older workers (Bamford and Dale, forthcoming). Age relations, like gender relations and race relations, are highly visible and charged with moral expectations that derive from estimations of the relative moral worth of different age groups, and they are manifest in acts of deference and derogation. The elderly are largely conceptualised as of low moral worth – evident from the 'social problem' focus and from the more general image of the elderly as poor, disabled, dependent and passive. But how does social class influence these age relations? We have only to consider the Queen Mother, the House of Lords and many elderly judges and politicians to realise the sharp contrast they provide to the more general image of the elderly.

Although the elderly may live almost exclusively in the 'private sphere' of their home, to what extent and in what ways do they remain tethered to the 'public sphere' through their previous position in the labour market? What is the extent of inequality among the elderly and to what extent is it market-determined? Gender, also, must not be lost sight of: are there greater gender inequalities between men and women in retirement than during working life?

Why Have the Elderly Been Neglected?

At the time that Marx and Weber wrote on stratification, the elderly posed few problems for their theoretical concepts and analyses. This is not the case today. The major changes which have occurred this century are summarised in Figure 1. The early theorists did not have to consider the elderly any differently from other men in adulthood, because most elderly men continued in paid work (Townsend 1981). Retirement at sixty-five is an invention of the twentieth

Coursework suggestion 2

Research on the elderly poses interesting problems for sociologists in terms of access and of invisibility. On one level, most of us are familiar with older people through our families, but researching into the lives of our own grandparents raises issues of subjectivity and of replicability. However, we may use our elderly relations to gain access to other older members of society, through any friendship networks, clubs or support services they might be connected with. You may gather a small sample of elderly people through this snowball sampling method, whom you can informally interview on a topic of sociological interest. For example, you might explore how 'peripheral' or 'marginal' they feel to society, as suggested by the Arber article.

However, there are several problems associated with doing this type of research. Firstly, most people are not sociologists and therefore do not know what is meant by peripheralism or marginalisation. You as the researcher have to formulate the questions which will gain the information you need without using jargon which your informants may not understand. Secondly, questions on these issues are likely to be very sensitive and could produce strong emotions in your informants. You will therefore need to be very tactful in dealing with them, and know when to stop asking questions even if this means that the interview loses its value for your research. Thirdly, you will need to sort out the **ethical** problems associated with this form of research, asking yourself, for example, whether you have the right to ask questions which might upset your interviewees. Lastly, you will need to invest time and energy in gaining the trust and agreement of your informants. You cannot just rush in, ask a few questions and rush out again. This is a practical as well as a moral issue.

Nevertheless, this sort of in-depth research can often be very rewarding as you build a rapport and empathy with your informants. However, this creates its own dangers and you need to include in your evaluation a report on your own feelings when carrying out the research.

century. Actual retirement from paid employment today is increasingly below age sixty-five, but it may be disguised as long-term unemployment or disability. There is also the massive reduction in early mortality which has taken place during this century. These two opposing trends have given people a longer span of life after the end of their paid employment – somewhere between ten and twenty-five years for the majority of elderly men.

In the past, most elderly people shared their households with younger kin. As late as 1945, only 10 per cent of the elderly lived alone, and 30 per cent with their spouse (Dale, Evandrou and Arber 1987). For this reason, the class position of the elderly who were not in paid employment could be measured by the occupational class of a younger household member. By 1980, 34 per cent of elderly people lived alone and 45 per cent lived with their spouse. For the vast majority of elderly people it is no longer possible to assign them to a class on the basis of the current occupation of a younger household member.

A number of current labour-market changes are likely to increase inequality between elderly people, making the study of class among the elderly more important than in the past. First, there are class-based differences in the likelihood of 'premature exit' from the labour market; that is, a higher proportion of men leave employment before they reach the age at which they qualify for the state pension. Second, there has been a rapid expansion in private occupational pensions, and schemes differ markedly in the nature of their provision. To what extent is well-being in later life tied to occupational pensions and the nature of previous labour-market position?

These changes have produced two extreme positions among stratification theorists writing on the elderly:

1 **Proletarianisation theory** This sees the elderly as homogenous, and is concerned primarily with age relations, and the general poverty and disadvantage of the elderly. From this standpoint, the elderly constitute an 'underclass'.

2 **Labour-market continuity theory** This emphasises inequalities among the elderly which are based on previous labour-market position. Some writers argue that these inequalities are the same as during working life, while others claim that they have moderated or are greater in later life.

The latter position would expect a continuing influence of the labour market to be apparent in (a) the *likelihood* and *form* of premature exit from the labour market, and (b) differences in material circumstances

Early this century	Today
1 Men remained in paid employment after age 65.	Men leave paid employment at 65, and increasingly before age 65.
2 High mortality – average expectation of life was 49 years for men in 1901.	Lower mortality – average expectation of life is 71 years for men (in 1986). Elderly men often live for 10–25 years after paid employment.
3 Most elderly people shared households with younger kin.	80% of elderly people live either with their spouse of alone.

Figure 1 Elderly men in the past and today.

among the elderly. The proletarianisation thesis would not expect any such class-based continuities, but would expect substantial differences in material circumstances between the elderly and people of working age.

This article uses data from the *General Household Survey* for 1980–82 to examine these two competing theories. Clearly, there have been labour-market changes since the early 1980s, particularly those increasing the level of 'premature exit' from the labour market, but these changes are likely to have reinforced the trends found in 1980–82. Today there are likely to be greater inequalities than in the early 1980s. Although my analyses are restricted to *men* over the age of fifty, it is important to consider how gender intersects with the continuities of the labour market into later life. I will return to this issue at the end of this article.

Premature Exit from the Labour Force

Exit from the labour force is no longer a discrete event at a given point in time. There is now greater diversity in the age of 'retirement'. At the same time, the likelihood of 'premature exit' is socially structured. Over a quarter of unskilled men in their early fifties are not in employment, compared to only 2 per cent of higher professionals. None of these men define themselves as retired. However, it is unlikely that many of the 11 per cent of unskilled men who are 'permanently disabled' or the 15 per cent who are 'unemployed' will work again.

Among men in their late fifties, a different pattern begins to emerge, with the highest proportion of 'early retired' (4 per cent) being among higher professionals. However, this form of 'premature exit' is dwarfed by

Evaluation exercise

It has been claimed that a recent development in the British stratification system is the growing importance of non-class factors in society, as opposed to the influence of class factors. An evaluation exercise you could carry out is to compare the relative importance of class and non-class factors in modern Britain.

You will need to decide which non-class divisions you are going to examine in trying to assess their importance compared to social class. There are plenty of clues in the article, from age and gender to ethnicity and region.

You must make a case for the importance of both class and non-class factors in your evaluation. You can apply much evidence from all three articles in this chapter to support your evaluation, but you should be looking for a balanced presentation in each case. For example, you might examine how class divisions are still important in modern Britain, drawing on a variety of evidence. This may take the form of arguments concerning the distribution of wealth in Britain, or studies by Westergaard and Resler arguing that there is still class domination in Britain today. A selection of appropriate

arguments and studies should be chosen.

You should also consider the evidence for the increasing influence of non-class factors. For example, if you take gender as a main focus, you might put forward the changing occupational structure or the increase in lone-parent families as supporting the idea that gender differences are just as important in Britain as class differences. You may use the theoretical arguments of the radical feminists or the empirical work of Crompton to support this point of view. While it is legitimate to focus on one non-class division, you should also show that you are aware of other divisions, such as ethnicity, by drawing upon appropriate examples.

However, having considered the evidence you must come to a conclusion and directly consider the relative importance of the two types of division. Your evaluation should be based on the evidence that you have included. It is little use showing all the way through your work that non-class divisions are important, if you then conclude that class divisions remain more important. Your evaluation must emerge from the balance of the evidence you have provided.

---

exit due to permanent disability and unemployment, both of which show a strong inverse class gradient: only 8 per cent of non-manual men are unemployed or disabled, compared with 25 per cent of men previously employed in semi-skilled manual work and 28 per cent of men previously in unskilled jobs.

This class difference in exit from the labour market is most clearly seen among men in their early sixties, who are approaching statutory retirement age. Early retirement is *positively associated* with occupational class – 28 per cent of higher professional men compared with 11 per cent of unskilled men are 'early retired'. On the other hand, exit because of disability and unemployment are *negatively associated* with class – rates varying from 6 per cent among higher professionals to 33 per cent among unskilled men.

The GHS data, therefore, demonstrate greater class differences in the *form* of exit from the labour market than in the *likelihood* of premature exit. The reasons which people have for leaving the labour market are very differently structured by class, and this has

implications for the current and future economic power of different occupational classes. Stratification theorists need to consider the ways in which the greater 'flexibility' or spread in the timing of the transition from employment lead to greater inequalities before statutory retirement age, and whether these differences in material well-being prior to the state retirement age leads to greater inequalities in old age. It is therefore important to consider the social structuring of both the *form* and *likelihood* of early exit from the labour market.

Inequalities Among Men Aged 60–64

Material resources among men aged between sixty and sixty-four are related to both their previous occupational class and their form of exit from the labour market (see Table 1). Older men without paid employment for whatever reason, have a considerably lower average income than those who are currently employed. Their average income is only £53 per week, which is under half the level of employed men, £110. This differential remains roughly comparable *within*

| | EMPLOYED | NOT IN PAID EMPLOYMENT | | | ALL |
		Unemployed	Permanently disabled	Retired	
	£	£	£	£	£
Upper middle-class	165	47+	61	95	78
Lower middle-class	119	65	50	66	62
Upper middle-class	106	45	50	60	53
Lower working-class	91	42	45	48	45
All	110	45	49	64	53
Income of lower working-class as a percentage of upper middle-class income	55%	89%	74%	51%	58%

Source: General Household Survey, 1980–82
+Base number under 20.
*Average income is the median in pounds per week from all sources. The median is the middle value after the income of all men (in that class/employment status) has been arranged in ascending order.

Table 1   Income per week by social class and self-defined employment status for men aged 60–64*

Interpretation exercise

Look at Table 1. Describe, **without using any numbers**, the income position of retired men aged 60–64 compared to other groups identified in the table.

each class. As a measure of class inequalities, the average income of men in lower working-class jobs has been compared with that of upper middle-class men. For men employed in lower working-class jobs, their income is 55 per cent of that of employed upper middle-class men, and for men without employment it is 58 per cent. The similarity in the size of these proportions illustrates the continuing importance of previous occupational class on inequalities among men who have left work before the state retirement age.

The *form* of exit from the labour market also influences levels of income, with the 'early retired' having the highest average income in each class, and the 'unemployed' having the lowest income. The differential between the 'early retired' and the 'unemployed' previously in upper middle-class jobs is two-fold, £95 compared with £47. Among lower working-class men the differential is very small: £48 compared with £42. Thus, the form of exit has most impact on material circumstances among men who previously worked in higher non-manual occupations.

The main reason for these large class-differences in income among men who have left the labour market early is their differential access to, and size of, occupational pensions. Table 2 shows that both the likelihood of receiving a pension and the size of that pension vary with previous occupational class *and* form of exit. Early-retired man from higher classes are most likely to receive a pension – 84 per cent compared with only 29 per cent of lower working-class men who are unemployed. The amount of pension received varies five-fold, from an average of £72 among early retired men previously in upper middle-class jobs to only £12 among unemployed men previously in lower working-class jobs. Older men who are unemployed, irrespective of their previous occupational class, receive only a small occupational pension. Form of exit from the labour market has a particularly strong influence on the size of the occupational pension among non-manual workers. Men previously employed in higher classes receive occupational pensions that are nearly four times higher than men in lower working-class jobs.

Labour market position also has a major influence on the accumulation of 'liquid' assets, which may cushion some of the effects of 'premature exit' from the labour market. Higher class men receive twelve times as much money from unearned income, such as investments and savings, than do men previously employed in lower-class jobs (see Table 3). Men who are 'early-retired' are in a particularly advantaged position compared with men who are permanently disabled or unemployed. Here again both the form of exit and the previous occupational class influence

	UNEMPLOYED		PERMANENTLY DISABLED		RETIRED		ALL NOT IN EMPLOYMENT	
	% who receive pension	weekly pension (£)	% who receive pension	weekly pension (£)	% who receive pension	weekly pension (£)	% who receive pension	weekly pension (£)
Upper middle-class	56+	—	56	37+	84	72	76	65
Lower middle-class	61	17+	56	26+	85	45	72	35
Upper working-class	40	16	48	13	70	35	54	21
Lower working-class	29	12+	40	17	56	17	42	17
All	40	17	47	19	73	44	57	28

Source: General Household Survey, 1980–82
+Base number below 20.

Table 2   *Occupational pensions by social class and self-defined employment status for men aged 60–64.*

	EMPLOYED	NOT IN PAID EMPLOYMENT			ALL
		Unemployed	Permanently disabled	Retired	
	£	£	£	£	£
Upper middle-class	4.9	—	2.9+	13.3	9.6
Lower middle-class	3.1	1.2+	1.7+	8.0	4.9
Upper middle-class	1.5	1.8	.9	2.9	1.8
Lower working-class	1.0	.6	.4	1.9	.8
All	1.9	1.2	.8	4.8	2.3
Income of lower working-class as a percentage of upper middle-class income	20%	—	14%	14%	8%

Source: General Household Survey, 1980–82
+Base number under 20.

Table 3   *Average unearned income to family unit per week by social class and self-defined employment status for men aged 60–64 (1980–82).*

financial well-being among men who have left the labour market before statutory retirement age.

Thus, it is necessary to consider both previous power in the labour market, measured by occupational class, and form of exit from the labour market when considering financial inequalities prior to state retirement age. The following section considers to what extent structural sources of inequality relating to occupational class persist among the elderly.

Inequalities Among the Elderly

Previous occupational class continues to influence financial well-being even among men over the age of seventy-five, over ten years after state retirement age. Lower working-class men aged between sixty-five and seventy-four receive 70 per cent of the income of upper middle-class men, whereas among older men (over seventy-five), they receive 85 per cent (see Table 4(a)). These are much smaller class-differences than those

	(a) Average income (£)			(b) Average Occupational Pension (£)			(c) Average Unearned income (£) of Family Unit		
	Age			Age			Age		
	60–64*	65–74	75 and over	60–64*	65–74	75 and over	60–64*	65–74	75 and over
Upper middle-class	127	57	41	65	32	29	5.8	9.8	5.9
Lower middle-class	93	49	40	35	16	17	3.6	2.5	1.9
Upper middle-class	83	38	36	21	8	8	1.5	1.2	.9
Lower working-class	71	40	35	17	8	7	.9	.8	.4
All	85	42	37	35	11	10	2.0	1.8	1.2
Income of lower working-class as a percentage of upper-middle-class income	56%	70%	85%	26%	25%	24%	16%	8%	7%

*All men are included, irrespective of their employment status, except for Table (b) ages 60–64, which only includes men not in paid work.
Source: *General Household Survey*, 1980–82.   Note: Social class is based on own (current or last) occupation.

Table 4   Financial resources received per week by social class and age for men over 60 (1980–82).

observed prior to state retirement age.

The continuing class gradient in income among the elderly is the result of class differences in two sources of income, both of which are the direct result of previous labour-market position – occupational pensions and unearned income (Table 4(b) and (c)). The size of the occupational pension received by men previously in higher class occupations is four times greater than that received by men previously in lower working-class jobs. The average unearned income received by the family is over twelve times higher for men who previously had upper middle-class jobs than for men previously employed in lower working-class jobs. The large class differentials in these two sources of income do not reduce with advancing age among elderly men.

Conclusion

This article has demonstrated the ways in which the 'fortunes' of older men are tethered to their previous labour-market position, in terms of the *likelihood* of premature exit from the labour market, and the *form* of that exit. Labour-market continuity theory is supported – with the strongest influence of labour-market position among men who left paid employment before state retirement age. Previous occupational class has a continuing effect on financial well-being, reaching well into old age (see Table 4). While these findings cast doubt on the proletarianisation thesis (i.e., that the elderly are a homogenous group which is in poverty

and can be considered an 'underclass'), it is important to remember that the average income of elderly men decreases substantially with age, and is considerably lower among men over retirement age than among men who leave the labour force before sixty-five. While the elderly continue to be structured by class, they are generally less well-off than those who are younger and in employment.

While demonstrating the continuities in labour-market power for *men* into later life, this article has neglected *women*. Since labour-market position is so closely associated with financial well-being in later life, it is important to consider whether women's weaker labour-market position will be manifest in relatively greater poverty among elderly women than elderly men. Gender inequalities in the likelihood of receiving occupational pensions, the size of those pensions, and the ability to accumulate capital during the working life, may result in increasing gender inequality among the elderly in the future. This is particularly likely if the provision of personal occupational pensions is promoted and replaces the state retirement pension as the main means of financial support for the elderly.

Notes

1 The General Household Survey (GHS) is a nationally-representative government survey, in which about 25,000 adults over the age of sixteen are interviewed each year (OPCS, 1984). The response rate is 82 per cent. To provide a larger number of people who have left employment before statutory retirement age, data from three years of the GHS (1980–2) have been combined for the analyses in this article.

2   Table 1 shows one exception to this pattern – unemployed men previously in lower middle-class jobs have the same median income as early retired men. The cell size is relatively small for this category (twenty-three), and therefore it may be an unreliable finding.

References and Further Reading

Arber, S., Dale, A. and Gilbert, G.N. (1986) 'The limitations of existing social class classifications for women', in Jacoby, A. (ed) *The Measurement of Social Class*, Social Research Association.

Bamford, C. and Dale, A. (forthcoming) 'Older workers and the peripheralisation of the work force', in *Ageing and Society.*

Crompton, R. and Mann, M. (eds) (1986) *Gender and Stratification*, Polity Press.

Dale, A., Evandrou, M. and Arber, S. (1987) 'The household structure of the elderly in Britain', in *Ageing and Society*, 7.

Finch, J. (1987) 'Family obligations and the life course' in Bryman, A. *et al.* (eds). *Rethinking the Life Cycle*, Macmillan.

Goldthorpe, J. H. (1983) 'Women and class analysis: in defence of the conventional view', in *Sociology*, 17.

Office of Population Censuses and Surveys (1984) *General Household Survey 1982*, HMSO.

Phillipson, C. (1982) *Capitalism and the Construction of Old Age*, Macmillan.

Phillipson, C. and Walker, A. (1986) *Ageing and Social Policy: A Critical Assessment*, Gower.

Scott, J. (1987) 'Women and class theory', in *Social Studies Review*, Vol. 3, No. 2.

Thompson, J. (1987) 'Ageing of the population: Contemporary trends and issues', in *Population Trends*, 50, OPCS.

Townsend, P. (1981) 'The structured dependency of the elderly: A creation of social policy in the twentieth century', in *Ageing and Society*, 1.

Structured question (25 marks)

a) With reference to extract C, what is the difference between the average occupational pensions of the eldest groups in the upper middle class and the upper working class? (1 mark)

b) Does sociological evidence support the idea that 'wealth and power tends to 'pile up' at one end of society' (extract A)? (4 marks)

c) With reference to extract A, to what extent do sociologists agree that 'wealth and power generally also determine the life-style and therefore, prestige and status in society'? (8 marks)

d) Using the information in extract C and Table 4, assess the view that the elderly are an 'underclass'.   (4 marks)

e) With reference to extract B, how far does sociological evidence support the view that 'the distinction between manual and non-manual labour [is] largely irrelevant'? (8 marks)

Introduction to Paper 2 Topics

The number of questions you are expected to answer from Paper 2 of the AEB examination depends on whether or not you have chosen to do coursework. If you have chosen the coursework option (syllabus 664) you will have to answer two essay questions from Paper 2. If you have chosen not to do the coursework (syllabus 639) you will have to answer four questions from Paper 2. The length of time allowed for Paper 2 varies accordingly: one and a half hours for two questions and three hours for four questions. The range of questions is basically the same whether you answer two or four questions but there are two extract questions on Theory and Methods (Section 1) which can only be chosen by candidates who are sitting the three hour paper. This is not as complicated as it may sound, especially if you take the trouble to go through some past papers. This will be especially useful at the stage when you are trying to decide whether to enter for the coursework option or to answer more essay questions from Paper 2.

All essay questions carry twenty-five marks. In your essay answers you are required to show the skills detailed in the **General Introduction** to this book. On Paper 2, equal marks are allocated to each of the main skills (1) knowledge and understanding (2) interpretation and application and (3) evaluation.

Essay questions on Paper 2 (and the examples included at the end of the articles in this book) are worded in such a way that they ask you to apply your knowledge and understanding of sociology to a problem or issue and to weigh-up competing explanations. It is important, therefore, to recognise that a good answer to an essay question in sociology requires much more than simple recall of information. You do, certainly, need to be able to recall your knowledge of sociological arguments and evidence but it is vital that you **understand** the information you are going to use in your essays and that you **apply** it selectively and appropriately. A good essay will be fashioned in such a way that the material it

contains is selected to meet the requirements of the question. You need to think carefully about which parts of your knowledge to present in an answer and to resist the temptation simply to write down all you know about a topic. It is essential to develop your skills of interpretation and application because these skills are central to the process of essay writing in sociology. You need to be able to identify what the essay question requires and to respond with arguments and evidence which meet those requirements. The **Guidance notes** at the end of each article in Part 2 of this book will help you with this.

It is equally important to develop your ability to evaluate the arguments and evidence you put forward and discuss in your essays. To evaluate sociological information you need to be able to assess the quality of the evidence on which a point of view is based and to weigh up its strengths and weaknesses or give arguments for and against. This means, above all, that you need to be conversant with theories and methods in sociology and you must be able to see things from more than one point of view. You are not given marks in the exam for 'taking sides' with one perspective rather than another – it is the quality of your argument that counts – but you are expected to express a sociological point of view about the issues you discuss in your essays.

It is particularly important that you develop an evaluation in the conclusion to your essay (though evaluation can be included earlier in the essay as well). Candidates often put themselves at a disadvantage by failing to include enough critical discussion in their concluding paragraphs. Remember that evaluation of sociological arguments and evidence carries a third of the marks for essays so you need to develop your evaluation skills to achieve a good total mark. The **Guidance notes** at the end of each of the following articles give some pointers about how to develop evaluation.

CHAPTER 6

Deviance

Editors' introduction

The sociology of deviance covers a wide range of subjects and issues, but central to this area is the question of crime and its control. Seldom out of the news, crime seems to generate endless theories about causes, ranging from the effects of additives in hamburgers to ideas on genetic make up. At the level of social policy, dealing with crime seems to have an air of hopelessness. Whichever policies are in favour at any one time, crime rates seem only to escalate and levels of reoffending (recidivism) continue to resist remedial action. Ironically, such patterns seem to have convinced some sociologists and criminologists that the only way of dealing with the problem of crime is to address its underlying structural 'causes', while for others the 'failure' of 'grand theory' even to dent the rise in crime has encouraged a concern with more 'practical' small-scale research projects on crime.

The subject matter of sociological interest in crime has also changed over the past twenty years or so. If, in the 1970s, the general focus in this area was on **why people offended**, in the 1980s it was the **consequences** of crime, particularly for its victims, which moved to centre stage. According to supporters of this move, the new approach helped to depoliticise some theorising about crime, to inject more 'realism' into sociological discussions about the phenomenon, and to take more seriously its damaging effects, particularly as they affected the old, the poor and female victims.

In the following article, two of Britain's leading experts on the sociology of crime chart some of the recent shifts in this area. Professor Paul Rock considers in some detail two theories about crime – control theory and situational theory – which have become more prominent as both practical pressures and changes in 'doing' criminology have begun to have an effect. Frances Heidensohn, for her part, signals the rise of feminist theorising about crime and its effects. She demonstrates that sex is probably **the** crucial variable in predicting criminality. She argues that, given the recent rise in interest in 'control' theories and a greater focus on the victims of crime, a more fruitful approach for policy and research might be to ask not why men commit crime, but why so few women do likewise.

New Directions in Criminology

PAUL ROCK

To a large extent, the sociology of deviance is preoccupied with an agenda that was established in the 1970s. It is made up of Marxism, feminism, symbolic interactionism and control theory, but those ideas have themselves become less sharp and distinct. There have been compromises and accommodations, less of a concern about intellectual purity, and more of an interest in practical problem-solving.

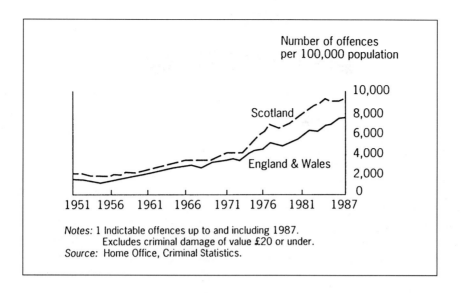

Number of offences
per 100,000 population

Scotland

England & Wales

10,000
8,000
6,000
4,000
2,000
0

1951 1956 1961 1966 1971 1976 1981 1987

Notes: 1 Indictable offences up to and including 1987.
Excludes criminal damage of value £20 or under.
Source: Home Office, Criminal Statistics.

From Theory to Survey

Let me explain how some of that has come to pass. One critical influence has been the appearance of new sources of information that have led to very major changes in the way in which the world of crime and deviance is viewed. Most specifically there have been crime surveys. The British Crime Surveys were conducted by the Home Office in 1981, 1983 and 1988, and there have been local crime surveys of Islington, Sheffield, Birmingham, Merseyside and elsewhere. The national British Crime Surveys entailed interviews in 11,000 households in England and Wales and one sweep of 5,000 households in Scotland. Interviewees were questioned about their experiences as victims of crime during the previous year, and their answers galvanised criminology. New facts were learned about the geography of crime (indeed a separate discipline arose bearing that title). Criminologists for the first time mapped the distribution of victims and they discovered how crime was concentrated in the inner cities, in council estates and in 'hard-to-let' estates and squats above all. They learned about lifestyles and crime. The typical victim of crime is a young male who goes out at times and to places that others hesitate to visit. Victims and offenders are often interchangeable. Criminologists learned about the psychological and social impact of deviants, crime and criminals, and more as to what we need to know in order to *do* something. It chimed remarkably well with the imperatives of policy-makers and politicians because, after all, that is the kind of criterion they apply.

In *The Causes of Delinquency* (1969), Hirschi revolutionised criminology by reversing its traditional question. He remarked that the problem was not why people commit crime but why the do *not* do so. He introduced what must be regarded as a curious assumption that anyone would commit a crime given the proper circumstances. It is that question that still gives a structure to control theories.

Leading Contenders

Control theories are quite diverse and they are still too new to have been systematised. Let me merely relate some of the arguments that are now on offer:

Travis Hirschi stated that delinquency occurs when the individual's bond to society is weakened, and that bond is itself make up of four elements: attachment, commitment, involvement and belief. Attachment is a matter of caring about others' opinions and wishes. Commitment is the investment which a person makes in such matters as getting an education, building up a business or acquiring a reputation for virtue. There is always a risk to such investments when delinquency is committed. Involvement is about *activity*: a person may simply be too busy doing conventional things to engage in delinquency. Belief concerns the *intensity* with which people believe they should obey rules. The non-delinquent is attached, committed, involved and strongly believing. The delinquent is not and he or she is free to deviate.

Steven Box in *Deviance, Reality and Society* (1971), identified the key issues in the removal of social restraint to be secrecy, skills, supply, social and symbolic support. Secrecy refers to the chances of concealing deviance; skills to the knowledge required for deviance; supply to the presence of the necessary equipment; social support to peer approval; and symbolic support to reinforcement from the larger society.

Harriet Wilson in *Parents and Children* (1978), and in 'Parental Supervision', an article published in *The British Journal of Criminology* (1980), reported a study of deprived families in Birmingham in which the critical variable in the prediction of delinquency was what she called 'chaperonage'. 'Chaperonage' is the supervision and protection that families exert over their children. It consists of fetching children from school, not allowing them to roam the streets, and enforcing rules about returning at night. Chaperonage sharply differentiated non-delinquents from delinquents. Parents who chaperoned their children tried to protect them from what they regarded as undesirable companions in an undesirable neighbourhood. Children were kept indoors, forbidden to play with certain others, and were allowed out only to places and at times that were approved.

Situational Theory

Situational Theory was introduced by staff working at the Home Office Research and Planning Unit in the mid-1970s. It embodies an emphasis on the immediate features of the environment in which an offence might be committed. Clarke, Cornish and Mayhew, three of its authors, were quite strongly opposed to what they called 'dispositional theories', theories that focused on the histories and motives of delinquents. They found it better to present crime and delinquency as if it were the behaviour of reasoning people making judgements in response to particular situations. Their view of the rational criminal corresponds to how many people, including the police and policy-makers themselves view and plan for action. Because it was based in a well-funded and busy research unit, situational theory led to a lengthy programme of research, exemplified best by Clarke and Mayhew's *Designing out Crime* (1980). The theory has at least two principal emphases: target hardening and surveillance

Target hardening is intended to make the commission of crime more difficult and it includes such measures as replacing vulnerable telephone coin-boxes with stronger ones; replacing telephone coin-boxes with those operated by credit card; property-marking; improved locks and bolts; stronger doors and so on. Bennett and Wright gave interest and focus to the idea of target hardening by playing videos taken from a passing van to imprisoned burglars (see D. Evans and D. Herbert (eds) *The Geography of*

Wilson claims that 'chaperonage' is the critical factor in predicting child delinquency.

Crime, 1989). They established what it was that burglars actually did when they surveyed potential targets: burglars apparently were concerned most about signs of occupance, being overlooked by neighbours, the possibility of concealment offered by shrubs, walls and other obstructions, and ease of access. The least vulnerable targets were mid-terrace houses, the most vulnerable were well-screened detached properties.

Surveillance refers to the informal controls exerted by people in everyday life. It was given prominence first by Jane Jacobs in *The Death and Life of Great American Cities* (1965), and by Oscar Newman in *Defensible Space* (1972). Jacobs and Newman pointed to the way in which the design of the built environment could aid or hinder the capacity of people to see what was happening about them, feel proprietorial about different spaces, and make decisions to intervene.

Considerable efforts have been made to transform large and confused areas of public space into protected pockets of personal space in which insiders have an interest and where outsiders feel uncomfortable. Tim Hope of the Home Office Research and Planning Unit, exploring influences on burglary in schools, identified two different styles of building. There was the large modern sprawling school of the country or suburbs that was set in generous grounds and the small, old and compact school of the city that was overlooked by adjoining buildings. Between 1978 and 1979, the average number of burglaries for the large and spacious school was 7.9, and for the small and compact school it was 2.2 (see Hope's *Burglary in Schools*, 1982).

The most vigorous defender of the surveillance approach has been Alice Coleman, whose *Utopia on Trial* (1985), tells of her efforts to remodel the physical structure of council estates by removing the walkways that she claims help to circulate crime, by reducing the number of points of access that led outsiders in, and by minimising public and maximising private space.

Conclusion

Control theory deals efficiently and provocatively with the commission of crimes in specific contexts. It *is* limited in what it covers and the problems it explores are not what every criminologist would choose to investigate. It does also 'bootleg' in an understanding of how deviants think and act – assuming that potential criminals follow a simple pattern – disembodies rationality, and its limitations may well be revealed when its predictions fail to match behaviour. A return may have then to be made to questions of history, context, motive and interpretation. It is certainly the case that Bennett and Wright have shown how that return might begin.

References and Further Reading

Box, S. (1971) *Deviance, Reality and Society*, Holt, Rinehart and Winston.

Clarke, R. and Mayhew, P. (1980) *Designing out Crime*, HMSO.

Coleman, A. (1985) *Utopia on Trial*, Hilary Shipman.

Downes, D. and Rock, P. (1988) *Understanding Deviance* (Ch.9), Oxford University Press.

Evans, D. and Herbert, D. (eds) (1989) *The Geography of Crime*, Routledge.

Hirshi, T. (1969) *The Causes of Delinquency*, University of California Press.

Hope, T. (1982) *Burglary in Schools*, HMSO.

Jacobs, J. (1965) *The Death and Life of Great American Cities*, Vintage Books.

Merton, R. (1957) *Social Theory and Social Structure*, Free Press.

Newman, O. (1972) *Defensible Space*, Macmillan.

Wilson, H. et al. (1978) *Parents and Children in the Inner Cities*, RKP.

Wilson, H. (1980)' Parental supervision: a neglected aspect of delinquency', in *The British Journal of Criminology*, Vol. 20.

Wilson, J. (1975) *Thinking about Crime*, Basic Books.

Gender and Crime

FRANCES HEIDENSOHN

Sex and Crime

The incidence of recorded crime is strongly linked to sex and to age. So are the rates of self reported crime and of victim or observer-recorded offences. All strongly suggest that crime is an activity carried out by the young, and more particularly by young, adult males (see Figure 1, p. 69).

Sex–crime ratios (that is the proportion of men and women offending) vary by offence, but of convictions for serious offences in England and Wales in recent years, over 80% have been males. Shoplifting, often thought of as a 'typically' female crime is one for which more males than females are convicted in Britain. The most dramatic differences, however, occur in crimes such as robbery and in recidivism rates. Women tend to commit less serious crimes and to do so less often. In consequence, there are far fewer women and girls in custody than there are males: in an incarcerated population of nearly 50,000 in Britain, fewer than 1,500 are female. This pattern, while it varies somewhat over time and place, is remarkably stable. In the USA as in England and Wales, about 80% of court referrals of delinquency cases are of boys and a survey showed males were 97% of all inmates in state correctional institutions – a proportion very close to that in Britain.

Figures from other countries, although they always have to be treated carefully and critically, are consistent with male predominance in crime. They only vary in the degree of that predominance. In India and Sri Lanka in the 1970s, males made up over 95% of convicted offenders, whereas the male share in many Western countries is closer to 80%. While the female share of criminality has risen slightly in some Western countries, in the later twentieth century, this share is still very small.

Hidden Female Crime?

Attempts to 'correct' this apparently stubbornly stable ratio in recorded crimes by revealing the hidden and secret crimes of women have not been successful. Self report studies, victim surveys, observational and other studies broadly confirm the picture of crime as a largely male activity (Heidensohn, 1985, Ch. 1). Many critics of criminal records have, of course, pointed out that they are not just an inadequate and incomplete account of all criminal activity, much of which must inevitably remain unobserved and uncounted. They are also fundamentally flawed since they mark police (and public) concern with only certain kinds of deviant acts or actors and not others. Armed robberies, which may net hundreds of pounds are carefully logged, publicised and pursued. Perpetrators are given long sentences, as are purveyors of illicit drugs. Yet these, it can be argued, are the crimes of the poor and the powerless. Depredations wrought by white collar criminals, huge embezzlements, elaborate computer frauds, etc. are often concealed or only lightly punished.

Undoubtedly, corporate crime is literally big business today and criminal law is selectively shaped and selectively enforced. Exposing these sections of the submerged 'iceberg' of crime would not, however, increase women's contribution to recorded criminality. On the contrary, it would, if anything, reduce their share, since they play little or no part in the hierarchy of organised crime syndicates nor indeed in the higher echelons of finance where such groups are possible.

The Hidden Crimes Against Women

One further point about concealed crime needs to be made at this point. There is little or no evidence of a vast shadowy underworld of female deviance hidden in our midst like the sewers below the city streets. On the contrary, as we have become increasingly aware in

modern times, quite the opposite is true. There is a great deal of crime which is carefully hidden from the police, from families, friends and neighbours. Much of this takes the form of domestic violence, abuse of children both physically and sexually, incest and marital rape. The overwhelming majority of such cases involve men, usually fathers and husbands injuring or abusing their wives and children. As Young (1986) puts it:

> professional criminals engaged in violent crime (are) a quantitatively minor problem when compared to domestic violence . . . the one most likely to commit violence is the man of the house against his wife. (Young 1986, p. 22).

Mothers do harm their own children and sometimes even collude in their sexual abuse. Nevertheless, 'private' crime seems to be even more male-dominated than public street crime.

Observations made when criminal records were first kept suggested that women were far less criminal than men. This is still true. As a classic text has it:

> Sex status is of greater statistical significance in differentiating criminals from non-criminals than any other trait. If you were asked to use a single trait to predict which children in a town of 10,000 people would become criminals, you would make fewer mistakes if you chose sex status as the trait and predicted criminality for the males and non-criminality for the females. (Sutherland and Cressey 1978, p. 130).

Gender, Crime and Criminology

Sex then is a crucial variable, indeed *the* crucial

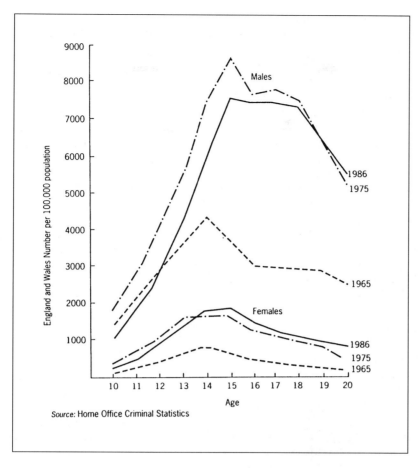

Figure 1 Persons aged under 21 found guilty of, or cautioned for, indictable offences per 100,000 population by age.

variable in predicting criminality. You might expect, therefore that students of crime, its causes, consequences and remedies, would have used this observation frequently in their work in explaining criminality. It provides an obvious touchstone for all theories of criminal behaviour, a vital litmus-test for the validity and reliability of all types of studies. The remarkable conformity of females, as well as the sex differences involved could be expected to stimulate considerable research. You might reasonably suppose these things but, at least until the late 1960s you would have been wrong.

New Studies

During the 1970s and 1980s there has been a flowering of new work. From a wealth of offerings we can note studies which depict girls' participation in gangs and fights and of the criminal careers of older women. A major, if distracting, theme has been that of the so-called 'liberation causes crime' argument, supported by Adler and Simon (1975) and vigorously attacked by many others. This view argues that as women become more assertive and more 'equal' to men in many spheres, so crimes by women also rise. One group of studies has focused on the criminal justice system, examining alleged bias in favour of women in it. This 'chivalry' thesis has been considered in relation to the law, the courts and the judiciary and found on the whole not to be proven.

It is only possible here to indicate part of the range of work in this field. While there remain many gaps to be filled, there has been a rich harvest and we can draw some broad conclusions about women and men and crime. First, women offenders often appear to be more stigmatised than males. Courts treat them as doubly deviant: as both role-bending because deviance is unfeminine, and rule-breaking because they are criminals. Social consequences for them, in the loss of their children, home, partner can be more severe. Damage to their reputation is also strongly felt by

Evaluation exercise

Although it has always been apparent that male criminality is more widespread than female criminality the differences in male and female crime rates were not, until recently, perceived as a problem that needed to be explained sociologically. The significance of gender differences in criminality have been highlighted particularly by feminist sociology with Heidensohn's work being a major contribution to the debate. In this context it would be very worthwhile to evaluate Heidensohn's observation that sex is *the* variable in predicting crime.

There are a number of variables which could be used to predict whether a person is likely to become a criminal or not, and to evaluate whether sex is 'the crucial variable' you will need to compare it with other variables such as social class, age and region. To begin with therefore you should explore all the possible variables which might help us predict the likelihood of a person becoming criminal. You will need to examine the evidence – especially statistics which relate crime to variables like class, age, region and sex (see **Cuttings** page, p. 74) – and to examine sociological explanations in some detail, including a range of studies which are referred to in other books. Heidensohn's article contains a lot of information that helps to support her own conclusion but you need to look at contrasting explanations as well, including Marxist accounts which emphasise social class inequality as the fundamental cause of crime. When you have been through the material and thought through your point of view on the evidence and arguments put forward by Heidensohn and others, you should be able to write an evaluation which highlights some of the most interesting issues currently being discussed in the sociology of crime and deviance.

Interpretation exercise

Explain what Heidensohn means by the statement 'girls and women experience more constraining social control than do boys and men in most societies'.

Make a list of five examples of such social controls. The quote refers to 'most societies' so be sure to give examples from different societies and different historical periods.

demonstrated their capacity to commit very serious, sometimes horrific, crimes such as terrorist murders.

A New Agenda

Recent events in several areas suggest that there is a new agenda in the study of crime and of policy in relation to it. Gender related issues are playing an increasingly important role in this. Most crucial has been the recognition of the 'gendered' nature of much personal, especially domestic, crime. On the whole (and with some exceptions) domestic violence is perpetrated by men against women and children. Awareness of the problems of wife and child battering, child sex abuse, rape and sexual assault has grown. Partly at least, this is due to the work of pioneers in this field who both studied them and helped to provide refuges and remedies (Stanko 1984).

While these topics are now much more widely acknowledged and are being given a much higher priority by police forces, the feminist analysis which attributes their causes to patriarchal power and its abuse in family and society is much more controversial. Nevertheless new agenda items have been set for discussion in which gender is one of the key themes. What, for example, constitutes 'normal' masculine behaviour for a father towards his children? How far can sexually harassing acts go before they become criminal?

Gender studies in sociology have often seemed to mean women's studies. Yet that is clearly nonsense. Gender has two aspects. It is as distorting only to look at the one and not the other. In the study of crime it was perhaps inevitable that, for a while, there should be an emphasis on female criminality. However, in criminology, and much more than in most other areas of social science, masculinity is much more of a problem both intellectually and socially, than is femininity. Most commentators agree, for example, that teenage boys' gang activities express their male

many women. Secondly, girls and women experience more constraining social control than do boys and men in most societies. Thirdly, women's offending has a much wider possible range than has previously been recognised. It is, like men's, mainly instrumental and related to economic goals. A few women have

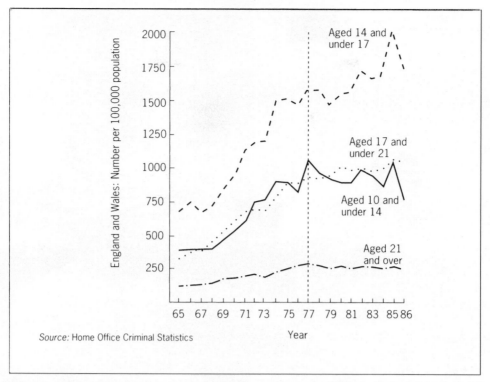

Figure 2 The peaks for female criminality: females found guilty of, or cautioned for, indictable offences, 1985–1986.

role and status in some way. But why must it sometimes be in violence and destructiveness?

Visible Women

Women and girls are on the whole, much more likely to conform than are men and boys. Gender has, albeit slowly, begun to be an issue confronted in studies of male as well as female crime. A study of young male heroin users acknowledges the importance of gender in their roles and lifestyles. Young and Matthews (1986) pay tribute to the critical importance of feminist work on the victims of crime in shaping the direction of their own development of 'realist criminology'.

A more extended approach is adopted by Dunning *et al*, (1988) in their research on football hooligans. In a chapter entitled 'The Social Roots of Aggressive Masculinity' they take the violence of football hooligans at soccer matches and its roots in lower working-class communities and cultures as a problem which they seek to explain. This distinguishes them from many earlier writers to whom such behaviour has seemed to be relatively unproblematic.

While there are new criminological and crime control agendas, on which gender is an important item, there are still many gaps. Text books increasingly cover gender as a key topic. Compare, for instance, the first and second editions of Downes and

Rock's book *Understanding Deviance* (1979 and 1988). The latter devotes a whole chapter to feminist criminology.

Gender has not been the only neglected variable in the study of crime. Race has also been widely ignored and the complex interactions of gender, race and class even more so. Gender is a distinctive issue in that exploring it leads to new understanding not only of offenders, but of victims and not only of crime and deviance but also of conformity and of social control as well. Gender analysis is thus an indispensable tool for social scientists who study crime.

References and Further Reading

Adler, F. (1975) *Sisters in Crime*, McGraw HilL.

Carlen, P. (ed) (1985) *Criminal Women*, Polity Press.

Downes, D. and Rock, P. (1988) *Understanding Deviance*, 2nd Edition, Clarendon Press.

Dunning, E., Murphy, P. and Williams, J. (1988) *The Roots of Football Hooliganism*, Routledge.

Eaton, M. (1986) *Justice for Women*, Open University Press.

Heidensohn, F. (1985) *Women and Crime*, Macmillan.

Heidensohn, F. (1989) *Crime and Society*, Macmillan.

Heidensohn, F. (1987), 'Questions for Criminology' in Carlen, P. and Worrall, A. (eds) *Gender, Crime and Justice*, Open University Press.

Prisoners at Wormwood Scrubs. Of convictions for serious offences in England and Wales in recent years, over 80% have been males.

Smart, C. (1977), *Women, Crime and Criminology*, Open University Press.

Stanko, E. (1984), *Intimate Intrusions*, Routledge.

Sutherland, E. H. and Cressey, D. (1978) *Criminology*, Lippincott.

Young, J. (1986), 'The Failure of Criminology' in Matthews, R. and Young, J. (eds) *Confronted Crime*, Sage.

Examination essay question

Control theory and situational theory are both recent approaches which stress the need for practical solutions to rising crime. Outline each approach and assess its advantages and its possible drawbacks.

Notes for Guidance

This essay title will allow you to focus on the article by Paul Rock and to consider what Jock Young has called the 'new realist' approach to the study of crime and deviance. Although it would be wrong to think that sociologists have left theoretical issues behind, the 'perspectival wars' between positivists and anti-positivists are less in evidence than they used to be. Sociologists have sought increasingly to find practical solutions to the misery and suffering caused by crime. In answering this question, therefore, you will need to present an accurate outline of each of the theories, drawing on additional material, as far as possible, from other sources, including the coverage given to these theories in textbooks. Heidensohn's article on gender and crime provides some other explanations and examples you could use. How you assess control theory and situational theory will depend on what you consider to be their advantages and drawbacks. Try to be imaginative and put forward criticisms of your own but don't feel that all the criticisms put forward need to be original ones. Paul Rock provides a whole series of points which you can use and develop to highlight the pros and cons of the two theories. Another way to develop the evaluation would be to think what would be missing from the sociology of crime if the only objective were to find practical solutions. What do theoretical frameworks such as labelling approaches or Marxism have to offer which is lacking in recent approaches which have a more practical emphasis?

Coursework suggestion

Given that sociologists are now placing an emphasis on tackling the consequences of crime and on finding practical solutions to the increasing crime rate, an interesting and valid approach to this area would be to conduct a victim survey or self-report study of some kind. Both types of study have been used by sociologists and others to investigate the 'dark figure of crime' – crimes which have either not been reported or for other reasons have not led to a criminal conviction. Whether you decide to interview victims of crime or try to get 'confessions' from those who have offended but not been caught, you will immediately run up against ethical issues and questions of confidentiality. What, for example, should you do if somebody admits to a crime when you are interviewing them? How far can you expect people to admit immoral or illegal acts just for the benefit of your project? These are difficult questions but shouldn't put you off doing this kind of research. You should certainly consult the ethical guidelines for A level coursework issued by the relevant examination board. As far as problems of confidentiality are concerned, you should try to explore them rather than thinking of them as a disadvantage. Many studies of deviancy have come up against such problems and the sociological literature provides useful experience you can draw on. The issue could in fact give you a very good way of developing an evaluation of the success or otherwise of the research you have done.

A survey of this kind will undoubtedly require sensitivity on your part, both at the stage of identifying those to interview and in the conduct of the interviews themselves. In the process however you may gain some valuable insights and be able to test one or more hypotheses about the under-reporting of certain types of crime and/or the ways in which crime rates are socially constructed.

Cuttings

The **Second Islington Crime Survey** (1990) argues that in many inner city areas, crime is the major concern among local people, many of whom have direct experience, or knowledge, of offences. In such locales, women are made housebound at night by the threat of crime, and confidence in the police is falling. With the UK currently housing a higher proportion of its people in prison than any comparable European nation, and few signs of the emergence of any effective deterrent to crime, solutions to the growing crime problem seem to be as far away as ever.

CRIME is always an attractive news story, but the recent disturbances on housing estates in Britain and the concern about 'hotting' or 'joyriding' in stolen cars has placed crime in the national spotlight even more than usual. The number of notifiable offences has been on the rise throughout the post-war period, but the last decade or so has seen an unprecedented explosion in the rise of 'official' levels of crime. Recorded crime has more than doubled since 1980 and now stands at over 5 million annual offences. Robert Reiner, Professor of Criminology at the LSE, argues that the scale of recent rises 'can be squarely blamed on unemployment and inequality' at a time when, unlike during earlier periods of hardship, official concern about joblessness and relative deprivation is perceived to be quite low (*The Observer*, 15 September 1991).

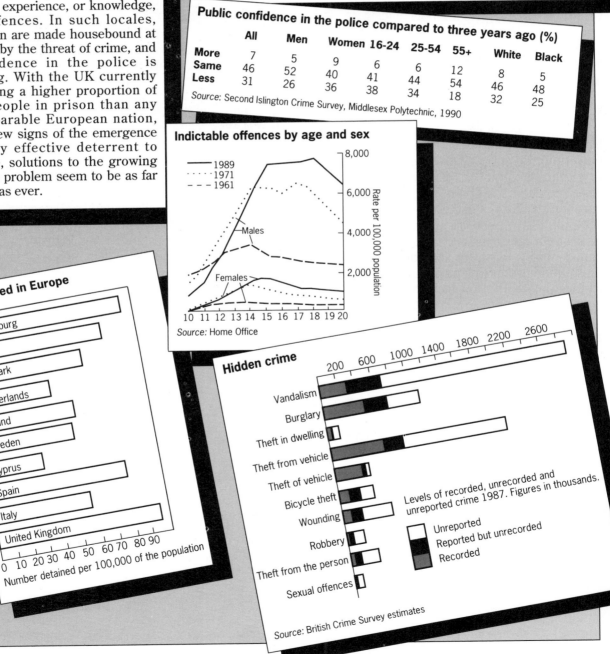

Public confidence in the police compared to three years ago (%)

	All	Men	Women	16-24	25-54	55+	White	Black
More	7	5	9	6	6	12	8	5
Same	46	52	40	41	44	54	46	48
Less	31	26	36	38	34	18	32	25

Source: Second Islington Crime Survey, Middlesex Polytechnic, 1990

Indictable offences by age and sex

Source: Home Office

Imprisoned in Europe

Luxembourg
France
Denmark
Netherlands
Ireland
Sweden
Cyprus
Spain
Italy
United Kingdom

0 10 20 30 40 50 60 70 80 90
Number detained per 100,000 of the population

Hidden crime

Vandalism
Burglary
Theft in dwelling
Theft from vehicle
Theft of vehicle
Bicycle theft
Wounding
Robbery
Theft from the person
Sexual offences

Levels of recorded, unrecorded and unreported crime 1987. Figures in thousands.

Unreported
Reported but unrecorded
Recorded

Source: British Crime Survey estimates

CHAPTER 7

Development

Editors' introduction

Modernisation theory and dependency theory are called upon each year for ritual confrontation in the classroom. Aidan Foster-Carter argues that this reflects a rather limited understanding of the scope of the sociology of development. He shows that the growth of the sociology of development was associated with a very practical concern to understand the hunger and famine so often found in the 'Third World' and the huge economic inequalities which exist between nations. Foster-Carter maintains that the theories which grew out of these concerns are no longer adequate. The breakdown of communist regimes in the 'Second World' of Russia and Eastern Europe has led to increasing international diversity and renders the whole idea of a Third World of under-developed countries problematic.

Foster-Carter documents some of the pointers to a re-orientation of development studies. He looks, in particular, at the contributions that can be made by social anthropology and geography. Social anthropology has always emphasised the importance of cultural factors and has looked at micro-sociological issues of face-to-face interaction in local communities. Geography has stressed the analysis of 'place' and location in space. Drawing on these ideas, Foster-Carter stresses the need for studies which are rooted in ethnographic detail and which show an awareness of the linkages between local and global processes. The over-arching framework for expanding these ideas is drawn from comparative and historical sociology, where a number of important works have formulated accounts of global processes of state formation and modernity within world systems. On this basis, he concludes, we might look beyond the traditional sociology of development to a broader comparative sociology which focuses on world-scale developments.

Development Sociology

AIDAN FOSTER-CARTER

The crisis and semi-collapse of the 'Second World' of communism render the popular term 'Third World' inaccurate in a literal sense. Even before this, such diverse phenomena as the rise of the OPEC oil exporters and the East Asian newly industrialised countries (NICs), or the growing gaps in economic growth as between Asia, Latin America and Africa (see box), had already begun to make the use of a blanket term like 'Third World' increasingly problematic.

Meanwhile, on the theoretical front, development sociology seems curiously stuck (not least at A-level!) in a presentation of self which all concerned agree is outdated and unhelpful. 'Modernisation theory' versus 'dependency theory' was always too simple a dichotomy the more so since those cast as the principal protagonists – those overworked war-horses Walt Whitman Rostow and André Gunder Frank – wrote their most influential works, respectively, more than thirty and twenty years ago.

In 1991, the 'new nations' are no longer new (some

Interpretation exercise

Foster-Carter suggests that the use of a blanket term like 'Third World' is increasingly problematic. With reference to the article, outline the reasons he gives to support his point of view.

never really were); the 'Third World' is no longer third; and the cold war is over. It may well be that the next decade, not to mention century and millennium, will require so radical a recasting of our perspectives that development sociology as we have known it could even disappear. If so, then so be it. This article attempts to identify some possible contenders to replace it

As a final introductory point, the focus here is on general frameworks rather than particular topics. By contrast, most of the latter – meaning areas like urbanisation or education or gender or health issues – have thriving literatures and debates of their own. My concern here is not with these, but rather with how now to define and frame the broader field of development sociology.

Average annual increase in real incomes per head, 1950–1989 (per cent)	
Asia	3.6
Latin America	1.2
Africa (sub-Saharan)	0.8
Source: Economist, World Bank	

Table 1 Increases in income

Beyond the 'Hunger Brief'

One of my former students at Leeds, Damian Tambini, coined an arresting phrase which pinpoints a major issue. In his view, development sociology is characterised by a 'hunger brief', in the sense that its implicit focus (whether in modernisation theory or dependency theory variants) is organised around issues of deprivation and want.

This insight enables us to pose what may seem a heretical or even a callous question. Is this necessarily the best or only way of doing the sociology of most of the world? Might other questions or approaches tell us other, equally important things? To avoid misunderstandings, this in no way implies that the horrendous poverty and hunger which still affect at least one billion people should not be a major object for sociological investigation – not to mention sheer

human concern, moral outrage, and political action. To the contrary, on both counts. Famine, for instance, is an excellent subject for sociological analysis; and I, like many others, went into this field because of a burning anger against the shame and crime of world hunger. None of that changes.

But maybe development sociology has set itself up to try do too many things at once. Despite being constituted from the start (as Preston 1982 has argued) in terms of practical problems, paradoxically it is practitioners above all who are increasingly disillusioned with what one of them has dismissed wholesale as 'the irrelevance of development studies' (Edwards 1989). Pointedly, in 1991 Oxfam and other non-governmental organisations (NGOs) began publishing a new journal, *Development in Practice*. Evidently, 'Rostow versus Gunder Frank' is of even less use to people *doing* development in the field and at the grass roots.

Anthropology's Attractions

At least some of development sociology's problems could be eased by more contact with what should be (but often has not been) a closely related discipline: *social anthropology*. Like development sociology social anthropology, too, is the (older) product of a particular place and time: in this case, the growth, from the late nineteenth century, of western awareness of and interest in non-western cultures, in the context of expanding imperialism and consolidating colonialism.

Although the link to empire has properly been the subject of much subsequent critique, modern social anthropology has evolved into a discipline whose virtues dovetail neatly with development sociology's vices. Three abiding merits, in particular, should commend anthropology to development sociology:

1 Cultures Social anthropology has always taken culture and cultures seriously, in all their specificity and diversity – unlike either modernisation theory, with its composite and pejorative notion of 'tradition', or dependency theory's virtual abandonment of (or hostility towards) this whole terrain in favour of political economy.

2 Acting subjects Neither modernisation theory nor dependency theory has ever had much room for the notion of Third World people as acting subjects in their own right. Using Haralambos's familiar trio of terms: if modernisation theory was the *functionalism* and dependency theory the *conflict* theory in development sociology, then where is the *interactionist* perspective? Almost nowhere, alas. By contrast, social anthropology has tended both to emphasise and to respect people's own definitions of

The gap is wide between theory and development work in the field.

their situation. In development sociology, as elsewhere, this could be both a key methodological complement and a valuable corrective against the excessively impersonal accounts of processes and structures in modernisation theory and dependency theory.

3 Micro-sociology Social anthropology can provide a much needed account of life at the grass roots: the micro-sociology of development, focusing on communities or even individuals as they are affected by – but also themselves effect – broader societal forces.

Although some sociology A-Level syllabuses and degree schemes include some anthropology, many do not. The above three points are really no more than good sociological practice; but each reflects a real problem in development sociology as it has come to be constructed. Here development sociology must learn from and cross fertilise with social anthropology, the more, and the sooner, the better.

Linking Localities

Coincidentally, one of these three anthropological virtues has also emerged separately by a confluence of interests among sociologists, human geographers and others in question of *place, space, and localities.*

The new sociology of space and place both resembles and differs from development sociology. Like development sociology, it is interdisciplinary, drawing as necessary on economics, politics, and history as well as geography and sociology. Unlike development sociology, it is mostly, thus far, done by, on and in the West. Above all unlike development sociology, it avoids any false opposition or one-way determinism between the global and the local – but rather insists on studying *both* the specificities of particular places *and* the broader forces which shape *and are shaped by* particular local circumstances and histories.

By contrast, development sociology (in both its modernisation theory and dependency theory variants) all too often viewed the Third World as a *tabula rasa*: one big empty slate, on which the implacable forces of modernisation or dependency (take your pick) irresistibly and everywhere wrote one single story. That may be an exaggeration, but certainly both of these mutual antagonists ironically shared the same twin faults: of homogenising the Third World, and underestimating particular places and people's capacities to make, at least in part, their own histories. Although some sociology of space and place can be deterministic in this way too, other work emphasises how (for instance) even something as general and powerful as capitalism itself is shaped by, and thus varies between, different social structures in different places. We return to this issue below.

Thinking Big

One striking feature of the recent sociological scene has been the welcome rebirth of *comparative and historical sociology.* Returning to both the themes and the scale of classical sociology, a whole series of authors have produced big books tackling large topics: moderninity, power, legitimation, state formation, revolution, nationalism, civilisations, empires, the world-system and more.

As the blanket term comparative and historical sociology indicates, all these works have at least two things in common. They are *comparative*, drawing upon evidence from a wide range of different societies, and they are *historical*, tracing complex social processes over time-scales less likely to be years or decades than centuries or even millennia. This, after

Some landmark works in the revival of comparative and historical sociology		
P. Anderson	*Passages from Antiquity to Feudalism*	1974
	Lineages of the Absolute State	1974
R. Bendix	*Nation Building and Citizenship*	1964
	Kings or People	1978
S. Eisenstadt	*The Political Systems of Empires*	1963
N. Elias	*The Civilizing Process (2 vols.)*	1978, 1982
E. Gellner	*Plough, Sword and Book*	1988
A. Giddens	*The Nation State and Violence*	1985
M. Mann	*The Sources of Social Power (Vol. 1)*	1986
B. Moore	*Social Origins of Dictatorship and Democracy*	1966
W. G. Runciman	*A Treatise on Social Theory (Vol. 2)*	1989
T. Skocpol	*States and Social Revolutions*	1979

all, was how Marx, Weber and Durkeim worked; hence, comparative and historical sociology could be described as sociology rediscovering its own roots.

Of course, comparative and historical sociology contains immense diversities of approach as well as of topic. Methodologically, most writers take individual nation-states as their units for comparative analysis, but Wallerstein criticises this practice and insists that countries can be explained only by looking at their position in the global hierarchy. Or again, Wallerstein's Marxist economic determinism contrasts with most other writers' more Weberian emphasis on the importance, in their own right of political and/or cultural factors.

And yet development sociology has much to gain from comparative and historical sociology. For one thing, comparative and historical sociology also studies social development – but without development sociology's baggage of presuppositions. Comparative and historical sociology has no 'hunger brief', nor does it feel obliged to deploy crude Procrustean categories like 'Third World' and 'First World'. There is no 'them' and 'us'. Very importantly, comparative and historical sociology makes it possible to deconstruct 'the West', seeing it neither as a given destination and reference point (as in the old modernisation theory), nor as a fixed focus of hegemony and exploitation (as in dependency theory). After all, 'the West' (like 'the Third World') is many societies, none identical or unchanging. In this sense, the comparative and historical sociology approach opens up issues and areas which development sociology (*in both* its major variants), had, in effect, closed.

To give just one example, many comparative and historical sociology writers employ some notion of *civilisations*. The plural is crucial: no racist ranking is implied, but simply the recognition that one way of looking at the world is as a whole series of interacting zones, each with its particular history and characteristics. For at least some sociological purposes (including development sociology), the compendium 'Third World' may now be less useful than its geographical and/or cultural components, e.g. Latin America, sub-Saharan Africa, the Middle East, the subcontinent, South-East Asia, etc. Importantly, such entities are not singular but multiple, and often they overlap. (Consider the different scopes of three such terms: the Middle East, the Arab world, and Islamic societies). Obviously, too, they change over time, and are the subject of manipulation and contestation by a whole range of social actors, from governments to social movements of many kinds. Yet they are real: they create identities and form bases for both co-operation and conflict. Sociology needs to resume this area of study, which development sociology tended to neglect.

Back to Modernity?

If my last point might seem controversial in some quarters, the next one may elicit a gut reaction too. Even within the already narrow development sociology perspective of 'modernisation versus dependency', every teacher knows that these two rarely get equal billing. On the contrary, modernisation theory is usually subjected to the same 'ritual slaughter' which Herminio Martins has described as the fate of functionalism: dragged on to the stage, only to be rapidly and unceremoniously booed and booted off again.

At least some of the older modernisation theories deserved this fate. Development sociology is well rid of both the teleology and ethnocentrism epitomised in

Daniel Lerne's famous quote that 'what the United States is, the modernising Middle East seeks to become'. (That was in the mid-1950s, when Ayatollahs were not yet in vogue.)

Yet there is a real risk that several babies have been thrown out with the bathwater here. For one thing, there was life after Rostow. More recent and often more interesting variants of modernisation theory, such as some of Peter Berger's work, are rarely discussed.

More important, however, is the fact that outside development sociology several adjacent rock-pools (notably those labelled 'theory' and 'culture') have recently come to be very interested indeed in 'modernity' – but with little or none of modernisation theory's ideological baggage. Giddens's four 'institutional clusterings of modernity' should be one case in point.

Events in the real world, as well as in sociological theory, suggest it would be timely for development sociology to reopen and reframe questions about modernity. Two key examples are the collapse of communism and the rise of East Asia. Both have a bearing on the once much debated but latterly neglected question of 'convergence'; yet intriguingly, they seem to point in different directions.

On the one hand, communism's terminal crisis would appear to support the belief that there is no alternative to capitalism as a viable form of moderninity. On the other hand, the spectacular success of Japan and the East Asian NICs suggests that there is more than one way of becoming and staying modern and capitalist. As has often been observed, contrary to old-style modernisation theory's presumption that 'tradition' must be an obstacle to modernity, East Asian capitalism may not only not be hindered but actually be powered in some degree by aspects of the region's older indigenous culture, notably Confucianism.

Maybe, then, we should speak of *capitalisms* and *modernities*, plural rather than singular. Reframing the issues thus avoids any risk of ethnocentrism or any presumption of convergence. It enables us fruitfully to reopen, without prejudice, classic Weberian questions about the relationship between cultural, political and economic variables in different places and periods: questions which had become twisted or lost in the modernisation theory versus dependency theory shadow-boxing, but which no development sociology can afford to ignore.

Going Global

The key word is *globalisation*. One way to introduce the issues is as follows. Suppose somebody suggested

Evaluation exercise

The theory of modernisation is not a popular one in sociology, partly because it implies that underdeveloped countries have only themselves to blame, rather like the culture of poverty theses. Many of the negative criticisms of modernisation theory are justified but, as Foster-Carter suggests, it is a theory that can also contribute positively by renewing interest in classical Weberian questions about the relationship between culture, religion and social change. Foster-Carter's article provides a number of interesting illustrations of the way religion has influenced the development of Japanese and East Asian societies. Using these examples as a starting point, it would be useful to identify and illustrate the positive side of modernisation theory by exploring the similarities between Weber's ideas and those of theorists like Walt Rostow. You will need to do some of your own research using textbooks and other sources to examine Weber's ideas about social change. Weber is said to have conducted a debate with the ghost of Marx because much of Weber's work was an attempt to refine and revise Marx's theories about social change. What you will need to explore are Weber's ideas about the Protestant work ethic and the suggestion that some types of culture and religion encourage enterprise and economic development whilst others inhibit them. As part of the process of evaluation you will need to formulate your own point of view on the relationship between culture, religion and economic development.

a research project on the 'Sociology of Surrey'. You might object that this would be fairly meaningless, inasmuch as most significant social processes of any kind in Surrey originate outside Surrey or across its borders – particularly with London. (You might care to consider whether the 'Sociology of Yorkshire', by contrast, would not be quite so meaningless – and, if so, why.)

What if something similar is happening even to the *nation–state*, which sociology (including development sociology) tends to take for granted as a unit of analysis? It is easy to list major trends and phenomena which transcend national borders. In *economics*, not only trade but also investment and production operate on a world scale. In *politics*, one could cite moves towards federalism in Europe, or manifestations of terrorism (e.g. hi-jackings), or the Rushdie affair. *Social* phenomena, too, are diverse, ranging from advances in communications to labour migration to drugs (the latter a nice example of Third World production for First World consumption). Above all, *environmental* issues – global warming, pollution, resource constraints – are no respecters of national boundaries. (In that sense, I have always found the idea of a 'nuclear-free zone' slightly ridiculous.)

A few concrete examples also may help give the flavour of what I am suggesting. New communications technologies make it all but impossible for governments to continue to police the ideas their citizens are exposed to, whether this be soft porn beamed via satellite TV, or fax communications between the Baltic States and their emigrés in the West. As a result, particular cultural forms and icons travel far and wide. Malaysia for a while banned heavy metal music; and the remote south-west of China, producing goods to smuggle into even more isolated Burma, does a roaring trade in Michael Jackson tee-shirts.

'One world' is not just a slogan but, increasingly a social fact. Not that this means equality, or lack of diversity (as we discuss below). But it does mean connectedness, and sociology (not just development sociology) must take it on board. This requires readjustment at three levels. First, all sociology ought already to be *comparative*. Knowing about Britain is simply not enough. To give an example close to home: you, the reader, are probably an A-level or college student. Do you know anything about your counterparts in France, Germany or the USA, their syllabuses, the organisation of their education system, the funding of their students? If you *do*, you'll be aware of the enormous diversity even between broadly similar western industrial countries. And adding in social anthropology, as discussed above, brings home an even greater range of variation in fundamental social arrangements.

All this should be at the core of comparative sociology in any case. Yet comparative sociology still pre-supposes that there are separate societies to compare. A second step towards globalisation would be to go beyond this and focus also on social processes and actors which themselves either *connect* or even *transcend* nation–states. Most of those listed earlier in this section would be cases in point. To take an obvious example, no sociology of drugs can focus solely on the ghettos of Brooklyn, the baronial estates-cum-laboratories of Colombia, or the peasants growing coca in Bolivia. The total phenomenon connects them all – and many others besides.

Two further examples will grow in importance. First, how can sociology cope with *trans-national corporations*: entities which are often bigger economic units than some entire Third World countries, not only selling but also producing on a global scale, and perhaps no longer possessing any particular national base or loyalties? Second, like capital, people move too – albeit more restrictedly. Labour migration is a major global phenomenon, by no means all aspects of which can be filed (as they usually are) under 'race relations' or the sociology of ethnicity. Key questions about labour market segmentation, citizenship, and the play

Child weavers in Lahore. Third World production for First World consumption.

of identities all arise here; and the issues, like the people, both cross and transcend national boundaries

The third and final step, then, is to abandon or bracket the nation-state and embrace *global society* as sociology's fundamental unit of analysis.

Finally – although this would require an article all to itself – *environmental* issues are global by definition; and, as these grow in real importance and urgency, so sociology will need to rethink its agenda. Particular forms and patterns of human interaction with nature, especially processes of industrialisation, may have effects – whether in depletion of rain forests or mineral or fossil fuel resources, or in effluents of pollutants such as CFCs (not to mention disasters like Chernobyl) – which extend out and on in space and time to affect millions, apart from the particular groups or societies which initiate these processes. If such issues pose urgent problems for political action (e.g. just whose business is it, if every Chinese peasant buys a fridge, and the hole in the ozone layer doubles?), they also require a recasting of social theory: one which must take as its primary object of analysis nothing less than the emerging *world society*.

Conclusion: a Farewell to What?

'Development sociology' as a way of looking at the world has been invaluable for the discipline, putting on to the agenda, as it has done, issues of both great practical urgency (the 'hunger brief') and analytical importance (how to explain the uneven development of societies).

Neither the practical nor the theoretical issues have diminished in the half-century or so of development sociology's existence. But changing social realities

always eventually burst through fixed sociological categories, and I think the 1990s are such a moment for development sociology.

A decade from now, as society and sociology enter a new century and millennium. I would hope to see our syllabuses recast in such a way that *world society* becomes a core concern. Beyond and below that, we will need a varied *comparative sociology*, which draws alike on the perspectives and themes of development sociology, social anthropology and comparative and historical sociology.

References and Further Reading

Useful introductions to some of the areas mentioned are:

- **Anthropology** Besides the many general texts. Long and Long (1992) are particularly good on 'acting subjects' and recent debates.

- **Space and place** Gregory and Urry (1985), and indeed the whole Macmillan *Critical Human Geography* series.

- **Comparative and historical sociology** Skocpol (1984) is a useful summary and critique of the big blockbusters.

- **Modernity** Giddens (1990) and Turner (1990). For ongoing debates, see especially the excellent journal *Theory, Culture and Society*, published by Sage.

- **Globalisation** Featherstone (1990) and Sklair (1991) are a useful collection and textbook, respectively.

Berger, P. (1987) *The Capitalist Revolution*, Gower.
Edwards, M. (1989) 'The Irrelevance of Development Studies', in *Third World Quarterly*. Vol. 11, No. 1.
Featherstone, M. (ed) (1990) *Global Culture: Nationalism, globalization and modernity*, Sage.
Foster-Carter, A. (1990) 'Development' in M. Haralambos (ed) *Developments in Sociology*, Vol. 6. Causeway.
Giddens, A. (1990) *The Consequences of Modernity*, Polity.
Gregory, D. and Urry, J. (eds) (1985) *Social Relations and Spatial Structures*, Macmillan.
Jones, H. (1990) *Social Welfare in Third World Development*, Macmillan.
Long, N. and Long, A. (eds) (1992) *Actor Struggles and the Social Construction of Knowledge*, Routledge (forthcoming).
Preston, P.W. (1982) *Theories of Development*, Routledge.
Sklair, L. (1991) *Sociology of the Global System*, Harvester-Wheatsheaf.
Skocpol, T. (ed) (1984) *Vision and Method in Historical Sociology*, Cambridge University Press.
Turner, B. (ed) (1980) *Theories of Modernity and Post-Modernity*, Sage.

Application exercise

Foster-Carter uses the following examples to support the view that sociological issues need to be understood in a global context: the trade in illegal drugs, labour migration and the policies of multinational corporations. In each case he shows that we cannot understand the problem properly by looking at a single link in the chain. As an exercise, try to think of at least one other sociological issue or problem and consider how a global perspective might be applied to it. You may find it useful to discuss this with a fellow student before writing two or three paragraphs to explain your ideas. Alternatively, you could use a flow chart to show the links between different countries.

Coursework suggestion

This area of the syllabus may seem an unpromising one for coursework, given that the opportunities for primary research in a Third World context are obviously very limited. However, project work could be based entirely on secondary sources if necessary. Furthermore, the increasing emphasis on a global perspective means that it should be possible to conduct relevant primary research anywhere in the world. The thing that would be distinctive about a project on development would be the kind of issues you examined and the global context within which you would examine them. Such issues are often vital ones, and there is a range to choose from, but health and education often stand out as key issues where development is concerned. They are interesting topics to investigate and ones about which there is a fair amount of information and some lively theoretical debate.

One way of approaching it could be to concentrate on one or more areas of the Third World to compare, as far as possible, health and education. A particularly stimulating and controversial perspective on these issues has been offered by Ivan Illich. His work on medical nemesis and deschooling society, when applied to a Third World context, brings into question the wisdom of Third World countries which have imported Western medicine and expensive forms of schooling and higher education rather than concentrating on, arguably more effective and low-tech solutions to problems of public health and literacy. Perhaps to begin you could read about Illich's ideas and Paolo Freire's. You could then try to apply their ideas to an understanding of health and educational issues in your chosen society or societies.

Primary research is certainly not out of the question. You might, for instance, be able to interview people with Third World experience and ask them about health and education policies. Whatever the method of research you choose, and even if your coursework is largely theoretical in approach, it is important to go through all the stages required from formulating a hypothesis to conducting an evaluation.

Examination essay question

'Neither modernisation nor dependency theory offers an adequate explanation of global development.' Critically discuss this view.

Notes for guidance
The quotation in the title of this essay is intended to move discussion about development and underdevelopment forward from the Rostow versus Gunder Frank debate and on to the type of global perspective Foster-Carter advocates when he comments that 'one world' is not just a slogan but, increasingly, a social fact. The section of his article on 'Going Global' will be particularly useful when you evaluate modernisation and dependency theories but initially you should summarise and outline the main features of each of them. For this, you will need to refer to other sources so that you represent the theories as accurately as possible. It would be appropriate, for instance, to discuss Gunder Frank's important critique of modernisation theory as part of your evaluation. However you must move on from this debate towards the type of perspective that views development globally rather than tying it to particular nation states. In this article, Foster-Carter has demonstrated the importance of such a perspective when discussing ecological issues or the influence of multinational corporations which can largely disregard national boundaries. Try, as far as possible, to use examples to illustrate your essay and aim to develop a critical discussion, especially towards the end of your answer, to show that you have formed a sociological opinion about the strengths and weaknesses of the theories you have discussed.

CHAPTER 8

Health, Welfare & Poverty

Editors' introduction

'The poor' have been a topic of persistent political debate and focus for sociological research. This research has all too often defined poverty in terms of some kind of subsistence standard. Researchers have held that it is possible to define the basic subsistence needs of individuals and families: a minimum diet, clothing, housing, and so on. Those whose standard of living falls below this defined level are said to be living in poverty. During the 1950s however, sociologists came to reject this idea of **absolute** poverty and replaced it with a **relative** concept. According to this new view, poverty must be defined relative to the prevailing standard of living in a society. The poor are those who are deprived of whatever is regarded as an adequate standard of living. Because these standards change over time, the poverty line cannot be defined in absolute ahistorical terms.

Ruth Lister reviews the arguments which surround these two views of poverty: absolute and relative. She supports the relative view, but argues that **all** views of poverty, even those which attempt an absolute definition, in fact employ relativistic ideas. Lister also examines recent debates over the existence of an 'underclass'. She sees this concept as involving a moral absolutism in which the social conditions of the poor are seen as a product of their attitudes and behaviour. Such an approach 'blames the victim' and stigmatises the poor. Lister concludes that an adequate view of poverty must recognise the individuality and autonomy of people and the fact that poverty involves a denial of their full rights of citizenship.

Concepts of Poverty

RUTH LISTER

A meeting took place recently which brought together people with experience of poverty an anti-poverty campaigners (OSP/Bradford University 1991). What we mean by poverty was an important area of discussion. Although it raised some difficult questions, those living in poverty were able to offer some simple and clear concepts. 'Poverty's when you haven't got ,' said one man from a Glasgow housing estate. 'Poverty means when you haven't got enough on the table in front of you', is how a woman from Newcastle put it. A common refrain is that poverty is about existing, not living.

Deprivation can occur in different forms in different spheres of life. Peter Townsend (1979) makes a basic distinction between material deprivation, which includes for example diet, clothing and housing, and social deprivation, which includes, for example, lack of employment rights, recreation and holidays; limits on family activities. Out of this, Townsend has constructed a deprivation standard comprised of a series of indicators. The argument is that as one goes down the income scale, there comes a point when relative deprivation, as measured by these indicators, increases sharply. That is the level, or band, of income that can be said to constitute poverty.

This argument has been the subject of some controversy and is but one of a number of approaches adopted by those who operate with an explicitly relative conception of poverty, the other main ones being the 'consensual' and 'budget standards' approaches to measuring poverty (Piachaud 1987).

It is possible to identify a number of key concepts in addition to the basic one of poverty and deprivation: exclusion from full participation in society; marginalisation and powerlessness. They are synthesised well in the following quotation from the *Faith in the City* report:

> Poverty is not only about shortage of money. It is about rights and relationships; about how people are treated, and how they regard themselves; about powerlessness, exclusion and loss of dignity. Yet, the lack of an adequate income is at its heart, (Archbishop of Canterbury's Report 1985, para. 9.4)

Poverty is also about people's life-chances or lack of them. It is important, therefore, to build in a time dimension. The length of time in poverty and whether or not a person can see any prospect of its end will shape her or his experience of poverty. For children, in particular, poverty can both stunt their childhood and cast a shadow forward over their future lives. It can, for example, affect their health and physical development, indeed their very chances of surviving birth; their educational opportunities and even their chances of growing up in their own family, as the great majority of children taken into care are the children of poor families.

I am reminded of a warning given by David Piachaud:

> If the term 'poverty' carries with it the implication and moral imperative that something should be done about it, then the study of poverty is only ultimately justifiable if it influences individual and social attitudes and actions. This must be borne in mind constantly if discussion on the definition of poverty is to avoid becoming an academic debate worthy of Nero – a semantic and statistical squabble that is parasitic, voyeuristic and utterly unconstructive and which treats 'the poor' as passive objects for attention, whether benign or malevolent – a discussion that is part of the problem rather than part of the solution. (Piachaud 1987, p. 161)

This article attempts to present some of the insights to emerge from that academic debate, without getting too bogged down in its complexities. It starts by looking, inevitably rather superficially, at how the debate has evolved and changed as new concepts have been introduced and old ones modified. It then suggests that the different meanings of poverty for certain groups, such as women and black and other minority communities, are often obscured by conventional definitions. It concludes by considering the language of poverty and in particular the newly fashionable concept of the 'underclass'.

Changing Conceptualisations of Poverty

Once upon a time, there was a relatively simple tale to tell. Traditional concepts of poverty, used by people such as Rowntree, were supposedly based on a measure of basic physical needs and people were said to be in poverty if they had insufficient money to meet those needs. This was known as the 'absolute' approach.

During the post-war period it was challenged by social scientists such as Peter Townsend, who argued that people had social and cultural as well as physical needs and that these needs are shaped by social and cultural changes, especially during periods of rapid technological development. Thus, new needs are created and old needs are met in new ways.

According to this 'relative' approach, poverty has to be understood and measured in relation to living standards which are generally accepted in the society in question at the time in question. Thus, the fact that poor people in Britain today have a higher absolute standard of living than their counterparts in the 1930s or in the Third World does not mean that they cease to be poor.

In fact, there is a long tradition in which it has been recognised that needs are determined socially and culturally as well as physically. Nearly two centuries ago, Adam Smith wrote that

> by necessaries I understand not only commodities which are indispensably necessary for the support of live but whatever the custom of the country renders it indecent for creditable people, even of the lowest order to be without. A linen shirt, for example, is strictly speaking not a necessity of life. The Greeks and Romans lived, I suppose, very comfortably though they had no linen. But in the present time . . . a creditable day labourer would be ashamed to appear in public without a linen shirt, the want of which would be supposed to denote that disgraceful state of poverty. (Smith 1812, p.693)

Indeed, John Veit-Wilson has argued that a careful reading of Rowntree shows that he, too, was operating with a relative conception of poverty (Veit-Wilson 1986). It has also been pointed out that all conceptions of poverty are relative in that it is not possible to divorce the determination of even basic physical needs from the conventions of the society in which they have to be met (Ringen 1988).

While the academic distinction between absolute and relative poverty has been shown to be rather

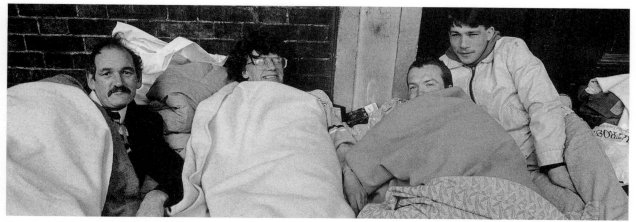

London's homeless bed down for the night.

blurred, there is still a distinction in many people's minds between a more subsistence-oriented and a more relativist notion. This came out clearly in answers to the British Social Attitudes Survey. The 1986 Survey found that only a quarter of respondents considered people 'who had enough to buy the things they really needed, but not enough to buy the things most people take for granted' to be in poverty; 55% defined having enough to eat and live but not to buy other needed items as poverty, and 95% accepted that not having 'enough to eat and live without getting into debt' spelled poverty (Taylor-Gooby 1987).

The old simple absolute/relative dichotomy has also been superseded by a series of more sophisticated approaches, conceptualisations and distinctions. Peter Townsend and others, for example, make a clear distinction between deprivation and poverty: between unmet need and the inability to participate in activities on the one hand and the lack of material resources that causes this deprivation on the other (Townsend 1987).

Hidden Dimensions of Poverty

What is lacking in all of these conceptions of poverty is any explicit recognition of how the meaning and reality of poverty and marginalisation might be different for those groups that are obscured by conventional definitions and official data, in particular members of the black and minority communities and women.

In an article in CPAG's journal, *Poverty*, Kenneth Leech and Kaushika Amin of the Runnymede Trust argue that 'there has been an increased racialisation of poverty: blackness and poverty are more correlated now than they were some years ago.' (Leech and Amin 1988)

It is not, however, just a question of the greater vulnerability of black people to poverty, it is also about how that poverty and marginalisation can be exacerbated by racism, both in the operation of the institutions of the welfare state and in the wider society.

Those members of the black and minority group communities who live in poverty, often because of the unfair burden of unemployment and low pay borne by them, can face a double exclusion and marginalisation.

So can poor women, for rather different reasons. The term 'the feminisation of poverty' had been coined to describe the increased incidence of poverty among women. In fact, women's greater vulnerability to poverty is nothing new. It is just that awareness of it is beginning to grow, at least in some quarters, and that it has become more visible because of the increase in the number of female-headed households.

There are a number of dimensions to women's poverty which are all too often **hidden**. They are summoned up by Jane Millar and Caroline Glendinning:

> The conditions under which women obtain access to resources, the levels of those resources, women's control over resources and their degree of responsibility for the welfare of others in deploying material resources – all these are factors which make women more vulnerable to poverty and which shape women's experience of the impact of poverty. (Millar and Glendinning 1989, p. 369)

For many women, poverty is closely related, either directly or indirectly, to financial dependency on men. What is partly at issue here is the distribution of resources, of the control of resources and of the

---

Interpretation exercise

Ruth Lister refers to 'the hidden dimensions of poverty'. Define what she means by 'hidden' poverty. Outline the explanation she offers for the hidden poverty experienced by (a) some ethnic minority groups and (b) some women.

consumption of resources within the family. A number of pieces of research confirms that, where women have no income of their own or only a low part-time wage, they cannot necessarily rely on a fair share of their male partners' income for themselves and their children.

Where income is not shared fairly, it means either that women and children may experience more intense poverty than men or that they are experiencing poverty when the man is not. This hidden poverty is not picked up by the traditional measures of poverty , which lump together the couple's income and implicitly assume that all members of a family have full access to that income and share the same standard of living.

Managing poverty – a task which largely falls to women – is also very time consuming. Time, and the fact that people with money can often buy time and may not realise the extent to which they do so, either through the labour-saving goods they buy or the services they employ, is a widely neglected dimension of poverty. It is a particular problem for lone parents, but women generally still have major responsibilities for unpaid caring and servicing work in the home, despite the rise of the 'New Man'.

The Language of Poverty and the 'Underclass'

The categorisation of poor people in the statistics is normally according to family and employment status. Traditionally, there has also always been a tendency to categorise poor people, albeit not statistically, according to their respectability of 'deservingness' i.e. according to moral rather than economic or demographic characteristics.

Recently we have seen a revival of such thinking on the New Right, spearheaded by US writers such as Charles Murray. They have criticised the liberal/left attempts to 'homogenise' the poor, so that the only thing which is said to distinguish them from the rest of society is lack of money.

In contrast, they are attempting to revive moral distinctions, using the concepts of 'behaviourial poverty' and the 'underclass'. However, in doing so, they are, themselves, introducing their own strains of homogenisation in lumping together all able-bodied poor people under the rubric of behaviourial poverty and dependency. In other words, it is argued that their poverty is the product of their own behaviour, such as having illegitimate children or avoiding work. This behaviour is then, the theory goes, reinforced by the social security system itself, which encourages and perpetuates dependency on the State (see Murray

1984). It is not, however, dependency *per se* which is of concern here; private dependency within the family is considered acceptable and even desirable.

Writers such as Murray have developed the notion

Evaluation exercise

One of the arguments you should be able to evaluate as part of your work on health, welfare and poverty is the culture of poverty thesis and theory of an underclass. The culture of poverty thesis was originally associated with the work of Oscar Lewis but has emerged again more recently, and in a slightly different form, with Charles Murray's theories about an 'underclass'. Lewis' theories, and now Murray's, have generated heated arguments about the causes of poverty and the social policies that might be introduced to deal with it. Some would argue that the notion of an underclass includes within it a number of moral judgements about how the poor ought to live and that it blames poverty on the poor rather than explaining it sociologically. Many of these issues are raised in Lister's article. Lister herself describes Murray's ideas as dangerous, imprecise and disturbing. As an evaluation exercise you should begin by reading through the relevant sections of Lister's article, noting down Murray's ideas and Lister's objections to them. You should also refer back to earlier versions of this debate by looking up textbook sources on the culture of poverty thesis and criticisms of it, including Marxist criticisms. When you have been through the material you will have the basis for writing an evaluation. Start with an outline of Murray's ideas and go on to discuss the criticisms of them. You will find Lister's criticisms very useful but don't take them at face value and don't apply them without thinking about whether you agree with them yourself. You are the person who is conducting the evaluation and you need to consider which of her criticisms of Murray are justified and which are not. If you believe that some or all of Murray's arguments contribute sociologically to our understanding of poverty, and you are able to justify your point of view, you should defend them against the sort of criticisms Lister and others have put forward.

Brixton on the dole. The jobless of all ages, sexes and races wait to 'sign on'.

of the 'underclass', which has become increasingly fashionable in this country too, and not just on the Right. It is used freely by the media, often as if it were synonymous with poor people generally. It is, I would argue, a dangerous concept (see Lister 1990). People tend to use it to mean what they want it to mean. Murray himself concedes that it is a waste of time trying to count the 'underclass' as 'it all depends on how one defines its membership' (Murray 1990, p. 23). In effect, it becomes a circular definition and it is impossible to prove that an 'underclass' exists or not.

The language of the 'underclass' is not only imprecise; it is also disturbing; it is the language of disease and contamination. Murray, for example, described himself in *The Sunday Times* as 'a visitor from a plague area, come to see whether the disease is spreading' (Murray 1989).

Language such as this encourages a *pathological* image of people in poverty as somehow different from other people and to be feared. The danger is that the concept of the 'underclass' is so imprecise that it gets stretched to describe the poor generally, and so value-laden and emotive that it stigmatises them as a group apart.

The language one uses in conceptualising poverty is important because it conveys images which can shape attitudes towards poor people and which can shape poor people's own attitudes and self-image. Indeed, the word 'poverty' itself is not without problems because of the stigma still attached to it, exacerbated by the glorification of success and enterprise in recent years.

People in poverty themselves therefore sometimes do not want to use the word. This ambivalence has been cleverly exploited by some politicians.

This creates a dilemma. Should one avoid the term and use instead the sanitised language adopted by the Government, such as 'the less well off' thereby implicitly agreeing with the idea that poverty no longer exists in this county? Or should one continue to use

Application exercise

In what ways does the evidence in the article and in the **Cuttings** page (p. 90) concerning health and poverty, debt and homelessness, support the view that poverty is caused by structural/material factors? In what ways does it support the view that poverty is caused by cultural factors?

Use the following headings to set out and plan your answer:
Evidence of **structural** causes of poverty
Evidence of **cultural** causes of poverty.

the words 'poor' and 'poverty' in the knowledge that some of the people to whom they refer do not want the label to be applied to them?

At the meeting referred to earlier, some people felt that they did not want to be labelled as poor. 'Labelling is for jars', said one woman. Others argued that poverty is nothing to be ashamed of and that one must not let the Government make people feel ashamed. Someone else asked how it was possible to give a value to being poor, without romanticising it, when what someone in poverty wants most is not to be poor.

Perhaps part of the answer lies in recognising that people in poverty are individuals like everyone else and that it is misleading to present them simply as passive victims. There is a distinction to be drawn between *powerlessness* and passivity.

While people in poverty are generally powerless in the face of deep-seated economic and social and social structural forces, this does not stop some of them from trying to gain more power and control over their own lives. As one woman who had been instrumental in the development of a credit union, said: 'The women have really pulled this estate up by its bootstraps. The credit union has given a new sense of pride, and dignity to the whole community.' (Dunn 1988)

Conclusion: the Language of Citizenship

It is important that conceptions of poverty have built into them a dynamic element that does not deny the individuality and action of people in poverty. The revival of notions of citizenship (not of the 'active' variety espoused by Government ministers) is helpful here. Poverty can be understood as *partial citizenship*, as a denial of the full rights of political, legal and social citizenship (Lister 1990). Nevertheless, people in poverty are still citizens of the same society. The challenge is to make a reality of that citizenship.

References and Further Reading

Report of the Archbishop of Canterbury's Commission on Urban Priority Areas (1985) *Faith in the City*, Church House.
Dunn, M. (1988) 'Strength in numbers: the story of Cowgate's credit union' in *Poverty*, No. 69, CPAG.
Leech, K. & Amin, K. (1988) 'A new underclass? Race, poverty and the inner city' in *Poverty*, No. 70. CPAG.
Lister, R. (1991) 'Concepts of poverty' in *Local Government Policy Making*, February.
Millar, J. & Glendinning, C. (1989) 'Gender and poverty' in *Journal of Social Policy*, Vol. 18 No. 3.
Murray, C. (1989) 'Underclass' in *The Sunday Times Magazine*, 26 November.
Murray, C. (1990) *The Emerging British Underclass*, IEA Health and Welfare Unit.
OSP/Bradford University (1991) *Working Together Against Poverty*, OSP/Bradford University.
Piachaud, D. (1987) 'Problems in the definition and measurement, of poverty' in *Journal of Social Policy*, Vol. 16 No. 2.
Ringen, S. (1988) 'Direct and indirect measures of poverty' in *Journal of Social Policy*, Vol. 17 No. 3.
Smith, A. (1812) *The Wealth of Nations*, Ward.
Taylor-Gooby, P. (1987) 'Citizenship and welfare' in R. Jowell, S. Witherspoon, L. Brook (eds.) *British Social Attitudes. The 1987 Report*, Gower/SCPR
Townsend, P. with Corrigan, P. and Kowarzik, P. (1987) *Poverty and Labour in London*, Low Pay Unit.
Veit-Wilson, J. (1986) 'Paradigms of poverty: A rehabilitation of B. S. Rowntree' in *Journal of Social Policy*, Vol. 15 No. 1.

Coursework suggestion

Whether poverty can and should be viewed as a relative concept is one of the issues raised most frequently in sociological discussions in this area. Evidence from different societies and historical periods suggests that it is very difficult to draw an absolute poverty line because what people consider to be poverty will vary considerably from place to place and from time to time. The relative nature of poverty therefore provides a useful focus for coursework.

You might begin by examining the sociological literature on the subject, drawing as far as possible from the cross-cultural and historical comparisons it provides. You might continue by conducting a series of in-depth interviews with people who have lived in other countries or interview a sample of elderly men and women with the aim of recording an oral history of poverty.

Choice of a sample is always important, even if it is very small. You will need to consider which cross-cultural and historical comparisons to highlight. You might, for example, have the advantage of being able to interview members of one particular ethnic minority group to draw a comparison between poverty in the UK and poverty in, say, Jamaica. Equally you may interview a particular age group to draw a comparison between, say, the 1930s and the 1990s. Either way it will be important, if you are using an unstructured approach, to ensure that you have a reliable way of recording the interviews and that you allow the data to speak for itself to some extent.

The skill of conducting an informal interview is to allow people to make a full contribution but to keep broadly to the original aim of the interview. In this way you should be able to formulate , refine and eventually test a hypothesis which is concerned with the relative nature of poverty. Evaluation of your own approach will be important, as always in A level coursework, and this should centre on an assessment of the sampling and interviewing methods you used, possibly highlighting the strengths and weaknesses of in-depth and qualitative methods.

Examination essay question

Outline and critically assess the argument which suggests that poverty is caused mainly by the lifestyle and culture of the poor.

Notes for guidance
This question gives you the opportunity to outline both the culture of poverty thesis associated with the work of Oscar Lewis and others, and more recent notions of an underclass. The Lister article contains a considerable amount of material about the concept of an underclass and the criticisms made of it. Explanations of poverty have tended to emphasise either the cultural characteristics of the poor or the structural and material conditions which create poverty. When you have outlined the first of these views you will need to consider how best to assess it.

The most important criticisms have been levelled by those sociologists who have put forward structural explanations of poverty. However, rather than simply putting forward a summary of structural explanations as an alternative point of view, you should aim, as far as possible, to use the structural explanation as a standpoint for criticising both the culture of poverty thesis and the notion of an underclass. Thus you should try to identify what Townsend and others would see as the shortcomings of a view of poverty which sees it as a consequence of the beliefs and attitudes of the poor. Major textbooks provide ample material on this area. Be selective in your use of them. Concentrate only on the sections which are really relevant to this particular question.

You will find some statistical evidence about poverty, as well as brief accounts of research done by Townsend and by others, on the **Cuttings** page overleaf.

Cuttings

Economic status of family heads of households below average national income, percentages, 1987.

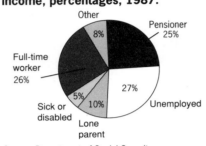

Source: Department of Social Security

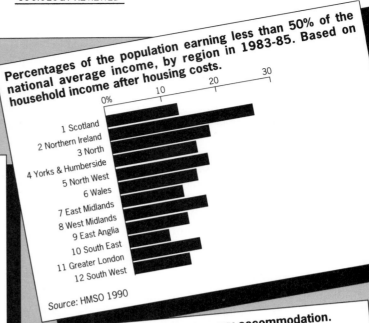

Percentages of the population earning less than 50% of the national average income, by region in 1983-85. Based on household income after housing costs.

1 Scotland
2 Northern Ireland
3 North
4 Yorks & Humberside
5 North West
6 Wales
7 East Midlands
8 West Midlands
9 East Anglia
10 South East
11 Greater London
12 South West

Source: HMSO 1990

Research conducted by Professor Peter Townsend and his colleagues at the Statistical Monitoring Unit at Bristol University suggests that between 1979 and 1989, the income of the poorest 20% of the population fell by 4.6% while that of the richest 20% rose by 40%. The Townsend study uses the government's own Family Expenditure Survey to demonstrate that changes in social security payments in 1988 have helped to worsen the relative position of the least well off and that specific kinds of households – state pensioners, single parents – have been hit worst of all.

Increase in households in temporary accommodation.

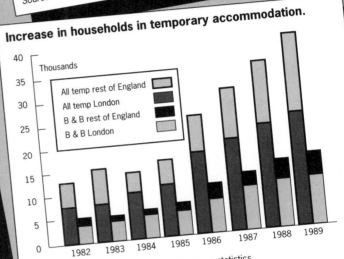

Source: Dept of the Environment homelessness statistics

In June 1991, the National Children's Home charity commissioned a survey on the eating habits of low-income families in Britain (NCH 1991). The results suggested that one in five parents 'regularly' denied themselves food through lack of money, and one in ten children under the age of five goes without enough to eat at least once a month. The report claims to have found a 'direct relationship between those on the lowest income and those with the poorest diet, and puts a lie to the argument that it is ignorance, not lack of money, that prevents families eating more healthily'.

The most recent focus for concern about the growth of poverty in Britain has been on the rise of long-term debt and of homelessness. A Policy Studies Institute report on Credit and Debt in Britain (1990) revealed that one in nine households struggles to make ends meet and that household debts totalled £3 billion. 2.4 million families are in debt arrears, with the average 'problem' debt being around £600. The poor, unemployed and single parents are the groups most at risk of falling behind in repayments, and while rich households use most credit, it is the poorer ones who go into increasing and unmanageable debt. According to the PSI, one-third of all households in which the head of household is unemployed is in debt.

CHAPTER 9

Mass Media

Editors' introduction

Perhaps the most convincing account of the persuasive powers of the media comes not from a 'factual' media report but from fiction. Just before the Second World War, the young Orson Welles produced a play for radio in the USA based on the science fiction novel, *War of the Worlds*. In the play, aliens from outer space overrun American cities, their progress being charted by a fictional, distressed radio reporter. In fact, some listeners tuning in to the play thought they were listening to a **real** news bulletin, and panic soon spread around major American towns and cities. A rueful Welles later apologised for the 'authenticity' of his production.

Why did this piece of fiction induce such hysteria? Well, for one thing, it was a convincing piece of drama! But social commentators attributed its startling effects to the existing fears among the American public about real alien threats from across the Atlantic in the shape of the rise of warring powers in Europe. In short, it was partly the fears and **expectations** which the **audience** brought with it to the broadcast which shaped the extraordinary response. A brief, but telling, tale.

Understanding the commercial and political interests which structure mass communication networks is a vital part of knowing how and why different media operate as they do. But, as Orson Welles discovered, what the audience brings to any media output is important too. In the short article which follows, Greg Philo tries to unravel the complex relationship between television coverage and its various audiences.

Philo points to the importance of individual, personal histories and to cultural and class experiences for interpreting media messages. In doing so, he argues for a rather more complex **interrelationship** between the media and its various audiences than is sometimes suggested by simple conspiracy theories, crude forms of Marxist structuralism, or those accounts which argue that the media is hardly influential at all in shaping our perceptions of the world.

Oh, and by the way, be careful what you listen to on the radio. . .

Seeing Is Believing?

GREG PHILO

We know that television affects us. TV news is our main source of information for national and international events. But what do *we* bring to our understanding of television? New research from the Glasgow University Media Group shows that what we understand and believe about the television message is influenced by our own personal history, political culture and class experience. In a new study (Philo 1990) groups of people from different parts of the country were given news photographs from the 1984/5 miners' strike. They were then asked to imagine that they were journalists and were invited to write their own news stories. They were also questioned about their memories of the strike and about what they believed about specific issues – for example, was the picketing that had taken place mostly peaceful or mostly violent?

One surprising result was the closeness of the 'news programmes' produced by the groups to original items which had appeared on the BBC and ITN. One year after the strike had ended, a group from Shenfield in Essex wrote the following 'news item':

> As the drift back to work in the mines began to gather momentum, violence erupted.

A group from Glasgow pursued a similar theme:

> On a day that saw an increased drift back to work . . . further violence was taking place . . .

While on the original news from ITN we had heard:

> Worst picket violence yet but miners continue their drift back. (ITN 17.45 12.11.84.)

It is very interesting that a phrase such as 'drift back' should have stuck so clearly in people's minds. At the time of the strike, some journalists commented on how such phrases became a routine part of news coverage. Michael Crick from ITNs Channel 4 news published his own diary of the strike:

> The national coal board's skilful propaganda claims that men are returning daily in hundreds, even thousands, and detailed figures are supplied first thing to news desks every day. Some journalists don't bother to attribute the figures to the board . . . and most have generally adopted the board's phrase 'the drift back' despite its suggestions of a continuous and inevitable process. (Michael Crick, *Reporting the Strike*, Granta, 1985.)

Application exercise

One of the main themes that runs through media research is that the content of the media is often biased and that social groups like strikers, for example, are depicted as a deviant minority. Philo's study examines not only the content but also the effects of the mass media. However for this exercise you should concentrate on how his evidence can be used to demonstrate bias and stereotyping. A good way to approach it would be to list some examples of bias and stereotyping in the reporting of the miners' strike.

What Does TV Tell Us?

The study shows that pictures and language can stick in our minds but it does not follow that we all believe what we have seen. For example, virtually all of the people who were interviewed thought that most picketing shown on television news had been violent, but whether they believed that most picketing was *really* like this was another matter. The extent to which they believed in the television version of the world depended on several factors, particularly on whether they had access to alternative accounts. No one who had actually been to a picket line thought that picketing was mostly violent. The police described it as being rather like a rugby scrum. 'A lot of it was good natured banter, and "Come on, lads, it's time for a good heave",' said one officer. Mostly, people who had been there described it as being very boring, nothing happening at all for hours on end, as they just sat around. But for those without such direct experience, television was more likely to be an important source of information. A woman interviewed in Scotland described how initially she had believed in the television account and then came to change her mind:

> When I first saw the TV pictures I thought it was terrible because I thought it was really violent. Every time it came on I would just walk away and not watch it. Then most of my friends at work, their husbands are miners at Polkemmit pit – they stood at the picket lines and there was never any violence, never any. The camera men must have deliberately filmed a violent bit for television.

Other people also found that their beliefs were affected by their work experience and personal history. A woman working in solicitor's office in Croydon, South London, wrote a very interesting news story, using the pictures provided. One of these pictures was of a shot - gun lying on a table. Most people in the groups associated the gun with the striking miners or pickets but in her story it is the police who use 'arms' and 'threatening behaviour':

> Serious disruption and fear was caused by the police today at the coal mines, as a result of them using arms and threatening behaviour towards the pickets and the coal miners.

At first sight, we might understand this as a simple critique of police behaviour, but in fact the writer gave a very complex explanation of how she had arrived at her 'news story'. From her professional experience in seeing court cases reported, she thought that the media concentrated on the sensational. The reporting of a strike would therefore focus on violence but she did not herself believe that most picketing had been like this. She had also written in her replies to questions that her attitude to the police was, on the

Catering workers in London study pictures before 'writing the news'.

whole, positive and that she actually believed that the gun belonged to a striking miner. I asked her how she could reconcile these beliefs with what she had written in her news story. She replied:

> I understand that the police do things which are not 'by the book'. It wouldn't surprise me if an officer had picked up the gun and used it. Things which I have been told by police officers which they have done to people taken in for questioning might surprise some people, but in certain circumstances it would be understandable. I can see why they do it.

I asked her, is she saw the police in this way, she described them as causing 'serious disruption' in her news story? She replied:

> In the miners' strike, I did see the police as a disruptive force. I didn't feel that all those police officers should be sent in. The miners and pickets may have sorted it out between themselves. When I see the police I associate them with criminals and the miners are not criminals. I do

have very mixed feelings , I do sympathise with the miners but I tend to see things from both sides. All my life I have had dealings with the police in my work and socially. My father was a police constable and my boyfriend was a CID officer.

The final comment about being a policeman's daughter comes almost like a punch line at the end to explain the complexity of her attitudes. Because she was so close to the police, she could both sympathise with them and know they might sometimes break the rules. At the same time, she had a clear and professionally defined view of what police responsibilities are. Through this extraordinary set of filters she was able to envisage a situation in which the police might fire unlawfully at pickets, while retaining sympathy both for them and the miners. At the same time she used her professional background both to assess how the police should be used and reject the media account of what occurred in the events.

People thought that most picketing shown on television news had been violent

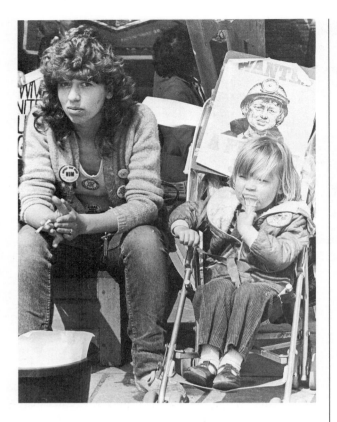

Peaceful pickets from Kent included miners' wives.

Using Personal Histories

In another case, a Salvation Army Officer from Beckenham, Kent used her personal history as well as religious material that she had read to inform her critique of news. As a child she had grown up in Durham, and she believed that those in mining communities were decent people who would not be involved in violence. She stated:

> With a TV camera you can take one shot and make it look like a hundred shots. You can take it from one angle and make it look like there are hundreds fighting – in short, cheat shots and manipulation.

She had read of this in a religious book, which had used the analogy of the manipulation of film images to comment on personal morality. As she said: if you didn't live your life correctly, you were doing cheat shots. The example which the book had used was of stunt photography in Hollywood. But the woman had applied the analysis to television coverage of picketing and had decided that it was a 'cheat shot'.

Some people used simple processes of logic to criticise what they had seen on television. They commented on the scale of the strike and the numbers involved, saying that people could not have been fighting most of the time. This deduction could apparently be made irrespective of sympathies with the strike. One woman from Penge in South London was very critical of the striking miners and said that she would have shot them if she had been a working miner. But she also argued: 'Because of the amount who were actually on strike . . . 'It can't all have been violent'. A print worker who was interviewed also commented: 'If they had been really violent, the police couldn't have coped. It would have been the army'.

Another reason for doubting television news was the comparison of it with other sources of information, such as the 'quality' and local press or 'alternative'

Aggressive picket? As seen on TV.

Interpretation exercise

Philo's research findings suggest that people have reasons for 'doubting television news'. Make a list of the reasons he gives.

Evaluation exercise

An early but influential model of the mass media was the 'hypodermic model' which, as the name suggests, compared the mass media with a hypodermic syringe, believing it to be a powerful influence capable of injecting the audience with its message. Although sociological explanations have moved away from the simple view that the hypodermic model represents, it is a view of the media which is still held by many members of the public and, not least, by 'television watchdogs' like Mary Whitehouse. Philo's research gives an opportunity to evaluate the hypodermic model by drawing up a list of arguments for and against it. What is special about Philo's study, marking it out from most other recent studies, is that he examines the relationship between the content of mass media – in this case the coverage given to the miners' strike – and its effects on audiences. Far from seeing the media as having a direct effect, Philo views the relationship between media content and media effects as highly problematic, as his findings show. To begin your evaluation, you may need to read about the hypodermic model in more detail than the brief references given in the article and then outline it. When you have done that you can make use of the examples from Philo's research firstly to demonstrate the shortcomings of the simple hypodermic model and secondly to consider how and in what circumstances the media might have the kind of direct effect that the hypodermic model implies.

Using the article, evaluate the hypodermic model of the mass media by drawing up a list of the points for and against the interpretation of media effects it puts forward.

current affairs programmes and radio. About 16% of the sample of people in this study made such comparisons. Some people also made comments on the tendency of television to exaggerate and focus on violence to the exclusion of other events. About 14% of the people made this criticism and gave it as a reason for rejecting what they had seen on the news. This is a relatively low proportion, given that the population is thought to believe, in general, that the media tend to exaggerate. But what is significant about this result is that even when such beliefs existed they were not always used to discount what was seen in the news.

Memories of the Strike

The study also analysed how memories of the strike were affected by personal history, by cultural and class experiences. All the people interviewed for the study were asked what were their key memories of the strike. This revealed sharp differences between the various groups. For example, women from working-class areas of Glasgow and London remembered queues for food and the loss of jobs in the dispute. But, in a group of women from the very middle-class area of Bromley in Kent, no one gave these as their memories of the strike. The effect of experience on memory could apparently last for many years. A middle-class woman living in Essex, married to an accountant, gave as her key memory of the strike the hopelessness of families and 'shortage of money'. She explained this by speaking of her own personal history as child in the steel works of Wales and the harsh consequences of unemployment for her own family.

It is clear that we can bring a great deal of our own history, culture and class experience to our reception of media messages. But we should not underestimate their power and especially that of television to influence public belief. Most of the people in this study did not have direct experience of the events of the strike and did not use alternative sources of information to negotiate the dominant message on issues such as the nature of picketing. Over half of the people interviewed for our main sample believed that picketing was mostly violent. Both television and the press were given as key sources of information, but people spoke of the special power of television, saying that its images were 'more immediate' and 'stuck

more'. As one resident of Glasgow put, 'Seeing is believing'.

This was apparently so for a large number of people, at least in relation to their beliefs about picketing. In all, 54% of the main sample had believed that most picketing was violent. The source of this belief seems very clearly to have been the media. It is something of an indictment of news journalism that after coverage virtually every day for a year, such a large proportion of people had apparently no idea what a typical picket line was like. In the course of the interviews for this research, I sometimes read out the eye-witness accounts which had been given by the police and others of experience on the picket lines. These were greeted with genuine surprise by many in the groups, who were convinced that what they had seen on the news was typical. Sometimes there was a sense of shock that they had been misled. As one women from a group of workers in London, commented: 'People always say don't believe what you hear in the media, but this really gives you something to think about'.

Conclusion

Where does this leave research into the 'effects' of mass media? The earliest mass communication researchers believed that the media had tremendous power to promote ideas and beliefs. They saw media power as akin to a hypodermic needle injecting society with ideologies and propaganda. Later it became apparent that *audiences* bring much of their own culture and history to their understanding of media messages.

However, our current research shows that at least some of the information which is used when these audiences think about the world is itself provided by television and the press. It is also clear that it can be very difficult to criticise a dominant media account if there is little access to alternative sources of information. In these circumstances we should not underestimate the power of the media.

References and Further Reading
Philo, G. (1990) *Seeing and Believing*, Routledge.

Coursework suggestion

Content analysis has often been the preferred method of research for sociologists who are interested in the mass media. A range of studies has been analysed for the content of media forms as varied as television, feature films, newspapers, music and children's books. Content analysis requires great care and an eye for detail. You need to know what you are looking for and the hypothesis and theoretical context of the study need to be clear before you start the research. Coursework based on content analysis at A level is all too often very simplified and does little more than point to the existence of bias without attempting to explain it or gauge its likely effects on audiences. You need to avoid that pit-fall. Themes you could examine are bias or stereotyped portrayals of social class in children's books or sexism in the lyrics of heavy metal music. There is an enormous range of potential material to analyse. Whatever area you choose, you should aim to interpret the findings within a sociological framework rather than simply describing the biases you may find. You should consider what social functions are served by stereotypes or bias in the media and who, if anyone, benefits from them. You could go further, however, and by taking the lead from Philo's research, use a questionnaire to investigate people's reactions to the media. Let's say you find that children's books do contain stereotypes of social class. You may then want to question whether such stereotypes actually have any effect on the children who read the material. If you were to discover that heavy metal lyrics are sexist, you might want to explore whether the fans are aware of it and whether they care. If you did decide to follow up your content analysis with a questionnaire your research would have to be in two stages with the design of the questionnaire left until you had completed the content analysis. This would require some sensitivity because you would need to reformulate your aims, to a certain extent, once you had identified areas to ask people questions about.

Examination essay question

Some studies of the mass media have emphasised their direct effect on audiences; others have stressed their indirect or mediated influence.

Compare and contrast these two types of explanation of the effects of the mass media.

Notes for guidance
Although the focal point of this question is the effect of the mass media on audiences, you are justified in broadening your answer to include discussion about media content and even issues of ownership and control. It will be vital, however, to keep bringing your discussion back to the issue of audience effects: this demonstrates your application skills. The obvious comparison to make would be between the hypodermic needle or manipulative models on the one hand and reinforcement models on the other (the latter being variously described as the two-step flow model, uses and gratifications model, etc.). You should certainly refer to such models in your answer but to concentrate on them alone would result in a rather old-fashioned essay (one which might have been written twenty years ago). It is important, therefore, to ensure that your source material is up to date. Philo's article should be helpful in this respect and you should also seek out references to Morley's study of 'The Nationwide Audience' which explores similar issues about audience responses. The question asks you to 'compare and contrast' so you should plan to draw out the similarities and differences between the two approaches. As far as evaluation is concerned, the thing to remember when you are asked to compare and contrast is that your comparison can be a critical comparison: one which highlights the strengths and the weaknesses of the approaches you are comparing.

CHAPTER 10

Community

Editors' introduction

'Community' was, for many years, a principal theme in sociological analysis. Classical sociology bequeathed to us a concern for the possible disappearance of local communities with the rise of large-scale modern society. The mechanical solidarity and 'Gemeinschaft' of traditional rural, agrarian societies, it was argued, would give way to the organic solidarity and 'Gesellschaft' of complex and differentiated urban, industrial societies. Such concerns were reflected in a spate of 'community studies' during the 1950s and early 1960s: studies of rural Devon, Wales and Ireland, and the fate of such 'communities' when they became absorbed into expanding cities. The growth of the city through expansion into the countryside created sprawling suburbs with little sense of place or community. The contrast was not always drawn so sharply and a number of cities showed 'survival' or re-creation of neighbourliness in the suburbs and new towns, but the general picture was clear.

Nick Jewson starts out from the concerns of the urban sociology which replaced the sociology of community, and he presents us with a rather more complex picture. He identifies three stages in the development of the city – the industrial city, the metropolis and the megalopolis. The industrial city, he argues, did not seem to involve the disappearance of communities, but the development of the metropolis (from the 1880s) began to change this as more central services came to be supplied through local political bodies. Such cities were, however, essentially **centralised** political and economic units. Within these cities were formed the 'traditional' working-class urban communities, such as those described by Young and Willmott (1962). These communities were, however, fragmented as post-war urban re-development created new urban areas and a 'privatised' family lifestyle.

Jewson documents the recent emergence of a more decentralised 'megalopolis' in which small-scale 'communities' once more become possible. Within the megalopolis, however, there is a growing polarisation between the declining and deprived 'inner city' areas and the more prosperous and cohesive suburbs. He concludes with a consideration of the political and economic context of inner city decay.

The Development of Cities in Capitalist Societies

NICK JEWSON

Capitalism has radically transformed the character and quality of the environment in which we spend our lives. In pre-capitalist societies the vast majority of people lived in rural surroundings and small settlements. Cities were typically small and always housed only a fraction of the population (10% at most).

Capitalism and Urbanisation
In capitalist societies, in contrast, cities are home to the mass of the population. What is more, the impact

of Western capitalism on the Third World has triggered off rapid urbanisation processes in many of the so-called 'underdeveloped' societies. All this has occurred in a remarkably brief period of time. In 1800 less than 2% of the world's population lived in cities. In 1900 Great Britain was still the only truly urbanised society. Today, about half of the population of the world are city-dwellers; by 2025 that proportion will have increased to around two thirds. In just two centuries we have become an urban species.

Capitalism not only creates cities, it also destroys them. It is the most restless and innovative economic system known in human history. There is a ceaseless search for new markets, commodities and technologies – resulting in frequent changes in work skills, production processes, transport systems and communication methods. New environments, communities and lifestyles are raised up, only to be torn down in the course of further innovation. Familiar streets, landmarks and buildings are demolished, taken over by new inhabitants or recycled for new uses. Capitalist cities are, then, in a state of change and flux.

Three phases can be identified in the development of cities in capitalist societies: 'industrial city', 'metropolis' and 'megalopolis'. These correspond to the three epochs in the development of capitalism itself, described by James Fulcher (*Sociology Review*, Vol. 1, No. 2, pp. 2-5). Fulcher terms these three epochs 'anarchic', 'managed', and 'deregulated' capitalism. The phases of city development are typical of cities in many capitalist societies (they are 'ideal types' in Weber's meaning of this term) but, for the sake of brevity, they are illustrated here by reference to Great Britain.

Industrial City

In Britain the 'industrial city' predominated for the first two thirds of the nineteenth century. It corresponded to an era, in the capitalist economy, of small firms, unfettered markets and weak trade-union organisation. The urban environment was dominated by the 'Smoke stack' industries of the early industrial revolution.

Factory-based production demanded large, spatially concentrated labour forces. As a result there were high rates of urbanisation in this era; masses of people flooded into hastily constructed or expanded industrial towns to take up employment in new kinds of labour markets. The proportion of the population living in cities increased rapidly. In 1800 about one fifth of the British population lived in cities; by the early twentieth century this had risen to four fifths. Many towns grew very quickly. Bradford, for example, had 13,000 residents in 1801; by 1851 they numbered 104,000.

'Industrial city' was characterised by a new physical fabric, a newly urbanised population and new urban ways of life. Many inhabitants experienced a profound 'culture shock'; social commentators frequently remarked on the impersonal, anonymous quality of city streets and the indifference to others of passers-by in the vast urban crowds.

There was very little (local or central) state intervention in urban life. Planning legislation, publicly financed housing and local services (such as street cleaning, water supply, sanitation and road repair) were either totally inadequate or completely non-existent. Indeed, in many rapidly growing towns of nineteenth-century Britain there was no effective system of local government. In these circumstances, cities grew in an unplanned, 'higgledy-piggledy' way; there was little spatial segregation of social functions. Workers and their families lived in housing close by the noise, dirt and pollution of factories, railways and commercial premises.

'Industrial city' was the place of William Blake's 'dark satanic mills' and Charles Dickens's *Hard Times*. It was characterised by appalling material and environmental deprivations; poisoned rivers, foul water supplies, hopelessly inadequate sanitation, toxic industrial wastes, choking fumes, enveloping 'smogs', grotesque overcrowding, jerry-built houses, narrow streets, lack of amenities, and epidemics of infectious diseases (Engles 1958). There were sharp class inequalities in adult and infant mortality. Furthermore,

Interpretation exercise

The article describes three major processes of social change: industrialisation, urbanisation and the development of capitalism. Explain what is meant by each of these terms and highlight the differences between them.

Industrial City

- rapid rate of urbanisation
- newly created urban environment, lifestyle and population
- minimal state intervention
- spatially mixed social functions
- poverty and deprivation
- communities of the oppressed
- riots and collective violence

the death rates of town-dwellers, both rich and poor, were substantially above those of the equivalent social classes in rural areas.

Whilst many city crowds might have seemed impersonal, in working-class neighbourhoods networks of family and community ties were forged out of the hard practical necessity for mutual support to ensure physical survival. In the absence of a welfare state, such communities provided a ragged safety net against poverty, unemployment and old age (Anderson 1971).

Uprooted populations, the geographical concentration of deprived people and strong community bonds provided the conditions for violent protest – as did the breakdown of traditional systems of social control and deference. Most poor people had few or no institutionalised or legitimated channels for the political expression of grievances. As a result, much of their political action took the form of sporadic street riots, machine breaking and attacks on property. These were met with bloody repression.

Metropolis

In Britain, the second phase of capitalist urban development unfolded from the 1880s through to the 1960s. It accompanied a period of increasing

---

Application exercise

In what ways does Jewson's analysis of the development of cities support the view that a loss of community has led to the decline of the traditional working-class family structure?

Each of the main sections of the article refers to the effects of urbanisation on family structure so you could make use of the following headings to organise your notes:

- Industrial City
- Metropolis
- Megalopolis

---

centralisation of economic and political institutions, increasing scale of business operations, the rise of a managerial/interventionist state, growing trade union organisation and the emergence of corporatist political solutions.

In the era of 'metropolis' the rate of urbanisation slowed down and eventually halted. By the mid twentieth century the overwhelming majority of British people were born and brought up in cities; an urban

Metropolis

- slow down and halt in rate of urbanisation
- very large, very centralised conurbations
- increasing state intervention and regulation
- spatial differentiation
- rise and fall of traditional working class communities
- political incorporation of the working classes

way of life was the only one they knew. Cities themselves became very large, covering hundreds of square miles and comprising millions of people. By the 1930s seven great conurbations contained, on their own, some 40% of the entire British population. Such cities were highly centralised. They dominated whole regions with a massive web of centralised social relationships, covering production, distribution, exchange, communication, education, health care, leisure, government and a host of other matters.

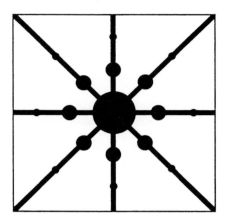

Figure 1 Metropolis – a centralised web of social relations.

State intervention in and management of the urban environment grew rapidly and took many different forms. In Britain, a new system of local government was established in the second half of the nineteenth century (reflected in the construction of grandiose town halls). Soon after, localised municipal services rapidly developed, including water and gas supply, trams, buses, libraries, sanitation and drainage, swimming pools, sports facilities, parks and so on. Before and, more particularly, after the Second World War huge programmes of slum demolition and 'council house' building were carried through by local authorities. A battery of laws, statutes and regulations concerning planning, housing standards and public health emerged in the first half of the twentieth century, adding considerably to the powers of central and local government. In addition, a generous expenditure on the welfare state led to the redevelopment of the urban environment. Buildings housing social services (such as schools, hospitals and colleges) and the bureaucracies of an expanding state (such as Social Security, Job Centre and Inland Revenue offices) increasingly punctuated the skyline or dotted the suburbs. In this era the state was drawn, as never before, into the provision of physical infrastructure, such as roads, railways and ports.

In this era, then, much of what we routinely think of as a city (roads, houses, offices) was increasingly provided by the state. The state shaped the fabric of everyday life.

The expansion of 'metropolis' was accompanied by spatial differentiation. Specialised geographical areas – devoted to commerce, industry, housing, leisure and services – became commonplace. In part, this was a product of the state-managed planning process. It also reflected the growth of suburbs (both owner-occupied and local authority) accommodating the burgeoning urban population. Processes of 'leap-frogging' and status-marking among home-makers accompanied, and manipulated, patterns of migration between communities and the movement of housing markets.

Gradual extension of democratic rights and welfare provisions led to the incorporation of virtually all citizens into the political process. Patterns of working-class protest and political mobilisation changed, becoming more bureaucratised and less violent. Many forms of social control altered in analogous ways; police stations, prisons, asylums and other correctional institutions became established aspects of the urban scene.

'Metropolis' encompassed both the high point of traditional working-class communities and the beginning of their decline. Their zenith reflected the accumulation of complex family and neighbourhood ties over several generations. Their break-up was presaged by: the emergence of the welfare state, which attenuated their survival functions; local authority demolition of slum areas, followed by dispersal of their populations; and changes in occupational structures which undermined the salience of 'smoke stack' industries (Young and Willmott 1962). In post Second World War Britain, a more privatised nuclear family increasingly characterised the mobile and affluent section of the working class (Goldthorpe 1969). This was based upon high wage employment and private consumption within the home, rather than upon communal togetherness in the face of adversity.

An image which symbolises many aspects of 'metropolis' is that of the London 'tube' map. This map was especially commissioned by London Transport in the 1930s, at a time when an integrated public transport system for the nation's capital was replacing a multiplicity of private operators. Its brilliant clarity of design reflects a corporatist ideal of service to the community. It shows a star-shaped, centralised railway network, whose dimensions clearly reflect patterns of suburban growth.

Megalopolis

The outlines of 'megalopolis' have emerged in the last

Evaluation exercise

Jewson's article can be used as a basis for assessing the view that there is an 'urban way of life', particularly if you have a number of questions in mind as you go through the material. Begin by making sure you have grasped the concept of an urban way of life, as put forward by the Chicago School – a number of textbooks provide summaries of it – and refer back to the following questions as you read through the article and other material:

a) Are the similarities among all city dwellers more important than the differences among them?

b) How important are differences in social class and ethnic background in cities? Are they more significant than the similarities there are among city dwellers?

c) Are all urban lifestyles the same or do they vary according to a city's stage of development?

As one of Jewson's main aims is to distinguish between different stages in the development of cities, his findings are bound to suggest that there isn't simply one way of life associated with living in cities but a variety. Those living in industrial cities have quite different experiences and lifestyles compared with those, like many of us, who live in a metropolis or megalopolis. Cities now spread so far and wide that we need also to question whether there is any longer a way of life which could accurately be described as 'rural'. These and other issues need to be discussed in an evaluation of the suggestion that there is an urban way of life. Some sociologists have argued that class and other forms of social stratification such as race and ethnicity are more significant in determining life styles and life chances. References to their arguments would also need to be included in a full evaluation.

significance in the global capitalist system. A handful house the headquarters of the trans-national corporations; some host the new information, research and design based industries. Others, wedded to industries transformed by declining demand, automation of production or relocation to the Third World, have been less fortunate (Smith and Feagan 1987).

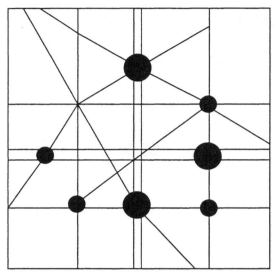

Figure 2 Megalopolis – a polycentric network of settlements linked by modern transport systems.

More generally, the outlines of a new type of city can be seen emerging; it comprises a sprawling, decentralised urban area. Cities become open, polycentric lattice-works of small-to medium-sized settlements, linked together by fast roads and high-tech electronic communication systems. There are green wedges in the spaces between built-up areas but, in a vast carpet of linked neighbourhoods, the distinctive boundaries of town and country disappear. The old central areas lose their commanding presence and appeal; there is no obvious focal point. Los Angeles is a case in point; British examples might include the M4 corridor (London–Bristol) or the M11 corridor (London–Cambridge).

In the midst of 'megalopolis' are to be found decaying 'inner-city' areas (Robson 1988). Their problems reflect processes of decentralisation of population, capital, employment, commerce and leisure.

From the 1960s onwards, conurbations in Britain experienced a decline in population, inner cities being particularly affected. Areas gaining population have included the suburban fringes of cities, small free-standing towns and rural areas. Residents remaining in, or drawn into, the inner cities were among the most deprived members of the population. They included

two decades. This era has featured the rise of 'post-Fordist' production, a decline in labour organisation, curbs on public expenditure, the 'rolling back' of the state and the predominance of trans-national corporations in the global capitalist system.

Some towns and cities have acquired a heightened

Retailing has decentralised.

the unemployed, one-parent families, the long-term sick, low-skill workers, the homeless and members of ethnic minorities. As a result, many inner-city local authorities, with dwindling populations of ever more needy residents, have encountered a 'fiscal crisis'. They face a decline in local tax revenues combined with an escalating need for local expenditure.

The movement of people was accompanied by the relocation of capital. Since the 1960s, inner urban areas have been dramatically hit by loss of jobs and of the smaller firms which traditionally provided them. Much

new investment has gone to suburban or 'green-field' sites, where land is cheap, buildings are up-to-date, motorway access is convenient and local labour is less unionised. Those investments which have located centrally have commonly generated professional and managerial jobs which do not employ local people. Retailing has decentralised to a significant degree. Suburban hypermarkets, often located close to motorways, offer easy parking and consumer goods in myriads of designer, or imitation designer, styles. Leisure facilities (such as skating rinks, multiple cinemas, bowling alleys) increasingly seek similar locations.

As householders, consumers and workers, the more affluent two thirds of city-dwellers tend to be suburban. They have no need to enter the decaying inner cities. They find their identities in consuming innumerable status goods and participating in the fashions of mass popular culture. Urban culture becomes 'post-modern' (Featherstone 1991, Harvey 1989). The out-of-town, drive-in, trans-national hamburger restaurant becomes a symbol of the age.

In 'megalopolis', central state intervention in many aspects of the urban environment has been decisively reduced. Council house building has been virtually halted and over a million council houses have been sold off to private individuals at subsidised rates.

Megalopolis

- de-urbanisation
- huge polycentric lattice-work of settlements
- decentralisation of capital and jobs
- decentralisation of retail
- decline of inner cities
- fiscal crisis of inner city local authorities
- rolling back of state intervention
- consumer culture as personal identity
- urban riots

Central government has encouraged owner-occupation as the normal form of housing tenure; council housing becomes an increasingly marginalised form of tenure catering (Willmott and Murie 1988, Jewson 1989). Planning legislation has been relaxed. Enterprise zones (in which controls on economic activities are greatly reduced) were the favoured method of Thatcher governments for 'kick starting' declining urban economies. Local authorities, especially those inclined towards 'local socialism' or 'local Keynsianism', have been subject to cash limits, competitive tendering of services and rate/charge capping. Others have been abolished altogether. Privatisation and deregulation have removed large swathes of the urban fabric from state provision. Even infrastructure developments, like the Channel Tunnel, have been undertaken with private capital.

Many inner-city residents are too isolated or too desperate to contemplate collective protest about their plight. For them life is circumscribed by fear, intimidation or defeat (Harrison 1983). Others pursue criminal or delinquent solutions to their problems. Some, however, have generated community ties reminiscent of earlier times. Ethnic identities, and the *de facto* denial of citizenship rights, have often played a critical role in defining and mobilising such communities (Rex and Tomlinson 1979). Since the early 1980s, urban riots, on a scale unprecedented in Britain since before the First World War, have been an explosive expression of the citizens' experience of the development of capitalist cities (Jewson 1990).

References and Further Reading

Anderson, M. (1971) *Family Structure in Nineteenth Century Lancashire*, Cambridge University Press.

Engels, F. (1958) *The Condition of the Working Class in England*, Blackwell.

Featherstone, M. (1991) *Consumer Culture and Postmodernism*, Sage.

Fulcher, J. (1991) 'A new stage in the development of capitalist society?'. *Sociology Review*, Vol. 1, No. 2, pp. 2-5.

Goldthorpe, J. (1969) *The Affluent Worker in the Class Structure*, Cambridge University Press, Vol. 3.

Harrison, P. (1983) *Inside the Inner City*, Penguin.

Harvey, D. (1989) *The Condition of Post Modernity*, Blackwell.

Jewson, N. (1989) 'No place like home: sociological perspectives on housing', *Social Studies Review*, Vol. 4, No. 4.

Jewson, N. (1990) 'Urban Riots: economic deprivation, ethnicity and citizenship', *Social Studies Review*, Vol. 5, No, 5.

Rex, J. and Tomlinson, S. (1979) *Colonial Immigrants in a British City*, Routledge.

Robson, B. (1988) *Those Inner Cities*, Clarendon Press.

Smith, M. P. and Feagan, J. R. (eds.) (1987) *The Capitalist City*, Blackwell.

Willmott, P. and Murie, A. (1988) *Polarisation and Social Housing*, Policy Studies Institute.

Young, M. and Willmott, P. (1962) *Family and Kinship in East London*, Penguin.

Coursework suggestion

One of the themes which runs through the sociology of community is that all communities are segregated internally in some way, for instance by social class, age or ethnicity. This theme could be an interesting starting point for a project based on observation of various sites within a locality. You might, for example, concentrate on trying to identify sources of integration and segregation between pupils who attend different schools in a village or district, or you could examine the influence of age and/or class differences on participation in an arts or sports centre. Pubs and clubs would be another set of contexts in which patterns of segregation or integration could be observed.

This approach to research has a long and distinguished tradition, a good example being Margaret Stacey's study of Banbury.

If you are going to approach coursework in this way it will be essential to read around the subject so that you can draw on previous research. The method used in such studies has often been participant observation which yields rich descriptions of community organisations and ways of life. With a project of this sort there may be a case for doing some observation in the field before testing a specific hypothesis. Your hypothesis could emerge from the observation you are conducting.

Examination essay question

Assess sociological explanations of the social problems associated with inner city areas.

Notes for Guidance
Examination questions about inner city areas have often tended to attract answers which are non-sociological in approach and based on commentary from the popular press rather than sociological research. However there is a wealth of sociological evidence in this area and no reason at all why your essay should not be well-documented and critical in approach. Jewson's article, amongst others, provides a lot of useful sociological information which could be applied to discussions about the inner cities, including his analysis of changes in the nature of working-class communities and the process of suburbanisation which has resulted in affluent sections of the population moving out of central areas of cities.

Other writers have suggested that a process of gentrification of inner city areas has occurred and that this has its own problems. You could discuss a range of social problems in your answer, including poverty, crime and social conflict. A problem you should also address, but may not have considered until now, is the way the expression of urban protest has changed. It would be relevant to discuss explanations of the 'riots' in British cities during and since the 1980s. The article will help you with this. Most A level sociology syllabuses encourage you to make reference to current events in your essays but do make sure that when you discuss 'riots', racial conflict or other social problems you combine your references to current events with references to evidence from sociological studies. Be sceptical of purely journalistic accounts which often speculate about the causes of problems without using sound evidence.

CHAPTER 11

Organisations

Editors' introduction

The sociology of organisations is often seen as a discrete and self-contained specialism, concerned mainly with issues relevant to managers and managerial control over workers. According to this view, it is simply a sub-area within industrial sociology. Glenn Morgan clearly shows the inappropriateness of this view. He demonstrates how a concern for the organisation of economic life – and of social life more generally – permeated the classic works of Marx, Weber and Durkheim. Morgan also examines its continuing centrality in modern social theory, especially in the work of critical theorists rooted in Marx and Weber.

Morgan uses his theoretical considerations to raise a number of contemporary issues in the sociology of organisations. He starts by looking at the issue of 'organisational culture', the framework of ideas and values through which organisations are shaped. He shows the centrality of gender to these cultural conceptions and how 'culture' is integrally linked with issues of power and control. Morgan also looks at the issue of inter-organisational networks and, in particular, of the trading and commercial relations, national and international, that tie organisations together. Finally, Morgan considers the comparative analysis of organisations, highlighting studies of Japan and other societies of the Far East. Stewart Clegg – one of the critical theorists discussed by Morgan – has recently pursued this question of Japan's 'post-modern' organisation (*Sociology Review*, **6**, 4, 1992).

The Sociology of Organisations

GLENN MORGAN

Our everyday life is dependent upon the ability of organisations to provide us with goods and services which would have been unimaginable just 150 years ago. We need only to walk into our local supermarket to find things from all over the world. For these products to be available to us, a vast complex of organisations and people needs to be managed and co-ordinated. Even in our leisure time, we depend on technology produced in Japan (televisions, videos and compact disc players), films produced in Hollywood, sports events sponsored by multi-national companies, football teams with Stock Exchange listings, holiday companies with aircraft and hotels around the world. Moreover, many of us work in large-scale organisations, whether they are companies, central and local government, the health service or educational institutions. In whichever direction we turn, we find ourselves dealing with organisations. It is impossible to escape from their influence and, in a modern industrial society, it is difficult to see how we could survive without them.

For these reasons, organisations are important to any social science discipline concerned to address contemporary issues. Not surprisingly, there are now specialist areas within disciplines such as psychology and economics which focus on organisational issues. Sociology is no exception. The sociology of organisations has been an accepted sub-section of the discipline since at least the 1950s. What have been its contributions and what is its future?

The Concept of Organisation

As individuals we have limited capacities. It is only when human beings work together that they become capable of the achievements of 'civilisation'. When we talk about organisation, we are referring to the way in which people have worked together in order to achieve a specific set of objectives. When we talk about organisations, we are referring to relatively enduring sets of social relationships of control, command and co-ordination which have been set in place with the purpose of achieving a certain limited range of objectives and have been accorded a legal identity, defining, in general terms, their rights, responsibilities, duties and powers.

Human societies have always been organised, in the sense of being dependent upon people working together. They have not, however, always been dominated by organisation. The grand architectural monuments of antiquity remind us that ancient societies were capable of great feats of organisation. What they lacked, however, was the great range of organisations, covering different aspects of life, which characterise modern western societies.

Organisations involve bringing together human beings and physical resources in a co-ordinated and controlled manner in order to achieve certain objectives. As these processes of control and co-ordination have become refined and rationalised, so the potential for organisations to expand beyond space and time constraints has increased. We are now used to the idea of companies developing five-year business plans in which they analyse their strategy and set their direction for years in advance. We are also used to the notion that a company will locate parts of its production process throughout the world; similarly, we expect companies to consider export markets and selling their products around the world. Whilst we would have different expectations of public sector institutions, we would still expect them to be run in a 'business-like' way and, indeed, many of them have taken this injunction to heart by producing their own equivalents of 'business plans' and 'strategy missions'.

Yet our familiarity should not breed contempt! It is only in the last 200 years that we have seen the growth of organisations on the modern scale. Furthermore, the establishment of these organisations has involved huge changes in and challenges to social, technological and political relations.

Sociology has a particular role to play in understanding these changes for two reasons. First, sociology has always been centrally concerned with the transformation from pre-industrial society. The social discontinuities of the eighteenth and nineteenth centuries became the core object of study for the classical sociological theorists such as Comte, Marx, Weber and Durkheim. The development of organisations was a central part of this process. Sociological analysis can, therefore, raise issues concerning how we achieved the organisations we have, how they differ across the world and what alternative types we can imagine.

Second, sociology has a particular concern with the relationship between individuals and social structures. Organisations raise this issue in sharp perspective. They are, on the one hand, structures of control and co-ordination, but, on the other hand, they are made up of people who are at times resistant to control and co-ordination. Organisations are made up of structures, i.e. stable relationships, but they are also spheres of action, in which change is always likely to occur. There is a tension between actors as individual subjects with their own goals and interests and the organisation as a structure of control and co-ordination which is trying to guide those actors to act 'for' the organisation as a system.

Approaches to the Study of Organisations

Historically, we can distinguish three main approaches to the sociology of organisations.

The classical theorists

Marx, Weber and Durkheim were all concerned with the nature of the transformation which nineteenth-century Western societies were undergoing. The best introduction to these authors and the relevance of their ideas for the sociology of organisations remains Albrow (1970).

For Marx, the process was best understood as the development of a capitalist mode of production. The central feature of organisations was their role in this process. Organisations in the economic sphere were concerned with the extraction of surplus value from the working class and its appropriation by the capitalists. Organisations in the political sphere reproduced this class domination. Thus, in the Marxist view, the study of organisations in capitalist societies is centrally concerned with how surplus value is extracted by management and the impact which this has on the class struggle.

Weber focused more explicitly on the changing nature of organisations. He argued that the development of the rational–legal bureaucracy created a new organisational type which was technically superior to any other. In traditional societies, organisations were frequently based on family and friendships, goals were weakly specified and processes of control and co-ordination were poorly developed. Industrialism was contingent upon the development of organisations where clearly expressed rules and a hierarchy of officials, paid salaries to perform specified tasks within a goal-oriented framework, were the order of the day.

Durkheim was concerned with the role which organisations would play in the formation of social solidarity. As individuals became more independent from one another, the potential for social pathology would arise; it was, therefore, vital that individuals should feel a part of something wider. As members of organisations, in Durkheim's view, they would participate in wider social decision-making; the organisation would act as a crucial intermediary, linking the individual with the wider society.

The approaches of the classical authors established certain themes that have continued to influence the sociology of organisations. From Marx, there is the theme of organisations and management as instruments of capitalist domination. The organisation is both a site of class struggle and a major contributor to the wider expansion of capitalist relations. From Weber, there is the theme of organisations as technically efficient means of producing goals. From Durkheim, there is the theme of organisations providing individuals with social value and position. For all these authors, the potential and the constraints apparent in society were revealed in detail within organisational settings. There was an inevitable and necessary link between organisations and wider questions of social transformation.

The analysts of bureaucracy

For all their strengths, the classical theorists were basically uninterested in any particular organisation. It

was only to be expected that eventually a focus would develop on organisations *per se*, and it was also likely that such a focus would disrupt the link between the sociology of organisations and wider processes of social change. This began to occur in the 1950s, when sociologists began to look in detail at what was actually going on inside organisations. At first, these studies were predominantly qualitative. In the USA, authors such as Merton, Gouldner, Selznick and Blau conducted case studies of the way organisations functioned (see Albrow 1970). In the main, they were inspired by Weberian themes concerning the degree to which organisations were functioning effectively, though this was taken at a micro-level (i.e. how did one particular organisation match up to efficiency expectations) rather than as a question about organisations and social development in general. These authors showed how the bureaucratic model could generate inefficiencies – bureaucratic inertia, 'red tape', the 'bureaucratic personality'. They remain influential for two main reasons. First, their case-study approach generated some of the best monographs on the sociology of organisations that have ever been written. Second, they addressed key issues about the extent to which the form of a bureaucratic organisation matched its practice: they showed that there was a gap between the two.

One of the problems with the case-study approach remains its lack of generalisability. In the 1960s, this led a number of authors to seek to develop an approach to organisations which was quantitative. The most sustained effort in this direction has come from authors in what is known as the Aston Group (see Pugh *et al.*, 1987). They sought to develop a detailed profile of an organisation by distinguishing its different features (How standardised are certain procedures? How centralised is decision-making? and so on) and developing measures for each feature. In this way, they were able to create profiles for each organisation studied. They concluded from their study that organisations tended to fall into a few basic models, which in turn, appeared to be determined by two main factors: size and dependence. Their overall argument was there was a basic 'fit' between an organisation's environment and its structure; by implication, if the organisation did not fit the environment, it could not survive or be effective.

The structured approach taken by the Aston Group could be replicated in many different industries and countries. Furthermore, it touched a chord with practising managers, in that it could be developed as a prescriptive solution to problems of organisational efficiency. However, it also began to diverge radically from the sociology of organisations. It is not surprising

---

Application exercise

Using information from the article, show how the explanations of social change put forward by classical sociologists influence their theories about organisations.

Structure your answer according to the following headings:
1 (a) Marx's explanation of social change
   (b) Marx's theory of organisations
2 (a) Durkheim's explanation of social change
   (b) Durkheim's theory of organisations
3 (a) Weber's explanation of social change
   (b) Weber's theory of organisations.

that, at this time, the term 'organisation theory' began to be more commonly used amongst authors following the Aston approach. Lex Donaldson, one of the most vociferous defenders of the Aston approach in recent years, entitled his book *In Defence of Organisation Theory* (Donaldson 1985) and criticised the pernicious influence of sociology in this area. The Aston approach departed from sociology in that it seemed to ignore the human actor within organisations; it did not give much consideration to the choices involved in organising, or to the conflict that existed inside organisations; nor was it particularly interested in issues of wider social transformation. To some extent, sympathisers with the Aston approach might argue that this is beside the point. The authors never claimed that sociology was central to their approach; they drew on psychology, economics, decision-making and statistics as well as on sociology. Nevertheless, it was dissatisfaction with this style of analysis that resulted in a range of unequivocally sociological attempts to reorient the agenda of the study of organisations in the 1970s and early 1980s.

The critical theorists

During this period, there were a number of theorists who sought to re-establish the link between organisational sociology and issues of wider sociological concern. There were two strands to this. One strand emphasised the substantive themes of Marx and Weber, the concerns with class, conflict and social order. Clegg and Dunkerley (1979) and Salaman (1979) examined existing organisational sociology and criticised it for its failure to analyses the social foundations of organisation. They proposed an approach based on the centrality of class, conflict and the political economy of capitalist societies. The second strand was more concerned with the philosophical underpinnings of the subject. Burrell and Morgan (1979) sought to bring out the implicit assumptions about knowledge and society which were embedded in organisational analysis. They argued that, in the main, the subject area was dominated by the functionalist approach, which was sterile and limiting. They sought to encourage the exploration of other perspectives, which they labelled radical humanist, radical structuralist and interpretive.

Much of the work of the critical theorists was based on secondary analysis of the existing literature. Whilst it was successful at re-establishing the link between organisational sociology and areas of wider theoretical concern, it rarely involved any empirical research on organisations themselves. Nor was it altogether clear what research in this mould would be like. By the mid 1980s, an outside observer could have been forgiven

for believing that organisational sociology in Britain was becoming irrevocably split. On the one hand, there were those authors working on empirical research, many of them drawing on the Aston approach, and uninterested in wider sociological issues; on the other hand, there were philosophers and theorists, who concentrated on critiquing the foundations of existing research without offering much in the way of an alternative.

Organisations have become increasingly concerned to motivate their workers by making them feel part of the organisation.

Of course, the situation was never this clear cut and, in the last few years, a number of areas of empirical research have emerged, which integrate key theoretical questions with detailed analysis of specific organisations. (This can be seen by comparing the textbooks of the late 1970s with those that have recently been published, e.g. Clegg 1990, Morgan 1990, Thompson and McHugh 1990).

During this period, new areas of interest have been established which draw on many of the traditional themes of organisational sociology but extend them in new directions. This has gone along with an expansion

Interpretation exercise

Morgan makes the distinction between empirical and theoretical approaches to the study of organisations. Identify an example of each type of study and explain why its approach is 'theoretical' or 'empirical'.

in empirical research which feeds back into the process of theory formation. Overall, it is to be hoped that this is promoting a much healthier dialogue between researchers, based on competing theoretical perspectives and empirical work.

Current Issues in the Sociology of Organisations

Inevitably, any selection of current issues will reflect the interests of the author. In my view, however, we can consider three main levels of renewed interest in empirical research.

1   The organisation

Authors have begun to examine in more detail the internal workings of organisations, but linking them to wider issues of social structure. One of the central themes to emerge is the importance of organisational culture. Over the last decade, organisations have become increasingly concerned to motivate their workers by making them feel part of the organisation. This has been done by creating company mission statements and logos, as well as by subjecting employees to intensive training. Organisational sociology, however, has shown that culture and symbols go deeper than simple manipulation by managers. Culture and symbols are an endemic part of organisational life and we need to examine how they affect people and management controls (Turner 1990).

One aspect of culture which has received attention is its gendered and sexual nature. All of social life is gendered and it is not surprising that this should apply within organisations as well. What is more surprising is that, until recently, this fact has been ignored. This area covers more than the ways in which routine organisational events contrive to restrict women's opportunities: it also concerns the domination of a male, machismo culture in most organisations, which shapes wider social relations between men and women (Hearn and Parkin 1987). These questions point to the need to expand our notion of organisation. It is not solely the area for rational, goal-oriented behaviour. All sorts of behaviour – non-rational, emotional, habitual – exist within organisations, and part of the interest is to focus on how management seeks to control and direct these energies.

The revival of Marxism in the 1970s created an interest in the detailed mechanisms whereby management controlled the work-force. This 'labour process' perspective, associated in the first instance with Braverman (1973), was the stimulus to a range of research concerning how mechanisms of control were changing. More recently, however, attention has shifted from the labour process *per se* to a concern

with the subjectivity of the actors concerned (Knight *et al*. 1989). In this argument, management control becomes more effective as it becomes less to do with objective constraints on action and more to do with the subjective internalisation by workers of a positive orientation to the organisation.

This links back to the issue of culture, as previously described, because recent managerialist texts have argued that tight systems of control and rigid hierarchies reduce individual motivation and that what is required is more leadership and inspiration from top managers (Peters and Waterman 1982). Critical organisation theory seeks to place this change in the context of new forms of control and discipline in modern societies. It thereby integrates theorising about the distribution of power and control in society

Evaluation exercise

Arguments about value judgements and bias are highlighted in the sociology of organisations because many of the studies in this area of sociology were conducted with the aim of improving organisational efficiency. The classic examples of this are the time and motion studies associated with the work of Taylor which were simply aimed at increasing the productivity of the workforce. Marxists like Braverman have in fact argued that most, if not all, studies of organisations are geared towards controlling the workforce more effectively and organising the workplace in a manner that is designed to maximise profits. From Braverman's point of view we should not be surprised if studies of organisations are more concerned with trying to solve the problems faced by management than those faced by the workforce.

As an exercise in evaluation you could consider how far the information in Morgan's article either supports or challenges Braverman's point of view. As part of your evaluation you will need to distinguish between different approaches to the study of organisations. Some approaches are quite obviously and unashamedly geared to the aims of management whilst others may be more difficult to judge because it is not immediately clear which side they are on. When you have explored the issues you should be able to reach a judgement about how valid Braverman's criticisms are.

with the analysis of particular organisational forms and management practices, in order to explain how new forms of social order are produced.

2 Inter-organisational networks

These changes in culture, discipline and control are also impacting on the way in which organisations relate to one another. One of the inspirations for the emergence of this debate has been the work of the institutional economist, Oliver Williamson (1975). Williamson argues that economic actors choose whether to transact their exchanges through the market-place or through bureaucracies. Bureaucracies emerge in specific conditions where markets break down because of the lack of trust; similarly, bureaucracies become inefficient after a time and may effectively break down in terms of performing their original functions. Williamson's economics posed a considerable challenge to sociologists who had not really faced up to the question of how organisations decide what to produce and what to sub-contract out or purchase on the market. In the 1980s, when Western (and more lately Eastern European) governments were privatising and large companies appeared to be shrinking and subcontracting out a good deal of their work, Williamson's arguments were of great interest and have demanded a sociological response. In the main, this response has sought to argue that these decisions are not taken on solely economic grounds; they are derived from the perception and power of senior managers in organisations and the state (see Perrow, 1988; one of the best discussions on the subject). Thus, culture and subjectivity return to the agenda, but from the point of view of how inter-organisational relations are managed.

A related argument here concerns the way in which a dominant view of organisational rationality is transferred between organisations in different settings. The 'institutional' school of organisational analysis points to the way in which definitions of efficiency are socially constructed; actors learn what is understood to be efficient in a particular social context. They may then seek to apply these definitions in other spheres, with potentially disturbing effects, e.g. the application of business accounting systems to the National Health Service in Britain (see Morgan, 1990, Ch.3 and 4, on these issues).

3 The comparative analysis of organisations

Different societies have different expectations about how organisations and management should be structured (see especially Clegg, 1990). The rise of the Japanese economy and of other Far Eastern states has shown that forms of organisation can differ radically, even between 'successful' capitalist economies. Equally, the rapid demise of Communism in Eastern Europe has raised questions concerning how different social structures will adapt to these changes and what sort of organisations will emerge. Again, these issues relate to questions of culture, control and competition, particularly in the context of an increasingly international economy. The operation of multi-nationals and their relationship to national governments and supra-national institutions such as the European Community is also clearly important here.

Conclusions

The current period presents a host of threats, challenges and opportunities to the sociology of organisations. The main threat concerns its ability to retain a distinctive identity, separate from managerialist approaches which focus only on solving the problems of management. The challenge is whether the sociology of organisations can make itself relevant to areas of emerging public debate. The opportunities arise from the changing political and social climate, in which issues concerning the quality of life are now given a higher profile. The sociology of organisations has had a chequered past, but it has established areas of common ground and understanding which should enable it to meet the future with some optimism.

References and Further Reading

Albrow, M. (1970) *Bureaucracy*, Pall Mall.
Braverman, H. (1973) *Labor and Monopoly Capital*, Monthly Review Press.
Burrell, G. and Morgan, G. (1979) *Sociological Paradigms and Organisational Analysis*, Heinemann.
Clegg, S. (1990) *Modern Organisations*, Sage.
Clegg, S. and Dunkerley, D. (1979) *Organisations, Class and Control*, RKP.
Donaldson, L. (1985) *In Defence of Organisation Theory*, Cambridge University Press.
Hearn, J. and Parkin, W. (1987) *'Sex' at 'Work'*, Wheatsheaf.
Knights, D. *et al.* (1989) *Labour Process Theory*, Macmillan.
Morgan, G. (1990) *Organisations in Society*, Macmillan.
Perrow, C. (1988) *Complex Organisations* (3rd edn.) Scott Foresman.
Peters, T. and Waterman, R. (1982) *In Search of Excellence*, Harper Row.
Pugh, D. *et al.* (1987) *Writers on Organisation*, Penguin.
Salaman, G. (1979) *Work Organisations*, Longman.
Thompson, P. and McHugh, D. (1990) *Work Organisations*, Macmillan.
Turner, B. (ed.) (1990) *Organisational Symbolism*, de Gruyter.
Williamson, O. (1975) *Markets and Hierarchies*, Free Press.

Examination essay question

Outline and evaluate Weber's claim that bureaucracy is the most efficient form of organisation.

Notes for guidance
Weber's analysis of bureaucracy continues to be of central importance to this area of sociology and this essay will allow you to use material which is well-documented in most textbooks, whilst renewing and updating it with selective use of Morgan's article.

Morgan identifies a number of key studies and theories which have been developed since Weber's theories about bureaucracy were first written. Taking Weber's 'ideal type' as a starting point, you should aim to give a full and clear outline which locates Weber's model within his overall view of society and social change.

Try to explain why Weber considered bureaucracy to be superior to other forms of organisation. If you can write an accurate and detailed account of Weber's ideas you will be able to evaluate them all the more effectively. Criticisms have generally been of two types. Firstly, those which have pointed to the importance of informal social processes and questioned whether bureaucracy is necessarily efficient at all. Secondly, those which have raised questions about whose interests are served by bureaucracy. Weber believed that bureaucracy served everybody's interests but subsequent researchers have questioned whether that is necessarily the case.

Coursework suggestion

A recurring theme in the sociology of organisations has been that organisations – whether they be factories, schools, hospitals or offices – often run more efficiently if people are able to find ways around the rules, regulations and red tape. It seems that formal rules can, at times, work against flexible working practices and individual decision-making. There is a wealth of research on the role of informal processes in organisations, some of which Morgan refers to in his article, and this could provide a good starting point for an A level project.

There are a number of ways in which you might examine how rule-breaking can actually serve the interests of an organisation such as a school, college or place of work. You could, for example, investigate whether and why class registers in a school or college might be 'falsified' and students marked present when they are elsewhere doing assignment work or having a reading week. Another area to investigate might be the way employers sometimes turn a blind eye when children who are under-age work in part-time jobs. The question you will need to ask is how such informal processes benefit the organisation or certain people within the organisation. You might begin with non-participant observation before deciding on the most suitable method or combination of methods to use. A project of this type could address long-standing questions about how organisations work but you would need to be both inquisitive and tactful in your approach.

CHAPTER 12

Power & Politics

Editors' introduction

The sociological study of voting behaviour has tended to be a quantitative exercise, positivistic in its approach and based on studying the implications of changes in voting preferences, particularly when associated with shifting class relations. However, recent claims that class-based identities have been superseded by others, such as gender, ethnic backgrounds, region or 'issue-related' identities, have substantially changed sociological concern with party politics. The focus now is more on the complex and changing ties between interest groups or class fractions and particular parties. Voters, it is argued, are no longer so firmly aligned to one party or class interest but are more discriminating in choosing the party which best meets their current concerns. Modern voters 'shop around' before casting their vote, and do so on more rational grounds.

But under what conditions are these choices made? Does each party have a fair chance to present its case? What of those such as the poor and the unemployed, who may be squeezed out of this new 'consumerist' form of political attachment? Has class really disappeared from political affiliation quite as much as some writers would have us believe?

One consequence of the supposed rise in 'consumerist' voting has been greater sociological interest in how political parties present their case. If voters are making a choice, rather than just aligning their class and party interests, then the image presented by each party becomes more important. Some critics argue that personalities rather than policies now win elections, and many express concern about so-called media 'dirty tricks' campaigns at election time.

In this article, Michael Riley looks at a number of theories of voting behaviour and considers the importance of presentation and image to contemporary political parties. While reading the article, you might consider how you yourself make up your mind about voting preferences. How are **you** influenced by media campaigns or by the changing position of the parties on particular issues? How great a part will tradition or class play in your voting decision? Are you a 'shop-around' voter, or would you stick with the same party, come what may?

Theories of Voting

MICHAEL RILEY

The Consumer, Rational Choice Model

An influential model of changes in voting patterns emerged in the 1970s derived from a consumer image of the voter who chooses a party in a situation of democratic pluralism. It suggests that the electorate have become 'more open to rational argument than they were in the past' (Franklin, 1985). It claims that *class dealignment* (a diminishing link between occupation and voting) and *partisan dealignment* (declining support for both main parties) occurred over the years 1950 to 1979. A particularly interesting factor was the growth in individual, consumer politics. In short:

(1) Self-interest (a consumer value) is a modern basis for casting a vote.

(2) Party identification is conditional; benefits need to accrue to individuals if loyalty is to be maintained.

(3) The major parties recruit support via their skills in persuading electors that clusters of policies are valid. Leaders have to be acceptable and policies credible if political legitimacy is to be achieved.

One well-known example of this model is a longitudinal study (Himmelweit, 1985) that argued 'each election is like a new shopping expedition in a situation where new as well as familiar goods are on offer'. This rational choice model sees the voter as knowing what 'goods' she/he wants.

In explaining the electoral unpopularity of the Labour party in the defeats of 1979, 1983 and 1987 (Crewe, 1987) emphasis was placed on the unpopularity of policy issues stemming from the left-wing of the party. Signs of declining political partisanship were also evident: in 1951 80% of electors identified with the two main parties; by October 1974 this had fallen to 56%. Membership of both parties had nosedived. Few voters were zealots, most seemed marginal and choosier. In the late 1970s, research concluded that the potent combination of the electorate's critical view of Labour's perceived weak performance in office, and a careful consideration of the implications of the policy issues on offer were much more important than socio-economic factors like class background (Sarlvik and Crewe, 1983). Instrumental, rational choice had seemingly taken over from class cohesion. In the 1979 general election the swing in favour of the Tories was the biggest since 1945.

According to this interpretation, then, rational choices were being exercised with a vengeance. In 1983 the Alliance gave issue voters 'more choice' taking over seven million votes, and Labour's vote collapsed to well under nine million. The rebuttal of Labour was marginally less in 1987, and the Alliance romance (albeit fading) continued. But one curious point for this model to explain is that the Tories were issue-unpopular at the 1987 election, yet they won easily.

Issue Voting and the 1987 General Election: A Paradox?

In a 'post-mortem' of the 1987 election result it is suggested that 'class remains the primary shaper of the vote' but that an interesting reinforcement of existing divisions, and cross-class brand loyalties now

exist among a regionally-polarised electorate. Using Gallup Poll data Crewe isolated four points:

(1) The 'core' middle classes, that is the professional-managerial occupations, were 59% Tory, 14% Labour and 27% Alliance.

(2) Amongst the labour aristocracy of skilled manual workers, the 'C2s', a distinct further swing to the Conservatives occurred. Blue-collars NCOs were 43% Tory, 34% Labour and 23% Alliance. 'There could be no starker electoral testament to Thatcherism' (Crewe, 1987).

(3) Labour was still dominant and gathering some lost ground amongst the semi-and unskilled manual strata having 50% of their vote, but again 31% had voted Tory and 19% Alliance. Further evidence of issue-voting and dealignment.

(4) The nub of Crewe's thesis then is that the two broad tiers within the working class are now well cemented in place. A *traditional class*, living in Scotland and the North, often still housed in council property, employed in manufacturing or public sector work. If Labour were to organise a skilled electoral strategy, Crewe argues, those amongst this tier of supporters who have deviated from Labour since 1974 could be recaptured. The second tier, *the coming class of 'new' dimension*, is likely to be in privatised housing, often in the Midlands and the South, largely employed in the private sector and non-unionised.

Thatcherite issues of an egocentric kind are more appealing to this latter class tier than solidaristic, collectivist appeal. Crewe's prognosis for the Labour party in the 1990s is gloomy. *Freed from traditional constraints the salience of personal, calculative choice (self-interest) is dominant. The working class was no longer Labour.*

The difficult sociological exercise is to interpret the *causes* of these changes and to assess their significance. Long-term structural changes have taken place in the class system, loosening the bonds between manual workers and Labour in particular, and generally creating a more volatile electorate. As electronics have taken over from traditional manufacturing, and as the Conservatives in the 1980s have taken the political initiative in broadening share ownership, and owner-occupation, a more individualist, consumer-based society is allegedly on the march.

The paradox of 1987 was that *despite Labour's greater popularity in terms of the important policy issues* (bar defence) the Conservatives easily won the election. Crewe explains this 'contradiction' in terms of the relationship between public poverty and private

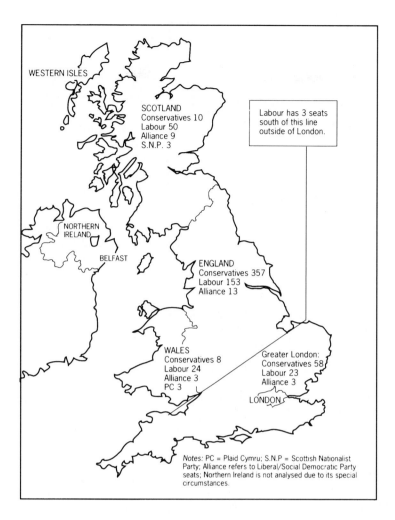

WESTERN ISLES

SCOTLAND
Conservatives 10
Labour 50
Alliance 9
S.N.P. 3

Labour has 3 seats
south of this line
outside of London.

NORTHERN
IRELAND

BELFAST

ENGLAND
Conservatives 357
Labour 153
Alliance 13

WALES
Conservatives 8
Labour 24
Alliance 3
PC 3

Greater London:
Conservatives 58
Labour 23
Alliance 3

LONDON

Notes: PC = Plaid Cymru; S.N.P = Scottish Nationalist
Party; Alliance refers to Liberal/Social Democratic Party
seats; Northern Ireland is not analysed due to its special
circumstances.

Figure 1 Disguising the trends to partisan dealignment: seats by country in the 1987 general election.

prosperity: 'When answering a survey on the important issues respondents think of public problems. When entering the polling booths they think of family fortunes. "Prosperity" is not an issue or a problem but a blessing and by a decisive majority (55% to 27%), the public regarded the Conservatives as likely to bestow it.'

He further asserts that voters 'believed' that the economy and family living standards were improving, and when these attitudes are set in the structural context of a regionally-divided working class – poorer and Labourite in the North, affluent and Thatcherite in the South – the Conservatives emerged as a party of *delivered* policies. Why risk change?

Criticisms of Rational Choice Theory

The first criticism is a methodological one. The model on which much empirical data collection is based derives from an orthodox occupational scheme following, in part, traditional categories used by the Registrar General's scale. It *offers a truncated view of the class structure.* If class is a sociological construct, not a 'natural' phenomenon, then it can be argued that it is important to consider its theoretical origin. Simply to take class as 'given', as a pre-existing category, is to leave us with a working class and a middle class. In the back of our minds then is the unresolved query – 'Where is the upper portion?'

The dichotomous (two class) model, then, reduces class to occupational strata hierarchically divided, and any idea that there may be a conflict of interests between income earners and wealth owners does not present itself. We see a model that takes note of income distinctions but not fully that of property ownership. Income is divorced from wealth in such an analysis, consumer values and attitudes and lifestyles are linked to voting behaviour, but *structures of power and domination are absent.* As a result the influence of elite groups is rendered invisible.

A second criticism is that this theory does not engage with the question as to *how the issue-voters' political preferences are shaped.* How is the agenda set? To concentrate on variables like occupation, housing tenure, income, trade union membership and so on is important if we are to quantify sociological data.

However, the correlations that emerge may not be causations. A danger with the collecting of 'facts' from poll data, or exit polls or panels of electors is that a kind of 'galloping positivism' occurs. Critics of embourgeoisement in the 1960s said it was incorrect then to correlate variables like possessions and housing tenure with class dissolution, and a similar point is applicable now. People's perceptions of political realities do not simply reflect their location in the class structure nor their new found skills of personal issue discernment. We have take into account the *mobilisation of bias* and the creation of *sustained impression management.*

The thesis about volatility being linked to rational choice takes less account of criticisms about the *source* of voting attitudes, concentrating more on the *consequences.* Attitude formation may well be a function of unequal ideological power that can build political imagery in an active sense between general elections. Certainly poll evidence showed considerable faith in the view that the economy was strong. Yet many senior economists of varied political views have continually expressed serious reservations about the Government's claims. The rational choice voter seems to have accepted, if we are convinced by Crewe's thesis, the logic of the Tory case. Critics assert that the operation of skilful and powerful mechanisms of legitimation is one likely explanation of the public's confidence (Dunleavy and Husbands, 1985).

The debate over the *continuation and acceleration of inequality* provides a third criticism. Recent evidence suggests *there is still continued resilience in social class attitudes*, and considerable potential remains for class political action. One relevant finding confirms that individuals often perceive it is very difficult to turn their social class identity along with their peers into effective political action. More social justice is seen to be desired but the means of obtaining it is considered impractical.

Conflict Theory – The Strange, Slow Death of the Labour Party

The unprecedented humiliation of the Labour party in the 1983 General Election may well have been short-term following the modest recovery in 1987 but it was profound. Its share of the total vote fell from 37% (1979) to 27.6% and Labour was reduced to 200 MPs,

Evaluation exercise

To a very large extent it was the consumerist model of voting behaviour which influenced sociological interpretations of changes in voting patterns during the 1980s. Although useful, particularly in updating our explanations of voting patterns, it was often applied uncritically because of the apparent lack of any available alternative explanations of the success of the Conservative Party during the Thatcher years. This lack of alternative explanations has, until recently, made it difficult to interpret recent patterns of voting behaviour in terms other than those put forward by Crewe or Himmelweit or other advocates of the consumerist point of view. Riley's article, however, provides us with an ideal opportunity to assess the consumerist model because it formulates two viable alternative explanations: the Marxist model and the interactionist model.

You should begin by studying the consumerist model because it is impossible to evaluate a point of view you are unclear about. To evaluate it effectively you should examine it from a Marxist point of view, indicating that the consumer model lacks an adequate explanation of power and fails to recognise the processes which shape voters' preferences and so on. Similarly you should highlight the criticisms levelled at the consumerist model by interactionists who point to the need for a dynamic view of the electorate as active participants in the political process. You need to examine these issues in some depth by exploring the article and information from elsewhere. To develop an evaluation you should identify strengths as well as weaknesses. And given that Riley can offer three different perspectives on voting patterns, you should be able to draw out and justify what you see as the strong and weak points in each model whilst concentrating on the consumerist model which is the object of this evaluation exercise.

its lowest total since 1935.

Over the long-term, Labour has lost millions of skilled workers' votes (in 1974, 49% of skilled manual workers voted Labour). 55% of trade unionists voted

Labour in 1974, but this was down to 40% in the last election. The issue here, then, for Marxist theorists is the 'strange death of Labour Britain'.

The Marxist Explanation of the Volatile Labour Voter

The simplified, essential fact of Marxist theory is that capitalism has always organised its economic relationships in such a way as to maximise income, wealth and power for the ruling and owning classes at the expense of the subject classes.

Marxist commentators (Hobsbawm, 1983) suggest that the Labour party's electoral popularity was shaped during the years from 1880 to the early 1950s. Its appeal to a natural, proletarian majority structured by the concentration of production in regions such as Lancashire, South Wales and Yorkshire forged a labourist, communal politics sympathetic to socialism's general appeal. Since that time, however, the restructuring of the economy, its labour markets and subsequent gender, ethnic, and class relationships has again moved on. Logically, therefore, the politics of those dependent upon this complex economic structure evolved.

Macro-capitalist forces such as the move towards electronics and robotics, the tendency to concentrate ownership of enterprises in the monopolistic hands of a smaller number of capitalists, the growth in large financial and administrative enterprises, constantly differentiated the labour market. The *nature of work changed profoundly*:

(1) An increased *feminisation of industry*, service work and the labour market both in terms of full and part-time employment.

(2) A *decline of traditional, labour-intensive* (i.e. essentially proletarian) *occupations*.

(3) The *transference of labour* from declining manufacturing centres and industries towards white-collar service and tertiary employment, and attenuated centres of economic activity associated with the old capitalist industries.

(4) The *Structure of the working class is not being homogenised*. Capitalist employers are fragmenting the labour market by emphasising a need for less demarcation and more fixed-term contracts; temporary work is increasing; subcontracting and a general casualisation of work is accelerating.

(5) There is a *hardening of sectionalist trends* within the workforce. This argument suggests that the old solidarity within the working class is in decline. Power workers in the nuclear industry are less interested in their comrades in the coal mines and more concerned with their own, immediate needs. This parallels a rise in consumer values.

This differentiated structure of inequality has been economically transformed by the decline in manufacturing employment (8.4 million employees in 1966; 5.4 million in 1984) *British society is seen by Marxists as still divided against itself but not simply by class. Gender, region, ethnicity and education, consumption and leisure impact upon politics, as do an awareness of common class-interests.*

Influenced by Gramsci, a number of Marxist writers have argued that the new elements of post-1960s Britain could be politically mobilised: the issues of ethnic settlement, of women's liberation, of sexual changes and the family, and of youth subcultures, were very prevalent in the 1970s. People affected by such post-war changes could be attracted by political campaigns that *could unite them along different lines to that of class*. Divergent groups can be ideologically shaped, and materially attracted to the party of the dominant class – the Conservative party. New hegemonic forces emerged (Hall, 1982).

'Thatcherism' (the ideology), it is argued, articulates a diverse national-populism recruiting more 'voters' during the post-1979 era. This is not the 'duped' voter 'suffering false consciousness', but it reflects a more subtle recognition of the complex links between people's economic position, culture and political perceptions.

The political reality of Labour's defeat is the consequence of deeper changes within capitalism as it has reorganised over the last two decades, dismantling Labour's coalition between the trade unions and the progressive middle class (drawn away to the Alliance). Despite a relatively poor campaign in 1987 on a controversial and damaging set of issues (the poll tax, educational changes and unemployment) the Conservatives retained their coalition of voters. To conflict theorists this is not the 'politics of affluence' posed by rational choice theorists, but clear evidence of a fragmented proletariat under ideological attack.

The hegemonic argument is perhaps supported by the various poll data which indicate that around 60% of the electorate had committed themselves *prior to the campaign* as to how they would vote. The Tory appeal to home ownership and share purchase, combined with its ideologically positive resonances of 'sound economic management' and 'lower taxes' has been skilfully prepared by economic and fiscal policies fuelling wage rises for many in the prosperous *core*

The engine of British capitalism.

workforce, matching and indeed outpacing inflation. It is a telling, coherent strategy where it counts; in the late-capitalist affluent regions. Labour's ability to reconstitute its political bases outside its heartlands, looks uncertain. Below the Severn-Wash axis Labour took 80 seats in 1974, the Liberals five and the Tories held 169. Thirteen years later Labour had collapsed to 26, the Alliance five, and the Tories were overwhelmingly ahead with 229.

In summary, Marxism concludes that *Thatcherism offers a post-1979 recession-settlement* similar to the Butler-Gaitskill consensus of class balance. *A new compromise between capital and labour is being constructed.* The core workers are its principal beneficiaries, the unemployed are excluded and the poor are 'managed' at low levels of benefit. Those conflict theorists 'crawling from the wreckage' of 1987 are fearful that Britain is *moving out of multi-party politics to hegemonic rule by one dominant political force* (Gamble, 1987).

The Interactionist Analysis of Voting Behaviour

This analysis sees the chief failing of the pluralist and Marxist explanations as being quite similar; that of having an uncritical allegiance to models of society that see political motivations within the electorate *that are simply not there.*

'Both have taken the Western working classes as the essential means to achieving liberal or (conversely) socialist political and social goals; both . . . share a common tendency to view present events as part of a pre-determined long-term historical trend' (Marshall, 1987).

One of the objectives of interactionist analysis is to attempt to comprehend the view of politics that electors hold *in their own terms.* It suggests that there is *no natural electoral majority* for Labour defined by class subordination, gender exploitation or ethnic differentiation; that Britain is being transformed into a white-collar society with some speed; and that relative inequality has long replaced absolute socio-economic division. Labour has done badly as much for *political* reasons as anything else.

To interactionists, voters will be moved by ideological appeals of course, but will respond realistically to policies that they see as favourable to themselves not because they are the prisoners of capitalist hegemony *but because it would be foolish not to.* (Looking from the point of view of tenants, particularly the manual stratum, a privatised council house means a large discount on a home and potentially quick and profitable capital gains. Why should the devil have all the best tunes?)

How Britain Votes: the Interactionist View

It is this very criticism that *the electorate's past experience does not shape its future politics* that has been tested by interactionists. Detailed research examined politics with a view to the actor in this process and it was concluded that class background shapes the *potential* for political affiliations. But also the issues, ideologies and performance of the parties themselves critically attracts or repels electors. This alone might sound obvious but Heath's *et al* model of the electorate derives from a five-fold class schema. The two-class model was rejected as not being a social class analysis but more a market research tool (Heath, 1985). Interactionists argue:

(1) The changing nature of voting is *not* the result of class dealignment. Absolute class sizes have changed but *relative* class inequalities still form the basis for much social conflict. Class cohesion and class potential remain as fertile ideological receptors.

(2) The sharp decline in Labour's vote between 1979 and 1983 was *political* rather than sociological. (The ineffective politics of Labour was the cause, not the fading or loosening of the class structure.)

(3) The *longer-term* reduction in Labour's electoral support is virtually half sociological (the decreasing size of the blue-collar rank-and-file) and the other half is political. Labour has been a poor political class party in performance.

(4) Partisan dealignment has occurred, as pluralists clearly point out – *both major parties* lost 'natural' supporters for political reasons. Interestingly the Conservatives – given the increasing size of the *salariat*, and other non-working-class strata – should be in command of more of the voters than they are.

(5) Interactionism also raises a potentially damaging methodological question mark against the rational, consumer theorists. Doubts arise about some of the data derived from polling analysis. Quoting a Gallup Poll question used in Crewe's analysis of the 1983 election results, respondents were asked 'Would you say which party you would think would be best at reducing unemployment?' The thorny question of how respondents interpret such questions is itself problematic. Voters can respond without having knowledge of policy issues. This question, of the validity of such data, and the reliability of such survey techniques makes any interpretation of such poll information less scientific than it appears.

To summarise the main position taken by interactionist writers: voters combine a facility to be both ideologically loyal, yet independent and rational. Class inequalities are structurally tight and visions of class loyalties exist. The economic market place, not

---

Interpretation exercise

Distinguish between partisan dealignment and class dealignment.

Identify the arguments in the article which suggest that 'Partisan dealignment lives, class dealignment does not'.

---

income, is the essential magnet for class loyalty and political action. Crucially, models used by much psephological analysis to locate people within this complex class system have been inexact, and as a consequence much data derived concerning the loosening of class identities is at best a restatement of election results, not a clear explanation of the cause of electoral behaviour. The lesson to be understood, is not to impose meanings upon respondents, nor to expect classes to fulfil sociological theories but to examine data generated from the perspective of voters themselves. Partisan dealignment lives, class dealignment does not.

Conclusions

In May 1989, according to a MORI poll, Labour had climbed to 43% and the Conservatives retained 41% of the electorate's loyalty. The Democrats and the SDP appeared to be low in the public's estimation. How is this explained? Interactionist research had suggested that Labour should turn away from its old class-based policies and revise its strategy along the lines of an

---

Application exercise

The three main explanations Riley examines are the consumerist model, the Marxist model and the interactionist model. It would be useful to apply each model to an understanding of support for the Alliance. You could start by explaining how the consumerist model might be applied to the Alliance with the observation that traditional support for the two main parties may have declined and that policy preferences have become a more important influence on voting behaviour. When you have developed the analysis of the consumerist model in more detail you should then go on to consider how the other two models could be applied to an understanding of support for the Alliance.

---

appeal to social justice. Purists in the Labour movement had seen major policy revisions taking place much to the chagrin of those on the left who refused to heed Hobsbawm's view that the solution to political dealignment lay not in changing the voters but the party. Critics of interactionist theory riposte that its class model is similar to the pluralist one; it recognises the importance of a petty bourgeoisie and a salariat – but again *no grand bourgeoisies is apparent*. Those who control, or own, the power structures are collapsed into an occupational schema, and little attention is given to their disproportionate ability to mobilise bias in favour of inegalitarian policies. Some are more endowed than others but they escape analysis. The pluralist view notes that Labour is moving towards popular demands and 'consumer led' issues and, as the Conservatives retrench on less popular policies, rational choice works against them.

The unresolved theoretical debate between conflict theory, pluralism and interactionism should not obscure one essential point. The theories of voting behaviour themselves reflect assumptions concerning the nature of power, the socio-economic structure, the validity and reliability of quantitative data as well as the problematic concerns of interpreting evidence. Psephological knowledge encounters the same methodological problems as any socially constructed data and its rich quantitative detail may obscure as much as it reveals.

References and Further Reading

Crewe, I. M. (1986) 'On death and resurrection of class voting: some comments on how Britain votes', *Political Studies*, Vol. 35; and Heath, A., Jowell, R. and Curtice, J. (1987) 'Trendless fluctuation: a reply to Crewe', *Political Studies*, Vol. 35.

Crewe, I. M. (1987) 'A new class of politics, *The Guardian*, 15 June, p. 9.

Crewe, I. M. (1987) 'Tories prosper from a paradox', *The Guardian*, 16 June. p. 4.

Dunleavy, P. and Husbands, C. T. (1985) *British Democracy at the Crossroads*, Allen and Unwin.

Franklin, M. N. (1985) *The Decline of Class Voting*, Clarendon Press.

Coursework suggestion

As the introduction to Riley's article suggests, the study of voting behaviour has tended to be a quantitative and highly positivist form of sociological analysis. A survey of the voting preferences of students in your school or college could provide a good opportunity for such research. Ideally the research should be on a fairly large scale, involving a representative cross section of pupils, but it is important to remember that the larger your sample, the more time it will take to collect and analyse the information.

Public opinion polls are widely used as a method of collecting information about voting preferences and it would be worthwhile to contact one or more of the organisations that are involved in national surveys of voting preferences such as NOP, Gallup or MORI to ask for background information about survey techniques.

If you intend to use an opinion poll of this type for your project it is likely that you will want to conduct structured interviews based on a questionnaire which has pre-coded questions. You will need to take great care over the selection of a sample so that it properly represents the wider population whose voting preferences you want to find out about. You may decide to use a quota-sample and it may even be possible to ask other students to act as interviewers. But remember that interviewers need to be trained and they need to be people you can rely on.

It is also important to remember that A level project work requires you to test a hypothesis and that this needs to be the basis of your questionnaire (for example, you might be setting out to test whether there is a relationship between the way students vote and the way their parents vote, or whether there is a relationship between gender and voting preferences). When you evaluate the findings of your study you should be able to draw on the numerous criticisms that have been levelled at the use of positivist approaches to sociology, including the interactionist criticisms that Riley outlines in his article.

Gamble, A. (1987) 'Crawling from the wreckage', *Marxism Today*, July, pp. 12–17.

Hall, S. (1982) 'A Long Haul', *Marxism Today*, November, pp. 16–21.

Heath, A., Jowell, R. and Curtice, J. (1985) *How Britain Votes*, Pergamon Press.

Himmelweit, H. *et al.* (1985) *How Voters Decide*, Open University Press.

Hobsbawm, E. J. (1983) 'Labour's Lost Millions', *Marxism Today*, October, pp. 7–13.

Marshall, G. (1987) 'What is happening to the working class?', *Social Studies Review*, Vol. 2, No. 3 (January).

Sarlvik, B. and Crewe, I. M. (1983) *Decade of Dealignment: The Conservative Victory of 1979 and Electoral Trends in the 1970s*, Cambridge University Press.

Examination essay question

Assess the arguments and evidence for and against evidence which suggests that social class is no longer a major influence on voting behaviour.

Notes for guidance
This question offers plenty of scope for using the material in the article and **Cuttings** page (overleaf) and combining it with source material from textbooks and elsewhere. One of your main tasks will be to draw together and sift through a considerable amount of descriptive and historical material in this area so that you can apply it directly to the question. Avoid the temptation simply to present a list of election results and studies. Aim to highlight concepts and theories as far as possible, concentrating on recent trends, and on the question of the extent to which class influences voting. The question takes us into the very heart of issues concerned with class and partisan dealignment, the argument that voting has become more volatile, pragmatic, etc.

The sign of a good essay will be the extent to which the material is applied directly to such issues. Think about factors other than social class, which have, arguably, begun to have a greater effect on voters' preferences than social class does. And when you weigh up the argument that 'class is no longer a major influence' you should try to consider alternative points of view on the matter in order to assess their strengths and weaknesses. After all, some sociologists argue that class is still the major determinant of voting patterns and that its influence remains as strong as ever.

Cuttings

	Con		Lab		Alliance	Lib/Dem
					1987	1992
	1987	1992	1987	1992	28	19
AB-Prof Managerial	60	59	10	20	27	20
C1-White Collar	51	52	20	24	26	17
C2-Skilled Workers	40	41	32	38	24	17
DE-Partly Skilled Workers	33	29	41	50		

Voting and Social Class: The 1987 and 1992 General Elections
Note: MORI figures for 1987; NOP for 1992.

The well known class-cleavages that continue to deliver Conservative votes in large numbers from the manual classes make short term factors important in the final decision as to how to vote. John Curtice in *The Guardian* on 13 April 1992 has noted the importance of the campaign, and the significant swing from Labour to the Conservatives in the final few days of the election. It is suggested by Curtice that Major succeeded in massaging the electorate's anxieties on the 'privatisation' of the NHS, and that although the government were seen as having mismanaged the economy, Labour did not persuade people that they could do any better. In short, 57% of the electorate are 'working class', but a significant element continued to vote for the Tories on issues rather than class or partisan loyalties.

Source: Mike Riley 'Winner takes all' *Sociology Review* Vol 2 No 1 September 1992

Parliamentary seats held

	1959		1987		1992	
	Con	Lab	Con	Lab	Con	Lab
North	77	72	88	63	93	53
Midlands	62	51	86	34	57	43
South	176	54	209	25	209	45

The Conservatives' regional dominance in England.

The 1992 General Election

	Votes cast	%
Con	14,231,884	41.85
Lab	11,619,306	34.16
L.Dem	6,083,661	17.88
SNP	629,552	1.85
PC	154,857	0.46
Green	171,703	0.50

	THE NEW WORKING CLASS				THE TRADITIONAL WORKING CLASS			
Party	Lives in South	Owner Occupier	Non-union member	Works in private sector	Lives in Scotland or North	Council tenant	Union member	Works in public sector
Conservative	46	44	40	38	29	25	30	32
Labour	28	32	38	39	57	57	48	49
Lib/SDP Alliance	26	24	22	23	15	18	22	19
Conservative or Labour majority in 1987	Con +18	Con +12	Con +2	Lab +1	Lab +28	Lab +32	Lab +18	Lab +17
Conservative or Labour majority in 1983	Con +16	Con +22	Con +6	Lab +1	Lab +10	Lab +38	Lab +21	Lab +17
Category as percentage of all manual workers	40	57	66	68	37	31	34	32
Change since 1983	+4	+3	+7	+2	-1	-4	-7	-2

THE DIVIDED WORKING CLASS: THE PARTIES' SHARES OF THE VOTE AMONG DIFFERENT GROUPS OF MANUAL WORKERS (%)

Note: Figures have been rounded to the nearest whole number, so totals do not always add up to 100%

Source: Ivor Crewe, 'Why Mrs Thatcher was returned with a landslide' *Social Studies Review*, Vol 3 No 1 September 1987

CHAPTER 13

Religion

Editors' introduction

Not very long ago, many sociologists discussing the socialising process would have been tempted to comment on the ever-declining importance of religion and the rising influence of the media in shaping the world view and beliefs of many people in modern societies. Today, these questions seem a little more complex. There is no doubting the powerful effects of the media, but in many matters of domestic and international concern the influence of religion seems far from spent.

In multi-ethnic societies such as Britain, debates about single-sex education, about free speech and about interpretations of history have all been deeply affected by differing religious beliefs. New religious movements have also eagerly tapped into more widespread concern about the earth and its diminishing resources. On the international stage, religious identities, as well as ethnic and nationalist identities, have moved dramatically therefore as discredited political regimes have collapsed in the old Eastern bloc. And, in the USA, religious affirmation seems widely – and commercially – popular in the face of economic, cultural and political uncertainties

at home and abroad. There have been campaigns ranging from the lobby for teaching the Biblical creation story in American schools to opposition to 'unGodly' lyrics in pop records. All over the world it seems, people are still 'getting' religion.

The two articles which follow provide very different examples of the continuing influence of religious movements. In the first, Roy Wallis looks at the rise of so-called 'New Religions' in the West, and their promise of 'solutions' to all personal and societal ills. The time-honoured nature of their appeal, he argues, seems to guarantee the rise of new movements when older ones fall on hard times. Steve Bruce follows with an account of the commercialisation of religion in the USA in the shape of the sharp growth in televangelism. He argues that the new charismatic religious leaders must look good on screen, present a sophisticated message and have business acumen. The religious message is largely the same, but the medium allows for communication with an enormous 'congregation'.

Worshippers of *Neighbours* move over!

The Sociology of the New Religions

ROY WALLIS

Introduction: the Variety of New Religions

In the 1960s and early 1970s a number of new phenomena appeared on the social scene. Some, such as the hippy movement and an enthusiasm for communal living, proved to be quite transient. Others, such as the recreational use of prohibited drugs which shifted from being an attribute of Bohemian life to a major social problem in most Western societies, proved far more enduring. Among these innovations was the emergence and growth of a wide variety of new religious movements and associated range of organisations and groups offering psychological salvation, that is relief from the anxieties and fears, the compulsions and constraints, in short the human

Traditional forms of religious worship.

Some movements were essentially new expressions of rather traditional forms of religion. These were typically more enthusiastic, more zealous and demanding, than the conventional forms of the traditions from which they came, and they often appeared in locations in which those particular religious traditions had no roots. They were *indigenous*, radical variants of prevailing Judeo-Christianity, such as the Jesus People, a movement which grew rapidly in the middle and late 1960s among young people in America and to a lesser extent in Europe. The Jesus People was the name given to a number of groups and organisations which offered a form of evangelical Christianity predominantly to young people. It combined elements of fundamentalism – that is, literal belief in the King James version of the Bible; a highly moral style of life excluding drugs, sex before marriage, alcohol, gambling and frequently smoking; an emphasis on converting others through an emotional experience of Jesus as Saviour; and a total commitment of one's life to the work of bringing others to Christ – with features of the youth culture from which it drew many of its members – long hair; hippy dress and speech; guitar music ('gospel rock'); and a communal life style. Thousands of young people joined various expressions of this movement, abandoning a life of promiscuity and drug-use to work on the land in agricultural communes established by some of the groups, or devoting their

Interpretation exercise

Using the examples from the article, explain what is meant by (a) fundamentalism, and (b) evangelism.

lives to witnessing on college campuses or at rock festivals, striving to bring others to salvation.

Other new religions drew on an *imported* religious tradition quite distant from their own. Hare Krishna devotees, members of the International Society for Krishna Consciousness (ISKCON), committed themselves to a sectarian form of Hinduism which demanded a radical break with the conventions of Western Society. Devotees adopted Indian dress and vegetarianism, again abandoning drug-use and promiscuity. Male followers were required to shave their heads, except for a top-knot. All, in the early years, lived in communal Temples, in which rigorous and ascetic regime was the norm. Members rose before dawn to undertake rituals and celebrations before the temple deities, and spent long hours chanting the Krishna *mantra,* reciting the names of God: 'Hare Krishna, Hare Krishna, Hare Rama, Hare . . .' Playing Indian musical instruments and wearing saffron robes, they could be found in many major Western cities in the late 1960s and early 1970s, dancing and singing the *mantra,* inviting interested passers-by to visit their temple and to abandon the world of *maya,* of corruption and illusion, for the spiritual life.

Similarly drawn from Indian culture, although with a far less demanding mode of life, was the Divine Light

Chanting disciples of the Hare Krishna movement in Washington DC.

Mission. Like ISKCON, the Divine Light Mission was led by an Indian guru, the Guru Maharaj-ji, but unusually, Maharaj-ji was himself only a youth, who offered followers through a relatively brief process of initiation the chance to see, hear and taste the transcendent world in their meditations. Still better known was the Majarishi Mahesh Yogi who also brought to the West a meditational practice, Transcendental Meditation (TM). TM secured hundreds of thousands of initiates and was widely credited with scientific validity for the major psychological and social benefits which it claimed to result from regular practice of its technique of meditation. This credibility was to falter in time, particularly when it announced that through the practice of more advanced techniques initiates could fly, elevating themselves from the ground by spiritual power alone. The few non-believers permitted briefly to witness this astounding phenomenon reported that they had only observed rather strenuous forms of hopping!

Some new religions, however, appeared to embody a synthesis of both Western *and* Eastern culture. The followers of the Reverend Sun Myung Moon claimed to be the fulfilment of Judeo-Christianity, but their beliefs and practices probably owe almost as much to Buddhism and Korean shamanism as they do to Christianity. The 'Moonies', as they are popularly known, believe that Jesus was sent by God to redeem the world, but that he was only partially successful in this mission. Jesus only succeeded in establishing a *spiritual* Kingdom, and thus the task of bringing about the physical Kingdom of God, of bringing the whole world to recognise God, remains to be achieved. Reverend Sun Myung Moon is credited with being potentially the Messiah who can establish the physical Kingdom of God, with the aid of devoted followers who have committed themselves to a rigorous life of service to achieve that end.

Although this idea appears strange to many people raised in the West, the idea of a Second Coming, in which Christ will return to establish the Kingdom of God on Earth, is a common theme within Christianity, even if it is not given great prominence in the conventional churches. But in addition to these Western elements, there are ideas and rituals drawn from the East relating to the importance of ancestors, and to the existence of a spirit world which can act for and against the mission which Moon pursues.

The Moonies have been particularly notorious as a result of their success in leading many young people to abandon their homes and education, frequently cutting contact with relatives and former friends when they joined the movement. In consequence, the Unification Church received much adverse publicity and experienced many episodes in which the families of members, often assisted by professional 'de-programmers', sought to kidnap back their offspring, and subject them to sustained pressure to abandon their attachment, to see 'the truth' about how they had been deceived and exploited, and to return to a conventional way of life.

In contrast to those new religions which drew heavily upon existing religious traditions, whether indigenous or imported, there also rose to prominence in the 1960s and 1970s a range of movements quite different in character, which seemed to owe more to the fringes of modern psychology than to the historic religious culture. Scientology is one such movement. It appeared originally in the form of Dianetics, a self-help psychotherapy, in the early 1950s. After a brief period of popularity it broke up and disappeared from view, reorganising itself as a spiritual philosophy and incorporating as a church in America. Scientology offered a wide range of practices designed to enable an individual to achieve his full potential as a human being and ultimately as a spiritual entity. It claimed to be able to eliminate psychosomatic and psychological illnesses and their effects, to increase intelligence, and to improve greatly the individual's functioning in interpersonal relations and in his career. In addition, it promised the committed follower the means to recover extraordinary spiritual powers which it was said that humankind had once possessed but since lost, powers such as the ability to see and hear things at a great distance, to be able to manipulate objects by purely mental means, to gain knowledge of previous lives, and to be able to dominate other beings. Scientology claims to be able to produce these results on the basis of training and 'auditing', a technique of counselling and mental and spiritual exercises. Training and auditing are provided at varying fees, but advancement in Scientology will normally cost several thousand pounds, or alternatively one may become a full-time worker for the movement, receiving training and auditing free or at low cost in return for working at generally rather poor rates of pay.

Erhard Seminars Training (usually known as 'Est') also offered to provide a kind of enlightenment in a rather more rapid fashion and at substantially less cost than Scientology (from which, however, many of its ideas were derived). Est purveyed a 60 hour training, taken over two weekends, the purpose of which was 'to transform your ability to experience living so that the situations you have been putting up with clear up just in the process of life itself'. This is clearly not the stuff of traditional religion. Such movements typically place little emphasis on collective ritual or worship. They focus on the problems of individuals, and market themselves as a service which individuals can purchase and consume at their convenience. Their practices are directed more to alleviating the problems of this life than to achieving salvation in some other worldly heaven. Such movements draw upon ideas current at the fringes of recent and contemporary psychology: from the more radical followers of Freud, such as Reich, Rank and Jung, and from their heirs, humanistic psychology and hypnotherapy. In addition, they may often draw upon ideas of a more occult kind, such as from Theosophy or vaguely Eastern thought. Hence one can perceive the origins of their view that the human being is perfectible, able to overcome all the inadequacies and deficiencies of life and to realise an essentially divine inner nature.

Not only is the content of these movements, ideas and practices distant from that of traditional religion, but so, likewise, is their organisational form. Rather than as churches or chapels, such movements typically organise themselves in the form of multinational business corporations, with branch offices and a sales force. They employ the techniques of modern marketing and advertising, providing their services with facilities for time payment or discounts for cash.

A Typology of the New Religions

We have so far looked at the new religions in terms of their origin in traditional religion (indigenous or imported) or in terms of more psychological ideas and practices. But, as it stands, this division is not sufficiently refined for sociological purposes, that is to permit the explanation of significant differences identified by the classification. While the psychologically-based movements seem to form a type, showing the common characteristic of accepting most of the goals and values of the wider society but providing new means to achieve them, the new religions which draw upon an existing religious tradition seem to be less homogeneous. A few – perhaps TM is the best example – also seem to be

---

Application exercise

Although Wallis is not primarily interested in the secularisation debate his article clearly has implications for the view that Western societies have undergone a process of secularisation. Read through the article, taking notes, and consider to what extent, and in what ways, the findings of Wallis' study can be applied to the secularisation debate. Consider whether his evidence tends to support or refute the theory of secularisation.

---

oriented to enabling people to achieve the conventional goals of this life (better jobs, higher IQ, greater success in personal relationships, etc). They must therefore be classified along with Scientology, Est and the like as constituting the category of *world-affirming* new religions. Others, like ISKCON and the Children of God (a movement which survived the disintegration of the Jesus People and took on a quite distinctive character), seem entirely different. They profoundly reject the world around them, seeing it as utterly corrupt and beyond piecemeal redemption. Such a world has to be entirely abandoned or totally transformed. These movements anticipate a spiritual revolution or the imminent return of Christ, and until that occurrence, separate themselves from the depraved world in communities of the faithful. Movements embodying this view of the world I shall refer to as *world-rejecting* new religions.

But there is yet another category on which so far we have not touched. I shall refer to this group as *world-accommodating* new religions. Movements in this category neither fully accept the norms and values of the surrounding society, nor entirely reject them by separating themselves off completely in communities of the like-minded. Rather, they feel that the secular world and even many religious bodies have slipped away from the God-ordained design for human life, but that individuals can redress this situation in their own lives without separating entirely from the secular world. Believers will normally continue in conventional jobs and family life, their religious practice reinvigorating and re-equipping them to face a degenerating secular world.

The World-accommodating group includes such movements as Neo-Pentecostalism and the Charismatic Renewal. These are themselves a collection of groups and organisations both within and beyond the major denominations which typically consist of individuals who were already committed Christians, but who felt something to be lacking in their spiritual lives, particularly an active *experience* of God's power in themselves and in the church. Neo-Pentecostalism and the Renewal Movement were attractive to such people because they claimed that the Holy Spirit was still active in the world and could be experienced through various charismatic gifts, most usually through glossolalia, the gift of tongues. Speaking in tongues consists of uttering language-like sounds, believed to be unknown or angelic languages, in praise, prayer or prophecy. Tongues-speaking forms part of a conventionally structured, but more enthusiastic, mode of worship than is normally found in conventional church services. Such groups are essentially a protest against the loss of vitality in

Children join in the chanting at a religious festival.

prevailing religious institutions, the cooling of their ardour and their abandonment of a living spirituality. The new movement restores an essential element to the spiritual life and returns to traditional certainties in a world where religious institutions have become colder, more bureaucratic and less certain of their role and even of their fundamental beliefs.

The world-accommodating category accounts for a few of the new religions which came to prominence in the 1960s and 1970s. However, it is important as a *direction* in which a number of new religions were to develop over the course of time.

The distinguishing features of the two main types are summarised in Table 1.

I now propose to turn to the questions of what the origins of these new religions are and what developments they have undergone.

Origins of the New Religions

The emergence of industrial society was one aspect of a process of *rationalisation* which has greatly affected the Western world. Rationalisation is the process by

	World-rejecting	World-affirming
Conception of God	Personal entity distinct from humanity	Element of every human life
Present world	Debased; its values all contrary to the ideal; in need of total transformation	Much to offer if one has the means to secure the good things available
Commitment required	Complete, including separation from family and career. Movement is a 'total institution'	Partial, a largely leisure-time pursuit while one continues one's activity in the world
Economic base	Wealth and labour of converts, supplemented by street solicitation of donations	Fees for goods and services marketed by the movement
Sexual morality	Ascetic (i.e. tightly regulating sexual contact) or antinomian (permitting promiscuous sexual relationships)	Largely indifferent to regulating general sexual conduct
Conversion	Rapid, abrupt after contact, attitude of 'surrender' required from outset	Typically a sequence of stages of progressive personal transformation
Leader	God's emissary or representative	Technical innovator
Social organisation	Communal	Corporate
Examples	Unification Church ISKCON COG People's Temple Manson's Family	Transcendental Meditation Human Potential Movement Est Silva Mind Control Scientology

Table 1   Characteristics of World-rejecting and World-affirming religious movements.

which life has become organised in terms of instrumental considerations: the concern with technical efficiency; maximisation of calculability and pre-dictability; and subordination of nature to human purposes. It therefore carries in its wake what Max Weber has called the 'disenchantment of the world', a loss of a sense of magic, mystery, prophecy and the sacred.

Rationalisation greatly affects our private as well as our public lives. The family is separated from production, children from adults (in schools and leisure pursuits), where we live from where we work, and so on. Modern life is therefore fragmented for many people, making it more difficult for people to identify fully with their public roles. Jobs have become more routine and mechanised, losing intrinsic interest and satisfaction for many workers. Moreover, achievement – what you can do rather than who you are – has become a major preoccupation for people whose image of how they should live, derived from the mass media, leads them to believe that comfort, happiness and satisfactory relationships are achievable by everyone. Old community structures have broken down and mobility, social and geographical, makes it increasingly difficult to recreate them in the anonymous world of the city.

Rationalisation in these various forms provides the backdrop to the emergence of the new religions. It particularly affects those experiencing the transition from home to the wider social world of work or college, thus most sharply striking those in late adolescence and early adulthood. It was precisely such people who reacted against the dehumanisation of the public world in the counter-culture of the 1960s and early 1970s. Through political protest, the hippy movement and the commune movement, young people sought to transform or recreate the world in which they lived. But political protest faced severe repression, and hippy culture and the commune movement largely disintegrated under the impact of drugs and exploitation. Young people committed to a sense that the world could be radically created anew came to see that such a transformation on the scale they sought could not be produced by human effort alone. Some had been led towards a more spiritual and mystical view of the world as a result of their drug experiences. By the late 1960s and early 1970s, then, many young people in America and Europe were available for a movement which claimed that some divine agency or power was poised to intervene in the world, that the millennium would be brought about by supernatural means if people would commit themselves zealously to the endeavour. The failure of the counter-culture was thus the principal source for those recruited to the world-rejecting new religions.

The world-affirming new religions had their origins in more pervasive features of advanced capitalist societies. Such societies create widespread aspirations for the values of power, status, personal attractiveness, happiness, etc, but distribute these resources unequally among the population. The world-affirming movements offered to provide either the recipe, technique or knowledge to reduce the gap between aspiration and actuality. In such movements as TM or Scientology, they would learn how to increase their abilities so as to be able to achieve their goals; in such movements as Est, the Human Potential Movement or the Neo-Sannyas Movement of Bhagwan Shree Rajneesh, they would learn that the present is the only moment there is, and that happiness lies in wanting, experiencing and celebrating what you get, rather than in getting what you want.

Those who joined or participated in these movements were typically from among the more comfortable sectors of Western societies, from among social groups who had benefited from above-average educations and incomes. This was particularly true for the Neo-Sannyas Movement – or Rajneeshism as it is now known – which advocates the abandonment of all striving, of all desire for power or achievement, of all ambition. Normally such attitudes will have little appeal for those who have yet to sample the good things that success and affluence may bring, and thus working-class people and other underprivileged groups are little represented among their members.

In an achievement-oriented society there develops a market for securing success. However, success is normally not achieved without cost. A high level of self-control, inhibition of spontaneity, and repression of instinctual desires is normally the price paid for the achievement of comfortable, middle-class jobs and life styles. When they have become successful in conventional terms, some people feel that they have done so at the price of repressing their 'real' selves, creating a mask or straightjacket around their expressive impulses, and forming barriers between themselves and others – even their own loved ones. Thus there arises a demand – met by some of the world-affirming new religions – for a context and method of liberating spontaneity, of contacting the 'real' self behind the masks and performances, of feeling and sharing intimacy and love (if only for a weekend before a return to the harsh reality of urban industrial life).

Development of the New Religions

What kinds of development have the new religions undergone? It is now clear that major changes affected the world-rejecting movements, particularly the disappearance of the counter-culture and the onset of recession. Fewer young people felt rebellious and wished to reject the materialist good life, and hence they failed to provide continuing cohorts of recruits. Members began to grow older and produce children. Some movements adapted to these changes in the time-honoured fashion of becoming less aggressive in their response to the world around them, more conventional in structure and appearance, more denominational in character, and thus drifted towards a more world-accommodating position. This can be seen in the Unification Church which has established a more conventional parochial ministry to service a constituency that may attend its services but which is disinclined to commit everything to the movement. Similarly, the Hare Krishna devotees have begun to find a new clientele and basis of support among the Indian community in Europe and America who are willing to donate funds and attend temple ceremonies and otherwise utilise the services and facilities of the movement, without a total commitment.

In other cases, the movement created so much hostility through the intensity of its rejection of the surrounding society that it mobilised a reaction which destroyed it – as in the case of Manson's Family in California – or which led it to destroy itself in anticipation of external attacks – as in the case of the People's Temple followers in Jonestown, Guyana. In other cases, reactive hostility from outside and the fear of severe control has led the movement virtually to go underground – as in the case of the Children of God or Family of Love. In short, such movements have either become more accommodating to the world or they have largely disappeared, the latter a consequence of the loss of their recruitment base and of social control measures evoked by their disregard for, and hostility towards, conventional society.

The world-affirming movements have not, in general, evoked such severe opposition, largely because they endorse many conventional social norms and values. The clientele for their service has also not disappeared; indeed, it seems likely to persist as long as there is unequal distribution of valued attributes and a widespread sense of everyone's right to possess them. However, these movements exist in a market for services and commodities of the kind they offer. They must compete with new brand names entering the market, names more effectively packaged or more closely geared to the latest market needs. The demand for means of self-expression and overcoming repression may be high when the economy is buoyant and everyone wants to relax and enjoy life. But when recession appears, movements too heavily committed to an earlier market trend may go to the wall – as did the Human Potential Movement – while other forms flourish which provide recipes for success in the corporate jungle when unemployment threatens.

Thus, some movements disappear only to be replaced by other suppliers, while other world-affirming religions such as Scientology and Est have diversified or modified their salvation products to attract a new clientele or to retain the brand loyalty of existing customers.

Conclusion

These two main forms of new religion in the West reiterate time-honoured preoccupations of humankind: the search for a recipe or remedy to cope with the world as it is, or for a supernatural transformation of the world into a Utopia free of pain, want and degredation. The desire for magic or the millennium has since time immemorial been the incentive for new salvational movements to resolve human suffering. Such movements may take new forms in each new historical and cultural location, appealing to different social groups and initiated by different social circumstances, but they form a persisting and recurring theme in our efforts to cope with life's vicissitudes and to secure escape or solace in the face of its difficulties.

References and Further Reading

Barker, E. (1984) *The Making of a Moonie*, Basil Blackwell.

Glock, C. and Bellah, R. N. (eds) (1976) *The New Religious Consciousness*, University of California Press.

Wallis, R. (1984) *The Elementary Forms of the New Religious Life*, Routledge and Kegan Paul.

Wilson, B. (1982) *Religion in Sociological Perspective*, Oxford University Press.

Pray TV: Observations On Mass Media Religion

STEVE BRUCE

The high profile of a number of American television evangelists during the Reagan presidency attracted the attention of social scientists who (mistakenly, as it turned out) supposed the 'new Christian right' to be a powerful political force. Recent changes in British broadcasting legislation has opened up the airways and made it likely that within the decade we will be able to watch 'holy roller' religious television programmes: programmes that differ from the present 'God slot' output in openly recruiting for a particular religious position, criticising the competition and persistently demanding that we give lots of money to Brother Bob or Brother Jim. The possibility of 'televangelism' in Britain worries the main churches, which fear that their liberal ecumenical religion will be pushed aside by aggressive fundamentalism.

The weakness, of 'Pray TV' as an influence can be seen from the very small numbers of the 'heathen' who watch it and are saved. The figures vary slightly from one study to another, but the conclusion of Stacey and Shupe's (1982) Dallas study can stand for them all:

> [televangelism] preaches to the converted who are already predisposed or self-selected, to seek out its message. These are persons who are members of fundamentalist congregations and/or persons with highly orthodox religious beliefs (Stacey and Shupe 1982, p. 299).

Why a medium on which so much money is spent is so ineffective in converting the unchurched is pretty clear when we consider the social bases of knowledge and belief. Much of what we know about the world we take on trust from others: in some fields there are 'experts' (hence, the white-coated scientist in the toilet-cleaner ads); in others it is personal bonds of friendship which most persuade us to try some new product or new idea. Some new possibilities we can test for ourselves. If a new kind of seed corn is supposed to give higher yields, we can plant it and compare the crop with that

The American Christian Broadcasting Network (CBN).

from the old seed; it works or it doesn't. But a lot of life, especially that dealing with the interpersonal, the emotional or the spiritual is outside that sort of testing. How, this side of the grave, can I know that 'getting right with Jesus' will bring eternal life? When the content of the message cannot be tested, how we respond has a lot to do with how we feel about the source of the message. To paraphrase McLuhan (1964), *the plausibility of the medium is the plausibility of the message.*

Parapersonal Communication

The importance of the personal bond in mediating impersonal communications is well known to television evangelists, who have pioneered techniques for pretending that their relationship with each member of their TV audience is, indeed, a personal one. Although the programmes are designed and produced by large bureaucratic organisations, they are usually built around the personality of the evangelist. Some are avowedly personality shows with the evangelist's name in the title, but even those which have a slightly more impersonal format – Falwell's *Old Time Gospel Hour*, for example, which is based on the Sunday morning service from his fundamentalist Baptist church in Lynchburg, Virginia – features the personality at the start and end of the programme and have him deliver the central sermon and usually the 'money pitches', the request for donations. When the evangelist invites the audience to write or phone, it is not to the organisation, but 'to me, Jerry Falwell'.

Televangelists are highly skilled broadcasters who devote considerable energy to appearing to be otherwise. In a medium which accords great prestige to those who display 'coolness' under stress, where the hero is the competent newscaster who continues to read the news while protesters break into the studio, religious broadcasters allow themselves frequent displays of emotion. Televangelists, such as the Bakers, Oral Roberts, Jimmy Swaggart and Pat Robertson, were all often moved to tears on screen.

The most advanced and impersonal technology – the computer – is used to simulate personal communication. When Oral Roberts says that he prays over your personal problems and prayer requests, what he means is that he prays over a computer printout of the names of those who have written to him. Typists scan the letters, feed in the name and address and a summary of the writer's problem (e.g. 'losing faith' or 'son on drugs') and the computer programme generates an apparently thoughtful reply with appropriate Bible texts (and a request for further donations).

'Parapersonal communication' neatly describes the end product of using high technology and a certain degree of masking to modify or appear to modify what is fundamentally an impersonal medium: a form of contact which lies between genuinely personal interaction and the entirely impersonal mass media. In its persuasiveness, televangelism conforms to what we would expect from previous research on conversion and influence. It develops a considerable loyalty between members of the audience and the evangelist, whom many feel they know as well as or better than they know people who they meet in the flesh. But it does not have the degree of 'plausibility' that will cause unbelievers to become believers or critics to become supporters. There is enough influence for people who already like conservative Protestantism to be convinced that they like *this brand* but there is not enough to shift people the greater distance from

How Popular is Televangelism?

Televangelists are notorious for claiming vast audiences and they certainly are popular. But how popular? It is actually very difficult to measure audience size. One can ask a sample of people to keep TV diaries, but many forget to fill them in. A more expensive way of finding out what people watch is to fit metering devices to a sample of television sets to record when the set is on and to what channel it is tuned, but this method does not tell us if anyone is actually watching the 'box' at the time. The most accurate way of measuring is to phone a sample of households at specific times and ask how many people are watching what, but this is too expensive to be used often or on large samples. Further, there are always uncertainties in generalising from a small sample to the whole country. A good estimate, using combinations of all three techniques, suggested that 40 per cent of households with a television watched 'six minutes or more' of a religious programme, which sounds like a lot until one realises that this is the figure for a whole genre. The same figure for 'sports programmes' or 'comedies' would be over 95 per cent. Reliable estimates in the mid-80s put the regular televangelism audience at around 15 million or some 8 per cent of the total American viewing public. The sex scandals which befell leading televangelists Jimmy Bakker and Jimmy Swaggart in 1987 and 1988 reduced that estimate by 3 or 4 million. Televangelism, although a significant cultural phenomenon, cannot be said to be sweeping all before it.

Evaluation exercise

Using the material from Steve Bruce's article, evaluate the statement that 'televangelism has swept all before it in a major religious revival'.

You could use the following headings to assess the statement: (a) arguments and evidence used by televangelists to support their statement, and (b) arguments and evidence which Bruce uses to challenge the statement.

mainstream Protestantism to fundamentalism or from unbelief to Christianity.

Secondary Pay-offs

Although it fails in its primary purpose, televangelism has an important secondary or latent function as a source of entertainment and 'spiritual nourishment'. Evangelicals and fundamentalists who want to hear good gospel music or listen to a celebrity talk about her religious conversion and her campaign against homosexuality can now turn to their favourite show. Those people who like talk shows can indulge in their secular pleasures, without missing 'added value' religion, by watching *700 Club*. In the sense of expanding the resources of the conservative Protestant milieu, religious broadcasting is as important as Christian schools, fundamentalist colleges, publishing houses or film companies.

Until recently, fundamentalists were 'dirt poor' and despised by cosmopolitan America, which sneered at their lack of education, wealth and culture. The creation of a technically sophisticated and glossy product – the production and distribution facilities of Pat Robertson's Christian Broadcasting Network are the equal of anything in the secular world – allows a previously marginalised group to feel that it has arrived. What comes through clearly in Hoover's (1989) interviews with regular watchers of Pat Robertson's *700 Club* is their pleasure in knowing that there are now people who think like them but who have status in the world. Mass media religion is no

longer some 'good ol' boy' in a bri-nylon shirt, healing the sick in a tent or belting out 'heart-felt, Holy Ghost, heaven-sent, devil-chasing, sin-killing, true-blue, red-hot, blood-bought, God-given singing of the gospel' (Swaggart, in Barnhart 1988, p. 128). As an interviewee told Hoover:

> We're very proud of Christian programming. We use it ourselves, in our witnessing, we're very proud that instead of just 'Bible thumping' as it used to be in the old days on TV – which was mostly embarrassing, really not that great content, it was mostly the salvation message and nothing much more, or something negative, something out of touch with society – now we're not ashamed because now there is excellent Christian programming that is very much contemporary, and in touch with society, and not afraid to discuss controversial issues. Hollywood and Madison Avenue will still try and make us look like a bunch of Elmer Gantrys and weirdos in general, but, basically speaking, people think it's OK. (Hoover 1989, p. 182)

Televangelism exists in America because private companies can buy air time to show their products and use that air time to solicit for funds to buy more air time, and because an awful lot of Americans are fundamentalists or evangelicals (about 25 per cent of the population). Rather than converting the heathen, it offers a high-quality product to people who already like that sort of thing and are prepared to pay for it. Unless televangelism can demonstrate a persuasiveness that the mass media have not yet shown, the rarity of conservatist Protestants in Britain (perhaps 2 to 5 per cent of the population) suggests that Pray TV will fail to follow soap operas and game shows into the affections of the British TV audience.

References and Further Reading

Barnhart, J.E. (1988) *Jimmy and Tammy: Charismatic Intrigue inside PTL*, Prometheus Books.

Hadden, J. K. and Shupe, A. (1988) *Televangelism: Power and Politics on God's frontier*, Henry Holt.

Hoover, S. M. (1989) *Mass Media Religion: the Social Sources of the Electronic Church*, Sage.

McLuhan, M. (1964) *Understanding Media*, Routledge and Kegan Paul.

McQuail, D. (1983) *Mass Communication Theory: An Introduction*, Sage.

Stacey, W. and Shupe, A. (1982) 'Correlates of support for the "electronic church"', *Journal for the Scientific Study of Religion*, Vol. 21, pp. 291–303.

Examination essay question

Assess the view that the growth of religious sects is a response to social deprivation.

Notes for guidance

There is a considerable amount of information available about the growth of religious sects which dates back to Weber and, more recently, Bryan Wilson's work and Eileen Barker's participant observation study of the Moonies (see References and Further Reading, p. 129). Such sources should be considered as they provide an invaluable source of evidence and argument on which to base your essay. Like any essay question, it has been worded carefully to point your answer in a particular direction. In this case, the question is asking about the relationship between 'the growth in religious sects' and 'social deprivation' so you must focus on that relationship rather than just describing religious movements generally. Whilst there is clearly a relationship between the growth of some types of sect and poverty this is not always the case. Consider whether there are other reasons for the growth of sects, for instance psychological deprivation. A number of sociologists, including Wallis, have developed typologies of sects which categorise different sects according to their origin and membership make-up. A knowledge of such typologies would provide a sound basis for this essay but you should also be critical in approach and comment on the different explanations you consider in your answer. It might also be worthwhile to question the assumption that people who join religious sects are necessarily deprived in some way. After all, the concept of social deprivation has been strongly criticized in studies of education and poverty so it ought to be challenged here too.

Coursework suggestion

The nineties have been described as 'the decade of evangelism' by some church leaders. You could take the question of whether a religious revival is happening in Britain as a starting point for a project (you will find useful data on the **Cuttings** page overleaf). One way to approach it would be to discover whether there is any evidence, at a local level, to support or reject the view that a religious revival is taking place. A range of methods could be employed, though you are almost bound to start with arguments surrounding church attendance statistics. It will be important to narrow your hypothesis down to one which can be tested at a local level, perhaps through the use of participant observation at churches or other religious organisations such as the Christian Union at your school or college. You might examine the attendance statistics for one or more churches and compare them with findings gained from participant observation. Such an approach, supplemented perhaps by in-depth interviews, would allow you to gauge the extent of the religious participation and begin to consider explanations. As with any project at A level, it will be important to interpret your findings within a sociological framework – in other words offer an evaluation of them. Evidence for or against a religious revival could certainly be interpreted in a variety of ways in view of the debates that have always surrounded the definition and measurement of religious beliefs and practices. A project of this type could be discursive in approach and assess a range of arguments and evidence.

Cuttings

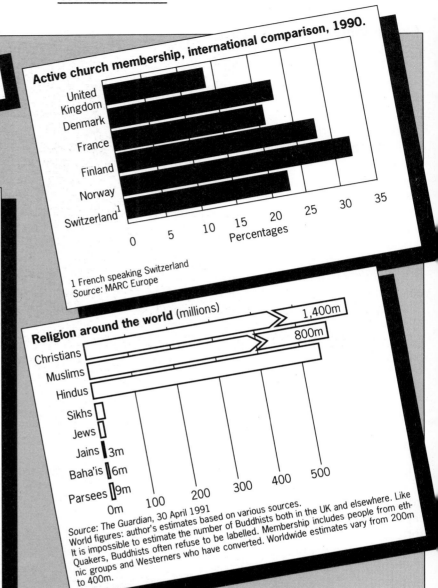

Active church membership, international comparison, 1990.

United Kingdom
Denmark
France
Finland
Norway
Switzerland[1]

0   5   10   15   20   25   30   35
Percentages

1 French speaking Switzerland
Source: MARC Europe

Religion around the world (millions)

Christians — 1,400m
Muslims — 800m
Hindus
Sikhs
Jews
Jains — 3m
Baha'is — 6m
Parsees — 9m

0m   100   200   300   400   500

Source: The Guardian, 30 April 1991
World figures: author's estimates based on various sources.
It is impossible to estimate the number of Buddhists both in the UK and elsewhere. Like
Quakers, Buddhists often refuse to be labelled. Membership includes people from eth-
nic groups and Westerners who have converted. Worldwide estimates vary from 200m
to 400m.

Church membership United Kingdom	Adult members (millions)	
	1975	**1990**
Trinitarian Churches		
Anglican	2.27	1.82
Presbyterian	1.65	1.29
Methodist	0.61	0.51
Baptist	0.27	0.24
Other Protestant Churches	0.53	0.65
Roman Catholic	2.53	1.96
Orthodox	0.20	0.23
Total	8.06	6.70
Non-Trinitarian Churches		
Mormons	0.10	0.15
Jehovah's Witnesses	0.08	0.11
Spiritualists	0.06	0.05
Other Non-Trinitarian	0.09	0.13
Total	0.33	0.44
Other Religions		
Muslims	0.4	1.00
Sikhs	0.12	0.22
Hindus	0.10	0.17
Jews	0.11	0.11
Others	0.08	0.24
Total	0.81	1.74

Source: UK Christian Handbook 1989–1990 Edition, MARC Europe, Social Trends, 1991 HMSO

Active church membership in the UK is rather lower than in other European countries, but the numbers of people who still consider themselves to be within a religious faith in the UK remains very high. Recent debates within the Church of England about the ordination of women, on links with other faiths, and on the stance of the Roman Catholic Church towards birth control, reveal an active and important struggle over the role and future of the long established faiths in this country. The 'modernisers' fear a continuing fall in active membership without change. The 'tradition-alists' suspect, instead, a fundamental betrayal of basic Christian tenets. The outcome may reveal a lot about the role and relevance of the church to a large proportion of the UK population.